FEAR, HATE, AND VICTIMHOOD

RACE
RHETORIC
& MEDIA

Davis W. Houck, General Editor

FEAR, HATE,
AND
VICTIMHOOD

How GEORGE WALLACE Wrote
the DONALD TRUMP Playbook

ANDREW E. STONER

University Press of Mississippi / Jackson

The University Press of Mississippi is the scholarly publishing agency of
the Mississippi Institutions of Higher Learning: Alcorn State University,
Delta State University, Jackson State University, Mississippi State University,
Mississippi University for Women, Mississippi Valley State University,
University of Mississippi, and University of Southern Mississippi.

www.upress.state.ms.us

The University Press of Mississippi is a member
of the Association of University Presses.

First printing 2022

∞

Library of Congress Cataloging-in-Publication Data

Names: Stoner, Andrew E., author.
Title: Fear, hate, and victimhood: how George Wallace wrote the Donald
Trump playbook / Andrew E. Stoner.
Other titles: Race, rhetoric, and media series.
Description: Jackson: University Press of Mississippi, 2022. | Series:
Race, rhetoric, and media series | Includes bibliographical references
and index.
Identifiers: LCCN 2021042928 (print) | LCCN 2021042929 (ebook) | ISBN
978-1-4968-3845-2 (hardback) | ISBN 978-1-4968-3846-9 (trade paperback) | ISBN
978-1-4968-3847-6 (epub) | ISBN 978-1-4968-3848-3 (epub) | ISBN 978-1-4968-3849-0
(pdf) | ISBN 978-1-4968-3850-6 (pdf)
Subjects: LCSH: Wallace, George C. (George Corley), 1919–1998. | Trump,
Donald, 1946– | Political campaigns—United States. | Presidential
candidates—United States. | Identity politics—United States. | Mass
media—Political aspects—United States. | United States—Race
relations—Political aspects.
Classification: LCC JK2281 .S77 2022 (print) | LCC JK2281 (ebook) | DDC
324.70973—dc23/eng/20220111
LC record available at https://lccn.loc.gov/2021042928
LC ebook record available at https://lccn.loc.gov/2021042929

British Library Cataloging-in-Publication Data available

To the memory of four men whose contributions made this work possible:
journalist and retired professor Steve Bell (1935–2019);
former Alabama governor Albert P. Brewer (1928–2017);
former US vice president Walter F. Mondale (1928–2021);
and journalist Dan King Thomasson (1933–2018)

CONTENTS

GEORGE C. WALLACE: A TIMELINE

August 25, 1919	Wallace born—Clio, Alabama
1935	Wallace wins contest to be Alabama State Senate student page.
1936–1937	Wallace wins two "Golden Gloves" boxing championships.
May 1937	Wallace graduates Barbour County High School.
August 1937	Wallace enters University of Alabama School of Law.
May 1942	Wallace graduates from University of Alabama School of Law.
October 1942	Wallace enters US Army Air Corps.
May 22, 1943	Wallace marries Lurleen Burns.
December 1945	Wallace honorably discharged from US Army Air Corps.
November 1945	Wallace named assistant state attorney general.
November 1946	Wallace elected to the Alabama House of Representatives.
July 1948	Wallace declines to participate in 'Dixiecrat' walkout of Democratic convention.
November 1953	Wallace elected judge of Third Judicial Circuit Court.
December 1955–December 1956	Montgomery Bus Boycott lead by Rosa Parks and Martin Luther King Jr.
June 3, 1958	Wallace loses Democratic gubernatorial primary in Alabama.
January 1959	Wallace acquitted on contempt charges in voting rights case involving US Civil Rights Commission.
May 1961	Mob violence against "freedom riders" at Anniston and Birmingham.

November 1962	Wallace elected governor of Alabama.
January 14, 1963	Wallace "segregation forever" inaugural address.
June 11, 1963	Wallace's "stand in the schoolhouse door" at University of Alabama.
September 15, 1963	Bombing of Sixteen Street Baptist Church in Birmingham kills four children and injures twenty-two others.
November 22, 1963	President John F. Kennedy assassinated at Dallas, Texas.
April–May 1964	Wallace enters Democratic presidential primaries in Wisconsin, Indiana, and Maryland.
June–August 1964	Three civil rights workers go missing, eventually found dead in Mississippi.
July 2, 1964	President Lyndon B. Johnson signs the Civil Rights Act of 1964.
March 7, 1965	"Bloody Sunday" as civil rights marchers beaten at Edmund Pettis Bridge trying to march from Selma to Montgomery.
August 6, 1965	President Lyndon B. Johnson signs Voting Rights Act of 1965.
September 1965	Wallace loses legislative fight to allow him to seek second term as governor.
November 1966	Wallace's wife, Lurleen, elected governor of Alabama.
Feb. 8, 1968	Wallace enters 1968 presidential campaign representing the American Independent Party, with name placed on all fifty state ballots.
May 7, 1968	Death of spouse, Lurleen Wallace—46th governor of Alabama.
October 2, 1968	Wallace names retired Air Force general Curtis LeMay his running mate.
November 5, 1968	Wallace finishes third in presidential election, pulling 10 million votes but winning only five southern states. Richard M. Nixon elected president.
November 1970	Wallace elected governor of Alabama.
December 1970	Wallace marries Cornelia Snively.
January 13, 1972	Wallace enters Democratic presidential primary race—wins primaries in Florida, North Carolina, Maryland, Michigan, and Tennessee.

May 15, 1972	Wallace shot, mortally wounded in Laurel, Maryland.
July 11, 1972	Wallace addresses Democratic National Convention at Miami Beach, Florida.
November 1974	Wallace re-elected governor of Alabama.
November 1, 1975	Wallace announces he will once again enter Democratic presidential primary, eventually wins only Alabama, Mississippi, and South Carolina.
January–June 1976	Wallace enters Democratic presidential primaries.
January 1978	Wallace divorced from Cornelia Snively Wallace.
March 1981	Wallace marries Lisa Taylor.
November 1982	Wallace elected to fourth term as governor of Alabama.
April 1986	Wallace announces he will retire from public life at the end of his term as governor.
February 1987	Wallace divorced from Lisa Taylor Wallace.
September 13, 1998	Wallace, seventy-nine, dies in Montgomery, Alabama.

ACKNOWLEDGMENTS

The author gratefully acknowledges the assistance and support of a variety of individuals and organizations for the completion of this work, including the Alabama Department of Archives and History, Governors George C. and Lurleen B. Wallace Collection, Mary Jo Scott, Montgomery, Ala.; the American Presidency Project, John Woolly and Gerhard Peters, University of California-Santa Barbara; Americanrhetoric.com; California State University-Sacramento, University Library and Communication Studies Department, Sacramento, Calif.; Ball State University Libraries, Archives and Special Collections, Muncie, Ind.; Steve Bell (1935–2019); former Alabama governor Albert P. Brewer (1928–2017); University of California-Los Angeles, Communication Studies Department Archives, Los Angeles, Calif.; Jimmy Carter Presidential Library, Atlanta, Ga.; Committee to Project Journalists, New York, N.Y.; C-Span Video Library, Washington, D.C.; former Massachusetts governor Michael Dukakis; Federal Bureau of Investigation archive, FBI Records: The Vault; Gerald R. Ford Presidential Library and Museum, Grand Rapids, Mich.; papers of former senator Barry Goldwater, Arizona Historical Foundation, Tempe, Az.; Dr. Richard Haney; Harvard University Archives, Cambridge, Mass.; papers of former vice president and senator Hubert H. Humphrey, Gale Family Library, Minnesota Historical Society, St. Paul, Minn.; Indiana Historical Society, Smith Memorial Library, Indianapolis, Ind.; Dr. Jacqueline Irwin; papers of former senator Henry M. Jackson, University of Washington Libraries, Seattle, Wash.; Lyndon Baines Johnson Presidential Library, Austin, Tex.; Mark Kennedy; Morgan Burns Kennedy; Peggy Wallace Kennedy; Maryland State Archives, Annapolis, Md.; papers of former senator George S. McGovern, Princeton University Library, Princeton, N.J.; University of Michigan, Special Collections and Archives, Ann Arbor, Mich.; University Press of Mississippi, Emily Bandy, Jackson, Miss.; former vice president Walter F. Mondale (1928–2021); Richard Nixon Foundation, Yorba Linda, Calif.; Ronald Reagan Presidential Library and Museum, Simi

Valley, Calif.; Bethany Crum Roush; St. Norbert College, Mulva Library, De Pere, Wisc.; Randolph Scott; C. Scott Sickels; Smith College, Special Collections, Young Library, Northampton, Mass.; Dr. Gerri Smith; Jonathan Swain; Dan King Thomasson (1933–2018); Judith Davis Turnipseed; former state senator G. Tom Turnipseed (1936–2020); University of Southern Mississippi, William D. McClain Library and Archives Special Collections, Hattiesburg, Miss.; University of Wisconsin-Stevens Point, Library and Archives and Division of Communication, School of Design and Communication, Stevens Point, Wis.; University of Wisconsin-Whitewater, Andersen Library, Whitewater, Wis.; and Youngstown State University, William F. Maag, Jr., Library, Youngstown, Ohio.

This research received support from a Probationary Faculty Development Grant, Office of Research, Innovation and Economic Development, California State University, Sacramento.

FEAR, HATE, AND VICTIMHOOD

INTRODUCTION

It didn't take long for comparisons between Donald J. Trump and George C. Wallace to emerge, surfacing basically from the moment Trump announced he was a candidate for president of the United States in 2016. Entering the fray with language that startled many—referring to the nation as a "dumping ground" and labeling Mexican immigrants to the United States (presumably documented and undocumented) as "murderers and rapists"—Trump rolled through a series of Republican presidential primaries with similar insults to his rivals with former governors in the race receiving pointed barbs: Jeb Bush was a "low energy loser," Rick Perry should "be forced to take an IQ test," and Bobby Jindal was a "substance-free narcissist." Opponents from the US Senate fared no better: Rand Paul was "a fake conservative"; Marco Rubio was "Little Marco"; and Ted Cruz and his family had alleged links to the Kennedy assassination, and Cruz was dubbed "Lyin' Ted." Even fellow business executive Carly Fiorina was a target because she possessed, Trump said, "a face" that "no one would vote for."[1] The aghast responses especially roared as Trump declared Senator John McCain (and Vietnam prisoner of war) was "not a war hero. He's a war hero because he was captured? I like people who weren't captured."[2] There would be many more moments where Trump's primary—and general election campaign in 2016 would cause sharp reactions—such as when Trump called for "a total and complete shutdown of Muslims entering the United States" in response to terrorist attacks abroad.[3] In short, rhetoric based in insult, resentment, xenophobia, and even anger was the guidebook for Trump's candidacy, and none of it seemed to slow down his quest for the White House. His voters, in fact perhaps nearly half of the voters taking a ballot in November 2016, excused such excesses as just part of the show, part of Trump "telling it like it is" just as they had four decades earlier for George C. Wallace. Even Wallace's daughter, Peggy Wallace Kennedy, believes Trump is channeling what her father tried to do over the course of four presidential campaigns between 1964 and 1976:

Trump and my father say out loud what people are thinking but don't have the courage to say. They both were able to adopt the notion that fear and hate are the two greatest motivators of voters that feel alienated from government.[4]

The contrasts and comparisons between Trump and Wallace are valid, and they are at the center of this examination. But beyond a reciting, however, of the instances where their speech and approaches broke new ground for political venom and contempt, a rhetorical analysis of the two men and their campaigns provides valuable insights. Such an analysis helps in understanding American politics in Wallace and Trump eras separated by almost half a century, but ones sharing the tumult and discomfort of profound change facing the nation. In Wallace's time, it was the march toward fully actualized civil rights for all Americans, most especially Black Americans, through federal court orders, new laws enacted, and growing attitudes that something had to change, that prompted dissonance among the nation's white majority. In Trump's time, the issues were similar, though not exactly the same. A rise in the diversity of the American populace, driven by immigration and other social factors (such as the role of women, rights for LGBTQ Americans) that presented cultural, political, and economic challenges to the white majority. Lest anyone believe an ideological basis exists for this approach, historian Dan T. Carter notes that the Wallace and Trump strategies and resulting tactics employed in response to such times have always been about "impressions" and "about a vague taking charge." He cites the change occurring in the nation in both eras and offers, "There are a lot of people who essentially want the world to stop and want it to stop changing. And when that happens, you look for a strong individual. And to me that's the big appeal and the big similarity between George Wallace and Donald Trump."[5]

A need exists, however, to move beyond the myriad comparisons that have been made between the two men that sent countless reporters, editors, and producers scrambling through news archives to revive memories of the Wallace campaign (most notably 1968). Considered through a frame of rhetorical analysis, especially one embracing ideas forwarded about "demagogic rhetoric," we gain a greater perspective on these two men, and what their campaigns mean about them, but also what they mean and represent about ourselves. Through the lens of ideas posited by rhetorical scholars, along with a deep look at primary and secondary sources from the Wallace years, we can begin to understand how we have arrived in the Trump era that seems so antithetical to what has come before. Chapter 1 explores the role ideas about "in-group" and "out-group" mentalities play out in politics. Chapter 2 reviews how anti-establishment views permeate much of the rhetoric in question. And chapter 3 reveals the seemingly paradoxical idea that while voters seek a powerful "say it like it is" leader, the rhetoric is wrapped in the expression of victimhood (even for individuals for whom privilege is well established).

In chapter 4, the role of "political spectacle" (or theater) in the process is examined, as well as the required co-opting of a logic-based media that struggles to respond to, let alone document, the demagogue and the performance of their toxic rhetoric. Campaign coverage in the Wallace and Trump scenarios is examined in chapter 5, where coverage is reduced to alarmed responses to the latest outrageous stunt or statement a candidate makes, and cast aside is little or no consideration of policies or ideas to address the problems being amplified. Even when media or political opponents attempt to counter the "show" with logical challenges to the fears and doubts being exploited, demagogic rhetoric is employed to cast such challengers as establishment figures who want to confuse, conflate, and delay "real" responses for "real Americans" who feel instinctually right. All of these elements were present throughout the career of George Wallace, who participated on the national political stage for more than a dozen years. As chapter 6 notes, ultimately, however, many believed the demagogic rhetoric of men like Wallace was eventually overcome by conventional political tactics that included strong policy positions, cordial and thoughtful exchanges of ideas, and the solemnity and reverence traditionally embodied in the process of asking for a person's vote. Donald Trump, however, turned all such ideas on their head and succeeded far beyond what Wallace ever knew. Whereas Wallace is easily relegated as "a four-time loser" and an interesting but troubling anomaly on the political landscape, he is perhaps more than that. Wallace, in fact, may simply be a prelude to a tune whose time had not yet come. Further, as Trump demonstrates, the messenger himself matters in making the demagogue's case, and Trump's aesthetic bested Wallace's southern-drawled persona on all levels. As others have noted, no one ever aspired to be George Wallace. Many have aspired to be Donald Trump, basking in the wealth of business and entertainment ventures that at least project the idea or aesthetic of success beyond what any governor of Alabama could ever achieve. Played out, then, is the idea that the Trump presidency is an actualized version of the Wallace presidency that never was. Though vast differences exist, the commonalities tied to the demagogic rhetoric of the two men provides a framework to understand these times—and perhaps a valuable warning about what is possible in our highly digitized information society.

CHAPTER 1

Politics of Crisis and the In-Group

A consistent, if not required, element of demagogic rhetoric as employed by men like George Wallace and Donald Trump is the creation of specific groups in which people reside. These groups are not some simple sorting of people but rather an essential demarcation of *good people* versus *bad people*. Further, once these lines have been drawn, a rich flow of disinformation, propaganda, deception, half-truths, and outright falsehoods is created that continually strengthens in-group thinking about those who are outside of the group. Not surprisingly, in the highly racialized context of American politics, race has served as a bright-line boundary between the good and the bad, the in-group and the out-group. This was especially so in the latter half of the twentieth century as America moved increasingly to a more urbanized and industrialized nation, with the rising dissonance between the promise of "all men are created equal" and the discriminatory reality many people of color faced was borne out. Into this hailstorm stepped an articulate, hard-working and determined Alabama native, George Corley Wallace, determined to stop or slow the rate of rapid change threatening the long-established borders of who was inside (white people), and who was outside (Black people).

It's unlikely Wallace ever sat down and conceptualized the manner in which he campaigned using in-group/out-group rhetoric so expertly. More probable is that he simply acted on instinct formed during a southern upbringing wrapped in bitterness and resentment in a South that came back from the destruction of the Civil War with a stylized (and counterfeit) history of the war, its causes, and its meanings. At the basis of the "rhetoric of resentment" that Wallace perfected was the erection of group lines and creating vivid, relatable crises and threats to the in-group, was the need to purge guilt of the immorality of a southern, slave-based society. As Anna M. Young noted, "guilt is purged through scapegoating a strawperson (extreme caricature) or imagined other" and is often coupled with "apocalyptic" oratory that constructs frightening threats to in-group identity and existence. Doing so creates a need to express the fear and anger that surface against out-group "sinners" who are believed responsible for the threats at hand. The threats can be real or grandiose fantasies—it appears to not matter to the followers of demagogic "leadership." As Moore wrote, "It does not particularly matter if grievances [threats] are manufactured or blown massively out of proportion, so long as it produces an us-versus-them siege mentality" among cohorts. Construction of this threat is a "performed, medi-ated, received, and circulated" phenomenon, Moore says, that sets up certain men (such as Wallace or Trump) as "champions of 'the people,' the savior who will deliver us from years of godlessness, brown people, and federal over-reach." The result then is the legitimization of xenophobia, ethnocentrism, and white nationalism.[1] In Wallace's time, "otherness" was defined almost solely on the basis of race and integration stood at the center of the issue. For Trump, immigrants supplanted Wallace's more narrow focus on African Americans. For both men, protestors, agitators, and anyone who questioned their govern-ment or sought change were part of an existential and/or perceived threat to the in-group majority. Wallace called such Americans "people who advocate for a breakdown of law and order" and said they were Communist-influenced traitors to the nation "who eventually wind up in Havana and Hanoi and Mos-cow." These same questioners, Wallace said, violently opposed law and order and he articulated the response to the threat he believed they presented, but in doing so promoted even more violence:

> If I were president today, you wouldn't get stabbed or raped in the shadow of the White House, even if we had to call out 30,000 troops and equip them with two-foot-long bayonets and station them every few feet apart. If you walk out of this hotel tonight and someone knocks you on the head, he'll be out of jail before you're out of the hospital, and on Monday morning, they'll try the policeman instead of the criminal.[2]

There was seemingly no incongruity in the contradiction of suggesting US military troops be turned on the American people to quell discontent, while lamenting acts of violence allegedly perpetrated by others. Wallace (like Trump in his four-decades-removed era to follow) embodied the contradictions, amplifying calls for "law and order" while also advocating violence via the ugly realities of raucous political rallies turned into melees. While Wallace would at least appear to try to calm the waters and quell outbreaks of violence, in his era, Trump openly advocated violence by his supporters, even once gloating he would pay any legal fees incurred by supporters for physical assaults on anti-Trump protestors who dared to enter the "Make America Great Again" domain he had created. Both Wallace and Trump personified a "rule breaking" machismo in politics that often attracts voters looking for what scholar Joseph E. Lowndes described as those seeking "new territories to delineate political discourse."[3] At the time, Wallace's words perfectly described who was good and who was bad. Trump took up the Wallace theme, but he expanded it to include forces from outside the United States. He articulated in 2016,

> The common threat linking the major Islamic terrorist attacks that have recently occurred on our soil . . . is that they have involved immigrants or the children of immigrants. . . . A Trump administration will establish a clear principle that will govern all decisions pertaining to immigration: we should only admit into this country those who share our values and respect our people.[4]

Both Wallace and Trump project a message based on "ethno-nationalist" foundations (according to Moore) that create in the mind of in-group adherents that "ideal" communities and times exist (but only in the past and in the "heartland") and that patriots who espouse American values are "true Americans" as opposed to questioning "traitors" or "fake Americans."

1964: An Articulate Protest

There was an almost visceral quality to Wallace's approach to creating in-group ideas and exposing the real or perceived threats to that group and how things have always been. Wallace knew how to speak to an audience and was driven to speak to anyone who would listen. His articulate abilities were on full display in the winter of 1963–1964 as he toured the nation in locales far removed from his duties back home as governor of Alabama. Speaking in Boston just two weeks before the assassination of President Kennedy, Wallace told reporters, "I came to New England because I was invited. But I think I can convert anyone with an open mind." Later, Wallace sat down for a thirty-minute televised "debate" on WNAC-TV with Vermont governor Philip H. Hoff, a fellow Democrat but a liberal who had introduced a civil rights platform of his own in 1961.[5] Wallace told Governor Huff and the television audience, "We Southerners just don't mind saying we don't believe in mixing the races in the school system," suggesting similar, but unspoken, feelings existed in the North.[6] Segregation was "a political, not a moral question," Wallace told Governor Hoff, and added,

"I believe sin emanates from the heart. If you segregate anyone because you hate him, that's sinful." The segregation he supported, Wallace said, was one he believed was in the best interest of whites and Blacks, and was therefore not sinful.[7] Wallace explained,

> The only difference in us in the South and people in other parts of the country, and I believe including Boston, is that we have *over the table said* that we believe in segregation. I am convinced in my heart about it. Millions of people feel that way. In other parts of the country they said we are for integration, but then they start about gerrymandering school districts and all sorts of other dilatory and undercover ways to provide segregation. We Southerners don't mind laying it on the table and saying we mind mixing of the races in the school system and that is [also] the case in other parts of the country.[8] [emphasis added]

Asked about violence that had erupted in his state as Alabamians wrestled with issues of civil rights bumping up against Jim Crowe traditions, Wallace responded, "I have never advocated anything but peaceful means [of protest]. . . . I do not believe in violence at all. In fact, I have prevented violence in my state in every instance in which I have been involved and there is less violence in Alabama today than we find in Washington or New York or Philadelphia."[9] Wallace's claim to have prevented violence in his state was a ludicrous claim on its face, ignoring the deadly bombing of a Black Birmingham church two months earlier in September 1963 (and subsequent violence during the "Freedom Summer" bus rides of 1964 and the March on Selma in 1965).

As he made his way to Harvard University for a high-profile address, Wallace stopped by the Massachusetts State House to call on Governor Endicott Peabody, another progressive Democrat, and the state's attorney general, Edward Brooke. Brooke later became the first Black man ever elected to the United States Senate (where he served from 1967 to 1979). In photos printed in newspapers across the northeast, Brooke looked stoic as he shook Wallace's hand, and Peabody looked on.[10]

For a speech in Tucson, Arizona, in January 1964, George Ridge, a reporter from the *Arizona Daily Star*, wrote, "The peppery little governor spoke out against the self-appointed social engineers and those in the news media who have obscured the master's hand of change being wrought . . . lulling the American people into a defensive position."[11] He reiterated by now-familiar themes of how the proposed 1964 Civil Rights Act would threaten free and uncontrolled use of private property, local schools, unions and even the right to a trial by jury. After his remarks, Wallace took questions from the audience, which often became pointed, including one query about educational opportunities for

Blacks in Alabama and a hypothetical question about whether "Jesus would sit by a Negro." Another questioner asked Wallace about the deadly bombing at the Sixteenth Street Baptist Church in Birmingham in September 1963. Wallace called the bombers "demented fools" who did not represent "the way of the people of Alabama." A more general question posed asked Wallace his personal view of "Negroes" he had known: "There are many Negroes I consider as members of my family," he said. "I have never said anyone is inferior. I have no animosity in my heart toward anyone."[12]

Despite the questions that served to revive troubling images of racial strife in Alabama (and across the South), a large portion of Wallace's remarks were devoted to an attempt to dismantle the law and reasoning behind the landmark 1954 high court ruling in Brown vs. Topeka (later known as Brown vs. the Board of Education). The governor likely calculated if cast correctly, the high court's decision to desegregate the nation's schools could be revved up into a threat that voters far outside of the South could feel—and respond to. The governor sought to reassure his Arizona audience that the people of Alabama were closer to "the problem" of school integration and warned, "We know the terrible price we must pay if integration of our schools is forced on us. We shall fight it to the last."[13] It was, once again, the raw rhetoric reporters had come to count on from Wallace and typical of the response one might expect from a "terrible price to pay" for school desegregation. Wallace declared the people of the United States, and particularly the South, "do not hate the Negro." Speaking of his white counterparts in the South, he offered a patronizing, paternal scenario where whites had "carried Negroes on their shoulders and have endowed them with every blessing of civilization that he has been able to assimilate. They want him to rise just as high as his capacities and his industry will carry him and the higher he rises the lighter will be their load and the happier their hearts."[14]

His words served to blunt any accusation or worry that the South—especially Wallace's heavy-handed "law and order Alabama"—had responded with brute force and violence against the protestations of Black Americans living there. If Wallace believed any part of his remarks would "win over" any northerners, the regressive and passively racist views underneath his closing remarks likely removed any doubt about that. In remarks that blamed the struggling position southern Blacks found themselves in as, essentially, their own fault, he concluded,

Remember, I am speaking of the African Negro, the Negro we have primarily in the South. He is our problem, not yours. He is a different problem from the sometimes highly educated, highly sophisticated and highly competent Mulatto who may attend your university. To argue that the Negro with whom we deal has the capacity of the white man is to argue that the mud and straw huts of Africa are equal to the cathedrals of France. To ask us to equate our children, classroom for classroom, with a race which is two years behind at sixth grade and three years behind at twelfth grade, is to ask us to deprive our children of the education to which they are entitled and in the effort to have this, we strain our resources to the utmost. It is our problem, not yours. Your problem here is yours, not ours. We ask that you believe that we are civilized humans and considerate of human rights. We give you credit for so being and we ask you to extend to us the same consideration.[15]

By distinguishing Blacks in the South as somehow different than Black citizens his northern or western audiences had encountered served to authenticate the threat he said they presented. His reference to "mud and straw huts in Africa" revived, no doubt, thoughts of tribal African Americans who posed a threat to regular democratic discourse. Further, rather than using the data that showed Black students in Alabama schools were underperforming their white counterparts as evidence that "separate, but equal" ideologies in the South had failed, he used it to advance ideas of Black inferiority and the resulting threat they may pose to "dumbing down" the entire educational system. Wallace had previously expressed similar views when trying to distinguish his views on voting rights from those of President Johnson and the 1965 Voting Rights Act the administration supported. Wallace said Johnson supported "universal suffrage without any qualifying conditions," but he favored a states' rights process by which states would determine who could vote and who could not. He believed,

> A person unable to read and write impairs and lowers the standard of political life. How can an illiterate vote intelligently in an increasingly complex world? The answer, in my opinion, is to make education available to all our citizens and not to lower qualitative [sic] standards. . . . I went on record as saying that in some few counties in Alabama, discrimination had taken place, but Negroes meeting Alabama's voting conditions were voting, and their numbers were increasing all the time. . . . [and that the Voting Rights Act] would destroy the constitutional system, and the cure would produce more evils than the illness.[16]

A month later, in February 1964, Wallace accepted a speaking engagement in Minnesota and did not shy away from using a provocative tactic to create an in-group identity for the audience and enhancing feelings of fear about persistent threats. In his remarks, he openly insulted Minnesotans, saying they were "hypocrites" on issues of race and said the people of Alabama "have done as much for the Negro citizen as anybody."[17] Wallace's words were as bold as they were false—but said with conviction over the murmurs of a sprinkling of audience members aghast at the audacity of the claim. His rhetorical successor, Trump, employed a similar trope when sending a Tweet that proclaimed, "My Admin. [sic] has done more for the Black Community [sic] than any President since Abraham Lincoln" and when he told mostly white Trump rally goers, "My administration is delivering for African-Americans like never before. No President has done more for our Black community."[18] At the base of the hypocrisy, Wallace accused northerners of possessing in general—and Minnesotans in particular—was "the Indian problem." Wallace told Cecil Newman, editor of the *Minneapolis Spokesman*, a Black newspaper in the city, "I am referring to Minnesota if you have Indians here on reservations, they aren't treated right."[19] It was a bluntness Wallace counted on getting away with (much like Trump's declarations that "our country is going to hell" or "America is weak and ineffective" or "America doesn't win anymore"[20]) because of what Ryan Skinnell describes as a "hard truths" or fatherly admonitions rhetorical approach that true believers are willing to accept for their own good.[21]

Wallace's forays outside of the South would serve as a preview of his coming plans to make formal his challenge to his party and the nation about what role he (and his fellow southerners) should play in the nation's future. While offering a southern perspective, Wallace sought to expand the boundaries of the "in-group" Americans he said were "put upon" by a fast-moving, ill-conceived civil rights movement that could threaten homes, families, schools, communities, and lives. As he traveled North to Wisconsin, Indiana, and Maryland in the spring of 1964, he carried with him a heavy agenda wrapped in sometimes crude, angry demagoguery mostly unfamiliar in the political discourse of most states.

Wallace's campaign started in Wisconsin, a state similar to Alabama in many ways—with a few large metropolitan areas, a vibrant coastline, and a strong mix of agricultural and manufacturing economic concerns. In 1964, 4.1 million people lived in Wisconsin (as compared to 3.4 million in Alabama), but only two percent of them were African American. In Alabama, almost 30 percent of the state's population was Black in the mid-1960s. These statistics likely appeared enticing to the Wallace campaign, which started its effort in the conservative Fox River Valley region of the state. Wallace arrived with some fanfare at Milwaukee's Mitchell Field on March 16 for campaigning in earnest before a small handful of supporters. He planned to spend the night in Milwaukee meeting supporters before setting off on campaign stops elsewhere. Perhaps expecting a poor welcome for Wallace in Wisconsin, the *Milwaukee Sentinel* reported, "There were no anti-Wallace demonstrators at the airport as the governor and his security and press aides got off the blue and white plane with a Confederate flag painted on it. The plane is owned by the State of Alabama."[22] At the Schroeder Hotel in Milwaukee (where Wallace lodged), campaign workers readied materials to distribute across the state, including photocopies of the civil rights bill, reprints of Wallace's 1963 inaugural speech, and leftover bumper stickers from his 1962 Alabama gubernatorial campaign. *Milwaukee Sentinel* reporter Richard Glaman, given a "behind the scenes look" at the fledgling Wallace campaign, noted, "Wallace will put on a short but intensive and apparently well-organized campaign in Wisconsin. . . . Wallace was obviously encouraged by his reception here and with comments he received from people he met in the hotel."[23] The next day, Wallace started campaigning in earnest in Appleton, close to the Grand Chute, Wisconsin birthplace of the state's infamous former Senator Joseph McCarthy (who had died seven years earlier). Wallace said, "I'm not campaigning against any race of people. I'm here to talk about the domestic issues facing our country and I don't intend to engage in personalities, either."[24] The governor's remark was an early attempt to dislodge claims that he was simply seeking to export his racist ideas outside of the South. Instead, he sought to use the progressive agenda that included civil rights to expand his base of Americans afraid of the threat such major changes could bring. Loading up one of his favorite lines, Wallace said he wanted to remind Wisconsin voters that "a vote for me in Wisconsin will shake the eye teeth of both national political parties and the people in Washington. We must bring an end to this liberalism."[25] In Wallace's world, liberals were procrastinating bumblers, policy nerds who never tired of discussing problems and proposed solutions, while he laid claim to possessing quick, easy-to-consume answers that shut down discussion and disagreement.

In Indiana, Wallace kept alive the threat facing American citizens, saying the pending civil rights bill (proposed, he said, "by a bunch of social engineers in Washington") had far-reaching effects that would "attack the free enterprise system, pose government control over farmers, labor union members, bankers and even fraternities and sororities." It seemed the civil rights bill posed a fearful threat to almost every aspect of American life. Exploitation of fear was a common Wallace technique meant to force his listeners to make choices and avoid compromise. "Wallace turned difference of opinion into differences of principle, principles that are antithetical to one another and admit no compromise, only unrelenting opposition," suggested scholar Lloyd Rohler.[26] At Butler University in Indianapolis, Wallace drew cheers from the students assembled as he made the threat to their own lives perfectly clear: "The government has enough to do without picking out pledges for a fraternity or sorority."[27] At Ball State Teachers College in Muncie, Wallace told students and faculty that the civil rights bill would turn over complete control of Indiana schools to the federal government. He also warned the bill would strip landowners of their rights regarding how to use (or dispose of) their property—and to whom—and as a result, it was a violation of their human rights. Further threats existed, he said, to union and workplace seniority rights that would move minorities ahead of others for promotions in the name of civil rights. Knowing he was in the heart of the Bible Belt and once fertile ground for the Ku Klux Klan, he reminded Indiana audiences that formal prayer had been banned from public schools, as had been reading of the Christian Bible. He even claimed singing all four stanzas of "America the Beautiful" was now illegal in public schools. Particularly pleasing to his Muncie audience, drawing loud applause, was a claim that Washington bureaucrats take money from states such as Indiana and Alabama and "throw it down rat holes."[28]

From Indiana, Wallace took his campaign to the eastern shores of Maryland, a state he surely saw as fertile ground. Wallace approached Maryland in the spring of 1964, correctly calculating that significant support existed for his states' rights pitch to not only slow down, but kill federal civil rights legislation. Wallace's team scheduled an early March news conference to announce his official entry into the Maryland Democratic primary. Given Wallace's showing in both Wisconsin and Indiana, reporters were certain another horse race was likely in Maryland as well.[29] As one of the nation's original thirteen colonies, Maryland's racial history had closely resembled America's history, dating back to when the state approved the US Constitution in 1788. Maryland's racial struggles were well known as it was one of four border states that remained in the Union as the Civil War opened in 1861 but still allowed slavery. The state didn't outlaw slavery until near the end of the Civil War in 1865. The state was also the birthplace of a famous figure in the fight for the freedom of slaves, Harriet Tubman, born into slavery in Dorchester County, Maryland, in 1822. She escaped slavery in 1849 and is credited with helping as many as seven hundred other slaves escape to the North via the "Underground Railroad" supported by sympathetic northern abolitionists.

The seat of Dorchester County is the city of Cambridge, a community that has never grown larger than 12,000 residents. In 1963, Cambridge and other key parts of Maryland had been targeted by in- and out-of-state civil rights leaders calling for change. Segregation remained firmly in place in Cambridge despite efforts by civil rights advocates and Governor J. Millard Tawes, a Democrat, to convince the state's legislature to outlaw segregation in public accommodations and other forms. Among the groups pushing hardest for change was the Cambridge Nonviolent Action Committee (CNAC), which protested restrictions on where Blacks could sit in theaters, what restaurants and other public accommodations they could patronize, what hospitals were open to them, and segregation in public schools. The efforts were met with strong resistance in many communities of Maryland, including Cambridge, where a deadly riot broke out in June 1963. At that time, National Guard troops were ordered to Cambridge by Governor Tawes and remained there for twenty-five days attempting to restore order.

Morris Cunningham, a Washington correspondent, offered a highly favorable assessment of Wallace's chances for Scripps-Howard Newspapers, asserting he was a man "with more of a grasp of the facts and issues" and "a keener understanding of the pending civil rights bill than most members of Congress."[30] Cunningham noted that "people are catching on to the spurious nature of the civil rights bill" and had the intelligence to convince Marylanders. Among the "spurious" aspects of the bill Wallace had begun highlighting was his analysis that it would remove requirements for jury trials and allow federal judges unfettered authority to jail or fine people. Cunningham added that Wallace's campaign answered "the racial question" in a "lofty and sophisticated manner" and noted, "He is reassuring people they can entertain certain beliefs without feeling depraved.[31] As part of his effort to reassure supporters that voting for him could be done with no sense of shame, and no taint of racism, Wallace frequently declared himself a nonracist. "I am not a racist. I am not a bigot and I'm not a hate monger," Wallace told an appreciative Baltimore audience. "We've got as much intelligence as the liberals have. In fact, we've got more, I think."[32]

In his only "debate" during the spring 1964 primaries, Wallace met with Senator Daniel Brewster for a television confab and repeated the threats he said the civil rights bill posed to education, employment, businesses, and property rights. Wallace said the bill would seek to correct "racial imbalance" by "transporting students across one section of the city to another, from one city to other cities of the union." He added the danger of job quotas that could cost white workers their existing jobs.[33] In a speech before supporters in Marlowe Heights, Maryland, Wallace expanded on the threat he believed the civil rights bill posed to workers, asserting that "the bill is so bad that an employer could hardly turn down any man looking for a job for fear he would go to jail."[34]

While the crises and threats Wallace attempted to conjure up for northern whites had gained him a lot of attention—and a troubling percentage of the Democratic primary vote in three states—it had not stopped progress toward passing the Civil Rights Act. It was another loss for Wallace, but a "symbolic" win of a type that Wallace was perfecting in his no-compromise approach—even if it meant he continued to lose the argument. As Michael J. Steudeman noted, it is more important to define "in-group identity"—clearly outlining who belongs in the tribe and who does not—than it is to actually advance any policy initiative. "Any effort to compromise, or acknowledge the shared humanity of the out-group, in turn, seems unreasonable," Steudeman writes.

"The traditional demands of democracy—acknowledging nuance, making sacrifices, living with difference—become threatening."[35]

Wallace played on feelings of powerlessness among voters, citizens who were convinced impactful decisions affecting their lives "were being made by people far distant from them and their experience." As Rohler noted, "A consummate campaigner, Wallace understood the price the social changes of the 1960s exacted on the political system, and he gave voice to those who felt threatened by it."[36]

Wallace's influence on political discourse for 1964, however, was not just a symbolic voice. Before long, conservative leaders who had successfully wrestled away control the Republican Party from "eastern establishment" leaders (such as Governor Nelson Rockefeller) demonstrated it was willing to co-opt the racially charged rhetoric Wallace had refined to promote the "threats" facing the American people. While normally more circumspect in one-on-one interviews and not incumbered by the racial politics of the past that haunted Wallace, the eventual Republican nominee for president in 1964, Senator Barry Goldwater, had moments where he appeared to be speaking from the same blunt text as Wallace. Before a mostly white audience in Warminster, Pennsylvania, a "white-flight" suburb of Philadelphia, Goldwater proclaimed, "Minority groups are running this country today. . . . They are benefitting from government handouts paid for by you." In case the reason for discussing minorities, benefitting from resources they had not paid for (and presumably did not deserve), was not clear, Goldwater expanded the idea to make clear the threat he believed existed:

> What kind of America will we have 20 years from now? What kind of America are we going to leave our children? Under the present [Johnson] administration, you are the forgotten Americans. Ninety-five percent of all Americans come under this classification. He is the one who pays the taxes and stays out of trouble. He is a member of the majority group. But the minority groups are running the country today![37]

While more blunt than other pronunciations on domestic issues, the Goldwater campaign earnestly attempted a "southern strategy" borrowing from the Wallace playbook to try and compete with a popular incumbent president. As one reporter noted, the Goldwater campaign successfully mimicked some aspects of the Alabamian's effort minus "the raw and vulgar 'n----- theme'" employed by Wallace. "The old, ugly and naked prejudices were clothed in the new right-wing semantic styles," noted *Los Angeles Times* writer Mary Reinholz, pointing to speeches by both Goldwater and actor-turned-politician, Ronald Reagan.[38]

Goldwater (and Reagan) successfully "dressed up" the agitating message of Wallace's campaign, fully cleansed it of any open racism, and sought to benefit from the resulting tension. In doing so, the audience is freed, in a sense, to actually own the still small voices in their hearts. As Leo Lowenthal and Norbert Guterman identified as long ago as 1948,

> the agitator appeals to predispositions which are still in flux; his function is to bring the flame the smoldering resentments of his listeners, to express loudly what they whisper timidly, and to lend social sanction to actions that might otherwise seem dangerous temptations. He works, as it were, from inside the audience, stirring up what lies dormant there.[39]

1968: Trying Again

His presidential aspirations fully ignited by his 1964 successes, Wallace undertook his campaign for president in 1968 in a manner that would be different than it was four years earlier. In 1964, he had staged a gadfly challenge to the establishment that had raised noise and some awareness but had done little else. This time, Wallace was determined to be a factor in the race for president and determined to do so outside the established political parties. A violent and troubling spring unfolded in 1968, with the assassinations of the Rev. Dr. Martin Luther King Jr. and Senator Robert F. Kennedy, along with the death of Wallace's wife, Governor Lurleen Wallace. Thankfully, Wallace was spared the need to campaign in spring primaries and eventually could turn his attentions toward the general election contest between himself and a former vice president and a sitting vice president—Richard Nixon and Hubert Humphrey, respectively. In preparation for 1968, Wallace continued his multistate speaking tours throughout 1967. The "prequel" tour was publicly touted as a "testing-the-waters" campaign, but it remained obvious to most that Wallace was running for president in 1968 regardless of any outside factors. Wallace's coyness about whether he would run faded quickly as he embarked on a full-court press in the fall of 1967 to prove something big—that he could gain ballot access in California, the nation's largest state, despite difficult state election laws that made third-party challenges nearly impossible. In order to do so, Wallace hired new media men to "tune up" his image for California voters and eventually a national audience. A campaign film was produced by a Texas film and adman, Norman E. C. Naill, titled *George Wallace & California: The Beginning* with snippets of it eventually used widely in Wallace television advertising throughout 1968. Directed by Jim Guillott (and using the narration of a familiar voice-over artist named Tom Paxton), the film touted Wallace's political appeal beyond Alabama and other southern states. The narrator proclaimed that Wallace's "down-home charm" and "his courage" were the basis of his appeal. The film, though featuring a rough country-and-western cover of the Roger Miller song "Walkin' in the Sunshine," made the case that Wallace was "a southerner who has universal appeal that is not clearly obvious at first glance" and that "he talks in a language that people can understand, and few politicians can match his uncanny ability to grasp the real issues and concerns of *real Americans* in any area. He is truly a man of the people."[40]

The Wallace film—devoid of any references to protestors or agitators who had become a regular feature for his campaign appearances—left out a May 1967 speech at Dartmouth College in Hanover, New Hampshire. That speech drew a lot of national attention to Wallace's return to the presidential political stage given a particularly rowdy crowd present with news reports indicating "Wallace was driven from the stage by the raucous hecklers" and "ran into more trouble outside the auditorium when the hostile group rocked his car, denting the roof and ripping off a radio aerial."[41] Even moments like this were used by Wallace to distinguish good people from bad. That his opponents had acted violently helped tremendously as the governor teed off on them by telling reporters he was not frightened during the altercations. He used their unruly behavior to further distinguish between good political discourse and bad, in other words, good people versus bad people. "That rocking the car business was nothing more than academic freedom," he said, mocking a claim his opponents often made in support of their antagonism to Wallace and his positions. Grinning, he added, "They said they were pacifists who don't believe in violence."[42] Wallace made similar moves to "out-group" his opponents while speaking in Buffalo, New York, before 8,000 supporters (and hecklers) in October 1968. He warned hecklers in his usual way: "You folks better have your day now because after November 5, you're through in this country." Even his warning to them stood as a reminder that "their days were coming to an end" and that "good people" would soon reclaim the political stage. He told his frustrated supporters who struggled to hear over chants of "Go home racist!"—"I know it's very difficult for you to hear because we have 'free speech folks' here who believe in free speech for themselves and not for anyone else."[43]

During the part of his Buffalo speech supporters *could* hear, Wallace told his audience that the American "working man is getting tired of a bunch of theorists telling him where he can send his children to school and of the Supreme Court's destruction of law enforcement."[44] His words were meant to cast doubt upon growing reforms in police agencies across the nation. Wallace, and many conservatives and southerners, remained skeptical and alarmed by a series of police reforms forced via groundbreaking Supreme Court decisions that would forever change law enforcement. Beyond that, many police agencies were beginning to embrace changes in patrolling, suspect handling, and even active recruitment of minority police officers. That these changes intersected with the growing civil rights movement across the nation added to the tension the reforms wrought. As law enforcement scholars Samuel E. Walker and Carol A. Archbold noted, "Two powerful forces engulfed the police in the early 1960s and exposed serious shortcomings of the professionalism movement." The court set in law, for all jurisdictions, basic constitutional standards required for searches and seizures of property and for interrogation of suspects. Further reforms pushed for changes in how police conducted investigative stops while on patrol and use of force. Many of these needed changes were highlighted later in the 1967 report of the President's Crime Commission (a frequent target of Wallace's criticism) and the subsequent 1968 Kerner Commission report, which examined issues related to riots in American cities.[45] Wallace cast the issue in much simpler terms, a classic rhetorical tool that relieved his audience of any thought or nuance to their positions. He told a Buffalo audience that what was needed was "backbone in the mayors and governors who have hampered and handcuffed law enforcement."[46]

The "law and order" focus of the Wallace campaign was getting noticed— even if it remained a veiled front to expressing concerns about racial politics in America without sounding like an open racist and came amidst the often violent and law-breaking demonstration of ugliness of clashes between Wallace supporters and protestors. The *Birmingham News* offered a "writer's analysis" by James Batten of Wallace's preparations for 1968 that suggested, "If there was a dominant theme running through Wallace's northern appearances, it was his decrying of 'crime in the streets'—a phrase now synonymous with Negro rioting and the generally high crime rate among Negroes."[47] Wallace used phrases such as "the breakdown of law and order" and proclaimed it "the gravest domestic problem confronting our nation." He said he would ask Congress to write legislation that would confront recent Supreme Court rulings—such as the landmark 1966 Miranda case regarding the rights of the accused. Such Supreme Court rulings, Wallace said, had "made it almost impossible for police to deal with criminals.[48] Wallace said the "moral support" of the presidency would "tend to prevent crime in the streets." He challenged his opponents who said they support law and order to be specific. He said,

There's not a dime's worth of difference between the Democrats and the Republicans. I'm tired of this silly kind of talk that they stand for constitutional government. They are going to have to be specific. They're going to have to say that they will put law violators where they belong. They're going to have to say they will return control of the schools and the hospitals and the labor unions and other domestic institutions to the people.[49]

Another threat frequently identified by Wallace (one that would remain a standard arrow in his quiver of epigrams used on the stump) was gun control. He warned a Dallas audience that only he stood between them and onerous laws that would take away personal gun ownership. "If you ever had a national gun control law that took away your guns, you would find that every law-abiding citizen in Dallas would not have a gun and every thug would have 10."[50]

Bruce Biossat, a national columnist based in Washington, DC, for the Newspaper Enterprise Association, offered a careful analysis of the threats Wallace promoted to his audiences. Biossat believed that Wallace's audiences didn't truly believe all of the wild claims he sometimes made—such as "dragging people about the hair, cuffing them around or slapping them into jail by the thousands" but found a strange solace in his brutish macho act. "In this time of incredible tension and turmoil, millions of Americans resistant to radical change, terrified by riot and crime and disgusted with protestors' violence on street and campus, find immense emotional release in Wallace's uncurbed language of retaliatory action. . . . Wallace has found a deep chord of response, a way of strumming hard on assorted discontents."[51] It was a similar inner need Donald Trump would seek to fill in later decades, perhaps best captured in his "trademark" line "You're fired!" from his canceled NBC reality show, *The Apprentice.*

The *Los Angeles Times* offered USC journalism major Pat De Graw a prime location on its editorial page as Wallace prepared to launch his 1968 effort. In it, De Graw analyzed the threat Wallace constructed for his supporters. De Graw had followed Wallace throughout the state and said he found many Californians feeling like "the country, it seems, is going down the drain" and Wallace casting himself as "the plug." He observed Wallace was happy to set himself as "the advocate of the man of the streets" who "knows his people" and "knows they are scared."[52] Likewise, Tom Wicker, a *New York Times* columnist, also followed Wallace around California and noted the candidate had

a gift that he can touch his shabby cause with a peculiar moral gloss. With unerring instinct, he can arouse latent racial antagonism while appealing to common sense and Christian duty; with vivid oratory he laments the vanquished righteousness of another day and paints every discontent and complexity of contemporary life in terms of a "pseudo-intellectual" plot against "the average man." His message is powerful medicine in the dry, drab small towns of Southern California, with their Okie heritage, their hard-working, God-fearing ethic, and their large numbers of old folks and southern migrants.[53]

It wasn't only Wallace who attempted to create threats to attract voters—the Republican nominee, Richard Nixon, succinctly summarized the same kinds of concern in his acceptance speech at the GOP's national convention in August. The speech, likely written by Nixon confidant Ray K. Price Jr., encapsulated cleanly the concerns of many Americans in a way Wallace had not, without the shadow of racism over his shoulder. Nixon had always been a conventional politician, dedicated and loyal to his party and its candidates, and a shrewd competitor who surrounded himself with conservative ideologues. Nixon told the nation:

> Let us look at America . . . we see cities enveloped in smoke and flame. We hear sirens in the night. We see Americans dying on distant battlefields abroad. We see Americans hurting each other; fighting each other; killing each other at home. And as we see and hear these things millions of Americans cry out in anguish. Did we come all this way for this?[54]

Nixon advanced the threat argument much further than Wallace ever did, inviting Americans to listen to "the voice of the great majority of Americans, the forgotten Americans—the non-shouters, the non-demonstrators." He emphasized, "To those who say that law and order is the code word for racism, there is a reply: Our goal is justice for every American." He assured Americans filled with the fears and doubt he articulated that they were

> not racists or sick; they are not guilty of the crime that plagues the land. They are the Black and the white, they're native born and foreign born, they're the young and the old. They work in America's factories. They run America's businesses. They serve in government. They provide most of the soldiers who died to keep us free. They give drive to the spirit of America.[55]

No better statement of "in-group" identity existed in 1968—Nixon successfully co-opting what Wallace had earnestly tried to do, but had failed to do. It was Nixon, not Wallace, who turned the corner from just articulating the concerns about "unprecedented lawlessness" and "unprecedented racial violence" and told the American people: "It's time for new leadership for the United States"—leadership for "the great group of Americans, the forgotten Americans"—promising "the long dark night for America is about to end." Unlike Wallace's, Nixon's words held out the idea of hope rather than just an accounting of the nation's wrongs.[56]

The third man in the race in 1968, Vice President Hubert Humphrey, reflected years later about the impact Wallace's demagoguery had had on his campaign.

Humphrey was affronted by the open efforts Wallace made to create visceral threats to concerned Americans. Humphrey described Wallace as

> a canny and shrewd politician who captured the vote of those whose fears and hates and alienation he had articulated.... [A] southern governor demagogued his way into the hearts and minds of those who wanted simplistic answers to difficult problems, justifiably concerned about violence and crime in the streets, and with less reason about job and neighborhood exclusivity.[57]

Humphrey said Wallace's "in-group" message appealed to lower- and middle-income Americans, factory workers, rural citizens, and first- and second-generation Americans who "felt resentful and threatened in virtually every aspect of their lives. In their view, their sons fought in Vietnam while 'hippie, long-haired kids' of the seemingly well-to-do demonstrated and cursed and smoked marijuana."[58]

1972: Necessary Updates

His impressive—but losing—effort of 1968 behind him, Wallace undertook a noticeable set of personal and professional upgrades for himself and his campaign as the 1972 presidential campaign approached. The agenda for Wallace was, however, centrally about one issue: busing. Unspoken but understood was the reality that busing was simply a straw-horse front for lingering worries about race. Wallace was a master of talking about race without saying the word "race" or any related terms. Rohler confirmed Wallace "carefully avoided the use of racial epithets in his political speaking, relying instead on code words to convey his meaning."[59]

Beyond avoiding the problematic racially charged rhetoric of the past, the Wallace campaign demonstrated a growing sophistication for the 1972 campaign, issuing policy or "white papers" on a variety of issues, including education, crime, foreign aid, the war in Vietnam, and economic issues—but the focus always returned to Wallace's call to end busing designed to desegregate the nation's schools—what he called "forced busing."[60] Wallace had correctly calculated that the issue of busing children from their neighborhood school to other schools across town in order to achieve racial balance was very unpopular. School corporations across the South and the North had moved aggressively to comply with federal court edicts that required desegregation of schools and an end to two "dual systems" of schools common (mostly in the South) where Black and white schools co-existed in a remnant of the "separate but equal" system that dominated for many decades. Busing was a ready-made issue for Wallace to exploit to his supporters and those he hoped to attract because it was highly relatable for all families. Wallace also calculated correctly that busing was unpopular not only among white parents but among many Black parents as well. Underscoring the irritation busing caused to both white and Black families allowed Wallace to step away from lingering racial overtones and gave his supporters "cover" that their opposition to busing was based on the best interest of students and nothing else. It was an old tactic, one scholars Leo Lowenthal and Norbert Guterman discussed as long ago as 1948, accusing political figures (such as Wallace) of engaging in "a psychological racket" that "plays on vague fears or expectations of a radical change." The goal is to "exploit existing discontent" and appeal to the built-in emotions change brings, such as distrust, dependence, exclusion, anxiety, and disillusionment.[61]

Veteran journalist and columnist Claude Sitton wrote at length about Wallace's fixation with busing for the 1972 campaign. He acknowledged the electoral success Wallace was finding in promoting the issue—especially with an impressive win in the Florida Democratic primary—but he also took note of the nuances in place: "The times and apparently Wallace have changed. Advocacy of school segregation as such is no longer fashionable, even in Alabama. So the governor's views have gone mod along with the length of his hair and the cut of his suits."[62]

Wallace's so-called plan to "end forced busing" was for the federal government to abandon its role and put the burden back on local school corporations to find ways to desegregate their schools—with Wallace asserting that he had "accepted non-discrimination" in the schools. Sitton noted, however, that Wallace's "busing plan" was little more than a slogan that would do little to relieve the burden on state and local officials attempting to address federal desegregation mandates.[63] It was a style-over-substance approach that Donald Trump would repeat more than four decades later by decrying issues as diverse as immigration, trade, and infrastructure but ultimately offering little specific policies to make a difference. The real issue was never busing for Wallace, or immigration or trade deals for Trump, but rather opposition to the authority of government.

For 1972, however, analysts wondered aloud whether Wallace could finally find electoral success in expanding the threat of busing by actually embracing the concerns of even Black families about busing children and thus ironically helping him expand his base with voters who previously had been repelled by the Alabamian. He was counting on that as he changed the threat—or at least the description of it—from an argument against putting Black and white children together in the same classroom to one of expressing concern for the wisdom of transporting so many children for so many miles. A typical take: "We should stop busing our little children and artificially polarizing people." To add incentive, Wallace said if he were to win the Democratic nomination, "President Nixon, within 30 to 60 days after the primary campaign is over, is going to end busing himself." He said he was counting on voters responding to his message to demand the federal government to "leave us alone" and stop trying to "take away control of a man's children from him."[64]

On the morning of the critical Florida primary, Wallace appeared on *The Today Show* and told NBC's Frank McGee that Florida voters would give him a big win and attributed his success to the busing issue and his willingness to speak directly about changing the process: "I have resisted for a longtime the takeover of the public school system by the federal government. I predicted that chaos would result, and it has resulted all the way from Michigan to Florida." Distinguishing his current effort from his previous "stand in the schoolhouse door" that had launched him onto the national stage, he clarified that he favored changing existing law: "Busing of our little school children is not the law. . . . I believe the vote in Florida is going to impress the politicians in Washington that the trafficking of the health and safety of both Black and white children in this matter is asinine and foolish," Wallace said.[65] He emphasized that the Supreme Court had not ordered busing to achieve racial balance in schools, only that dual or separate-but-allegedly-equal school systems had to go. "Schools are now open to anyone regardless of who they happen to be," Wallace said, implying that busing to achieve racial parity was unnecessary. He repeated his prediction that President Nixon would change his position on busing, asserting "a vast cross-section of the American citizenry, will show their displeasure and indignation, both Black and white."[66]

One person not convinced that Wallace's new take on busing—minus talk of racial issues—was George Lardner Jr. of the *Washington Post*. He wrote that "underneath the cosmetics, George Corley Wallace has changed very little."[67] Lardner said Wallace's trump card of busing that was hurting "the parents who own the chillun," was combined with a focused attack on the record of each of his DC-based Democratic opponents:

> Every single senator in this race voted against freedom of choice. I want to tell Floridians, black and white, rich and poor, that I am for quality education for every child, regardless of who they happen to be. But this senseless business of trifling with the health and safety of your child, regardless of his color, by busing him across state lines, and city lines, and county lines—into kingdom come—has got to go.[68]

On *The Today Show*, Wallace ended with a classic "in-group" assessment that "the mass of the American people feel that they have been deprived. The middle income average citizen is paid no attention as to his aspirations until tax-paying time. They have paid attention to the *exotic*, and as a consequence the middle class is ground into the dirt."[69] Wallace's use of the word "exotic" squarely connected with parents across the nation who feared they were powerless against court rulings that required integrated schools and busing. It was precisely the word Wallace needed to advance the idea that he was the man who would stand against an increasingly progressive Washington agenda that threatened the choices and lives of "real Americans." It was a message he'd used before and one he had nuanced and practiced to perfection. In these moments, Wallace can be seen as successfully transcending his roots in the crumbling segregationist movement to become what Lowndes described as "the more general 'Middle American'—the white middle-class male from every region who is pushed around by an invasive federal government, threatened by crime and social disorder, discriminated against by affirmative action, and surrounded by increasing moral degradation."[70] It worked well, with Wallace rolling up impressive primary wins in Florida, Tennessee, North Carolina, Maryland, and Michigan and respectable top tier finishes in Wisconsin, Indiana, Pennsylvania, Oregon, and New Mexico. A similar transcendence would work equally well for Donald Trump as he pushed opposition to foreign trade and immigration to escape his position of wealth and privilege to become the self-appointed voice and advocate of average, working Americans.

As Wallace predicted, the White House position on busing did shift slightly in the aftermath of his incredible showing in the Florida Democratic presidential primary. Sweeping a full field of progressive and establishment Democrats with 42 percent of the vote and winning every county, speculation began to turn to whether Wallace could pose a real challenge to Nixon from the right. Two days after Wallace's Florida win, Nixon addressed the nation "about one of the most difficult issues of our time—the issue of busing. Across this nation . . . states, cities and local school districts have been torn apart in the debate over this issue." Nixon said his opposition to busing "for the purpose of achieving racial balance in our schools" was well known:

> I have spoken out against busing scores of times over many years. But what we now need is not just speaking out against more busing. We need action to stop it. Above all, we need to stop it in the right way—in a way that would provide better education for every child in America in a desegregated school. The reason action is so urgent is because of a number of recent decisions of the lower federal courts. These courts have gone too far—in some cases beyond the requirements laid down by the Supreme Court—in ordering massive busing to achieve racial balance.[71]

Nixon said the nation faced the difficult question of "How can we end segregation in a way that does not result in more busing?" He noted "the purpose of such busing is to help end segregation, but experience in case after case has shown that busing is a bad means to a good end." He also called out those who said anyone opposing busing was "anti-Black"—such claims were "dangerous nonsense," Nixon said. The president proposed legislation "that would call an immediate halt to all new busing orders by federal courts—a moratorium on new busing." In addition, he was proposing a $2.5 billion "Equal Education Opportunities Act" that would increase federal school aid to assist school districts struggling to serve all students—regardless of race—equally. Nixon said his plan would "stop more busing" until a "guarantee" was in place that "the children currently attending the poorest schools in our cities and in rural areas be provided with education equal to that of good schools in their communities."[72] His attempt to change the subject of the debate from desegregation to uniformity of quality in public schools went nowhere. The Democratically controlled Congress ultimately took no action on Nixon's proposal, but one of his top aides, Patrick J. Buchanan, believed the speech and the proposal had been a political masterstroke. Buchanan noted that Nixon had successfully co-opted the busing issue away from the Alabamian (just as he had the "law and order" issue in 1968). "He had done what he set out to do—separate himself from George Wallace on desegregation, and separate himself from every liberal Democratic rival in opposing busing for racial balance," Buchanan wrote.[73]

While Wallace's rhetoric apparently had moved minds in the Nixon White House, he complained widely that his Democratic primary opponents were more than happy to steal his entire agenda. In Indiana, he told Democratic voters, "I was in your state in 1964 and again in 1968. Everything you and I said in 1968, they are saying now . . . taxes, welfare and other issues that plague the people of Indiana." He said it was ironic that his opponents had collectively served in Congress for 109 years, "and yet they've never offered the solutions I'm offering you until election year.[74]

1976: Counting Wallace Out

As Wallace's 1972 campaign drew to a tragic end—and far short of the Democratic nomination—most observers presumed Wallace's spot on the national political stage was ended. One of those who made such assumptions was the Democrats' 1972 vice presidential nominee (and a member of the Kennedy clan), Sargent Shriver. As speculation swirled about whether Wallace would make a fourth try for the presidency and enter the 1976 Democratic preferential primaries—30 of them in all—Shriver included Montgomery, Alabama, on his roster of cities as he tested the waters for his own possible run for president in 1976. While on Wallace's turf, Shriver told reporters the governor was "a brilliant politician" who can "successfully express the feelings of people who are unfairly treated" but was a man who offered few solutions. "He has not proposed anything to deal with the problems he talks about," Shriver said, capsulizing the phenomena that Wallace was effective at creating threats or concerns for his supporters, but "he brings people apart."[75] Shriver identified perfectly Wallace's demagogic rhetorical function in American politics to date wherein he created "in" and "out" groups in the nation for political gain, all while signaling that "establishment Democrats" were dismissing Wallace once again.

By 1976, one of the most painful issues "pulling Americans apart" was the now-ended war in Vietnam, culminating with the humiliating fall of Saigon to North Vietnamese communist forces in April 1975. *Washington Post* political columnist David S. Broder sought Wallace's view on the matter, despite describing him as "a politician who has built a career on the exploitation of divisive issues," and accused him of "fastening on to the tragedy unfolding in Indochina as his latest weapon." Regardless, Broder acknowledged that Wallace seemed tapped into the frustration of many Americans about the situation in Vietnam:

> There is going to be a great revulsion in this country against our going in there and not winning that war. The people of this country are going to remember the politicians who were intimidated by the loud noisemakers in the streets. This is an emotional thing. The people can't stomach a government that wasted all that money and all those lives for no purpose. They supported their government, because they're patriotic Americans, but if we weren't going to win it, we should never have gone in.[76]

It was a peculiar (if not insincere) position for the governor to take—given his broadly stated and vague positions on the Vietnam War while it was being fought. Wallace continually pledged that if he were president, he would follow what the Joint Chiefs of Staff would recommend in Vietnam, transferring the president's power to military advisers. There was ample evidence that both President Johnson and Nixon had done likewise on other occasions in attempting to prop up democracy in Southeast Asia but ultimately had failed to craft a sustainable democratic government in South Vietnam despite hundreds of millions of American dollars and more than 58,000 American lives. For Wallace, it was a predictable—if not nuanced—take on the war, blaming antiwar protestors and feckless Washington pols for the failure rather than forming any detailed or researched position on the conflict or acknowledgment of the commitment and strength of communist North Vietnamese forces who sought to form a united Vietnam. Regardless of the distinctions in the Wallace argument on Vietnam, bombast was still a part of the equation. sounding a lot like his 1968 running mate, General Curtis "Bombs-Away" Lemay, in the aftermath of the failure in Vietnam, Wallace was now declaring, "We ought to have bombed them out of existence up in North Vietnam. People say that would be barbaric, but if we had done it when some of us first said it, if wouldn't have cost one-tenth of the lives that have been lost, and we would have won. We should have bombed them into submission."[77]

While the morass in Vietnam was fresh on the minds of voters, it may not have worked as an issue to create a threat to in-group voters. Rhetoric about "what should have happened" in Vietnam likely fell flat for many Americans, most ready to lament the outcome but equally ready to move on from the ubiquitous conflict of the Vietnam era. As a result, Wallace shifted to other issues as it became obvious he planned to try again in 1976. He shared concerns about a new set of emerging threats to "real Americans," such as gun control and loosening of the death penalty in many states. A 1972 US Supreme Court ruling had nullified the death penalty as it was currently being administered, noting it violated Eighth Amendment protections against cruel and unusual punishment because it was inconsistently applied across the states utilizing capital punishment under state law. In the years that followed, thirty-seven US states enacted new death-penalty statutes that were later upheld. His death-penalty and law-and-order rhetoric echoed some of what he had used in 1968 but seemed now in conflict with how the issues were discussed. *New York Times* columnist Tom Wicker took up Wallace's opening salvos for 1976 and said the Alabamian had "lapsed back into his true gutter style" and had firmly "cast off the respectable robes" placed upon him by fellow politicians and the media following his 1972 campaign. Wicker took issue with Wallace's characterization of federal judges as "thugs" who sought "to create a hotel atmosphere" in Alabama's prisons by coddling criminals. Wallace said judges continued to ignore crime victims while "asking common citizens to foot the bill to make the criminal comfortable."[78]

While law-and-order issues—and cracking down on alleged welfare cheats—remained regular features, issues such as inflation and rising energy prices pressed in on the Wallace campaign. His response was to talk about Washington bureaucrats and rising taxes as the sources of the problem. There is scant record Wallace ever discussed at length any plan to address inflationary consumer prices or energy supply issues that were driving up gasoline prices for everyday Americans. He did, however remember to remind a Norwood, Massachusetts, audience in suburban Boston that they were part of the "downtrodden ordinary people" and added:

You who work and pay the taxes, you're the king and queen of American politics in this country. You have an opportunity to realign the political thinking of this country—of getting people back to work, getting the inflation matter solved, think about the regressive taxes that I'm paying and also quit this social experimentation on my children and my neighborhood.[79]

Referring to Washington bureaucrats as "parasites," Wallace asked, "What has the government done? They have ignored unemployment, inflation and recession." He said the nation's sagging economy was the top threat facing small businessmen, farmers, police officers and firefighters, auto workers, carpenters, beauticians, taxicab drivers—"the broad middle class," as he put it.[80] To Wallace, it was clear "the country's gone mad" and that too many Americans wanted the "government to solve everything" and that "we need to get away from getting something for nothing and back to old-fashioned morality" via a "spiritual revival" in the country. It was standard Wallace rhetoric, long on describing the concerns and short on specific answers. It also contained remnants of Wallace's past rhetorical devices, tough talk that he thought America needed to hear, all while reminding them they were a part of "an old-fashioned morality" that would likely respond positively to the idea of a "spiritual revival" in America.[81]

Wallace's entire pitch for the early Massachusetts Democratic primary in the spring of 1976 was crass and cynical. Before an audience at the Lithuanian Club in South Boston—an area of concentration for angry voters who wanted to put a stop to school desegregation and related busing orders, Wallace declared, "I'm your friend. I'm your friend now just as I was 14 years ago . . . I've been on your side long before you needed anybody to be on your side."[82] Joined on stage by Boston City Councilman Albert "Dapper" O'Neil and School Commissioner Pixie Palladino, two local leaders of the anti-busing efforts, Wallace said: "The government of the United States ought to put its mind to putting people back to work and controlling inflation and leave all this social experimentation alone." "Social experimentation" had become Wallace's 1976 code words for race and busing.[83] While the busing issue provided a ready pool of voters for Wallace, city and state leaders in Boston and throughout Massachusetts were attempting to deal directly with the issues at hand from a public policy perspective and promote a peaceful transition to fully integrated schools. Governor Michael Dukakis and Boston Mayor Kevin White were proactive, attempting to stage peaceful marches in support of local schools and parents—marches overshadowed by antibusing forces "who were almost exclusively white, carrying George Wallace signs," the AP reported.[84] Dukakis recalled,

We knew that Governor Wallace was trying to exploit the busing issue in many places, and of course that was so in Boston. In Massachusetts and Boston you had an awful lot of opposition to the school desegregation issue.... [T]he Boston of that time, the Boston that I grew up in, was racist, it was anti-Semitic . . . the city was really racially and religiously divided. The neighborhoods were segregated by race, but beyond that there were historic divisions between the Irish and Italians and so it could be rather tense politically. It really should be no surprise that there was a significant percentage of voters who liked Wallace.[85]

It was not a surprise to find Wallace searching for votes in the ethnic enclaves of Boston and its suburbs—he had successfully done so previously with white voters in Wisconsin and Indiana—but there were signs the Wallace appeal of earlier presidential political cycles was beginning to wane. Despite the "red meat" rhetoric offered at the Lithuanian Club in South Boston, only five hundred potential voters showed up to hear Wallace. Regardless, the Wallace camp thought the busing issue that had terrorized many Massachusetts communities could mean votes were up for grabs. As expected, heavy campaign spending emerged in Florida, a state Wallace won four years earlier. Florida television, radio, and newspaper advertisements were flooded with messages that echoed his successful 1972 effort, asserting, "Only George Wallace stands with the people of Florida on the 18 most important issues" in the state. TV advertisements showed school buses in heavy traffic and suggested to viewers, "Follow as your children are bussed all across town." The Wallace ads portrayed the issue as "forced busing" and quoted Wallace's pledge to Florida voters:

I support a constitutional amendment to outlaw forced busing. There is only one answer to forced busing. Stop it and stop it now. We must return to local control of schools without discrimination of any type and with freedom of choice. The social schemers who dreamed up forced busing admit it's a failure and 80 percent of our people oppose it. We should end it and never again tamper with our children's lives in such a ridiculous social scheme.[86]

Wallace had reason to work hard in Florida—two other candidates—former Georgia governor Jimmy Carter and US Senator Henry "Scoop" Jackson of Washington were making a concerted run in the state, both candidates with pedigrees that put them right of the ideological center of the Democratic Party. Carter was a particular threat, Wallace forces recognized, given that he represented what many viewed as "the New South"—a progressive southerner who wanted to move his state and region beyond the racially charged politics that had lingered for so long. Florida voters were seemingly on board with such ideas in their own right, twice electing governor Reubin Askew, a Democratic progressive who had also left racial politics in the past. Carter prevailed in Florida, many noting that the enthusiasm and energy of the Wallace campaigns of the past seemed to be missing.

The Wallace campaign limped forward to Illinois, a state where Wallace had spent little time since the fall of 1968. Speaking before 1,200 people at John A. Logan College in Carterville, Illinois, Wallace expressed his frustration with "the social experimenting" of Washington bureaucrats and called for welfare reform. "It's time we put the welfare rip-off artists off the pocketbooks of this state and the rest of this country."[87] In Rockford, during his remarks to a gathering of about five hundred people, reporters noted Wallace drew a mixture of cheers and boos from the crowd.[88] As *Decatur Daily Review* reporter Bob Sampson noted, for 1976 there were no longer loud and rowdy Wallace rallies, with the expected "foot-stomping, screaming frenzied audience" missing, replaced by polite applause "but no loud cheering or outbursts despite Wallace's efforts. . . . [T]he crowd didn't heat up."[89]

Again, Carter prevailed in Illinois as party insiders began to wonder if there was any way to stop this new "outsider" from the South, one with a lot more appeal and energy than Wallace could muster. Most believed Wallace's campaign was officially ended two weeks later as Carter scored an impressive win in North Carolina—a political "fire wall" the Wallace camp had counted on to get back into the race. Regardless, Wallace campaigned on, showing up in Wisconsin for its early April primary. For his Milwaukee opening, Wallace seemed to delight that the very first question asked of him by a reporter was about a final federal court order forcing Milwaukee's public schools to be fully desegregated. Wallace smiled and showed "mocked surprise" when he said, "I didn't know you had segregation in Milwaukee? Twelve years ago I was told that we had it [in Alabama] and you didn't. You had integration and we had segregation. I'm shocked and surprised."[90] Showing some of the bitterness of repeated losses to his fellow southerner, Wallace said voters should remember that Carter had been in Milwaukee days earlier touting a "voluntary school busing plan" he had developed to integrate schools in Atlanta. Wallace took issue with such plans, but not based on racial concerns, he said, but by decrying there was already "too much regulation on the lives of people."[91] Wallace appeared, once again, to be trying to soften his earlier stands on school desegregation by noting that he was not opposed to integration, but he objected to federal courts pressing the issue and "working out artificial methods, bringing about something through quotas and percentages, to destroy neighborhood schools by forced busing."[92] It appeared Wisconsin voters weren't listening, with Wallace gathering up an anemic 12 percent of the vote on primary day, finishing a distant third behind US Representative Morris K. Udall of Arizona and Carter.

A swirl of questions continued about why the Wallace campaign pressed on—mixed in with troubling reports that the candidate's health appeared to be failing him. Regardless, Wallace went to Indiana for its May 4 primary, where all eyes were on the Republican race heating up between President Gerald R. Ford and his determined challenger, former California governor Ronald Reagan. *The Economist* analyzed that the key to Reagan's success in Indiana

> was to tie up drifting Wallace voters set loose by the collapse of their former hero. Taking aim at his frustrated group searching for a new candidate to voice their angry concerns is proving an electoral master-stroke for Reagan's strategists. They are able to exploit the defection from Wallace in Indiana because the state's primary rules permit "crossover" voting. . . . In southern Indiana, Reagan scores well not only with Wallace Democrats, but with conservative Republicans who responded to his twin message that the federal government is far too big and spends far too little on defense.[93]

Author and journalist Garry Wills analyzed the inroads Reagan was making with Wallace voters in Indiana and elsewhere:

> Reagan's deepest appeal is to those who cheered George Wallace on but who felt a bit shabby and soiled after he worked them over, massaged their hate glands, made them queasy with the acrid emotions he sweated out of them. Reagan croons, in love accents, his permission to indulge in a functional hatred of poor people and blacks. Nothing personal about it. It is really an act of patriotism not to let the hard-working middle class be dragged down to *their* level.[94]

Reagan was going "all out" in Indiana, traveling the state with legendary actor Jimmy Stewart at his side and keeping the incumbent Ford on the defensive. Reagan's rhetoric in Indiana was a page torn directly from the Wallace playbook—a speech at Anderson being typical with Reagan arguing for a strong national military, opposition to gun control legislation pending in Congress, and clamping down on welfare cheats. Sounding a lot like a line George Wallace would offer, Reagan told Madison County Republicans: "If Joe Doaks is using his welfare money to go down to the pool hall and drink beer and gamble, and the people on his block are paying the bill directly, Joe is going to undergo a change in his lifestyle, or get off welfare."[95]

In a last-ditch effort to bring his Indiana voters back home, Wallace made an impassioned plea to a smaller-than-expected audience at Terre Haute, once the site of fiery Wallace speeches and rallies, urging Democratic voters to pick a proven conservative, such as himself, to an unknown outsider such as Carter. "The Democratic Party learned a good lesson in 1972 when they ignored Middle America and went to the exotic far left and lost," he said.[96] Wallace's appeals fell flat, however, as Carter rolled away with 68 percent of the Indiana vote, Wallace a distant second at 15 percent.

As rhetorical scholar Patricia Roberts-Miller has noted, successful demagogues possess likeable, charismatic qualities that draw in voters. "If condemnation of out-group behavior is performed by a very likeable person, then onlookers are likely to conclude that the rhetor would never engage in the behavior he or she is condemning," she wrote. Her suggestion that audiences want to focus on a "likeable" or "charismatic" leader could help in understanding why the bottom fell out from under Wallace in 1976. His rhetoric was essentially the same, and he *had* worked his way from being a fringe candidate and softened his edges, but he was also trying to do so as the first presidential candidate in American history appearing before voters in a wheelchair. President Franklin D. Roosevelt had not done so—with ready cooperation from the media—but those days were gone. Beyond Wallace's worn appearance (that left many wondering if he was physically able to meet the demands of the presidency), his rhetoric had not turned the page to hopefulness. Just as Richard Nixon had done with his 1968 RNC acceptance speech, Carter (and to an even greater extent Ronald Reagan) espoused his ideas with a smile and a cheerful confidence that drew in audiences. Carter and Reagan also did not carry with them the baggage of past racial battles—both having successfully navigated the governorships of their two states (Georgia and California) without the ugly bruises Wallace had inflicted upon himself.

Beyond the "charismatic" aspects lacking in the Wallace campaign, Carter, Reagan, and many others moved beyond the familiar demagogic territory Wallace still promoted. Wallace still carried the look and sound of a demagogue who rarely offered detailed problem-solving ideas (represented well in his repeated suggestion that the way to deal with protestors was to run his car over them). But had Wallace's followers, who had become well-trained in accepting the idea that "we need someone who is authentically one of us, who is passionately loyal to us" begun to see Wallace as used goods, and a candidate who couldn't win?[97] Joshua Gunn outlines how successful demagogues engage in rhetorical flourishes that convince audiences that they can bring order to chaos "by representing strength, resolve, and absolute autonomy." But had the assassination attempt on Wallace's life, his chronic pain, and bitter personal outlook rendered him ineffective at convincing audiences of his "invincibility and autonomy"? He continued to articulate problems well, but sans any explicit details and seemingly lacking any vigor to tackle the issues, his anemic approach was, sadly, as one writer noted, as powerless as his legs.[98] A key aspect of his effort had been to set himself—and his supporters—up as deprived, disadvantaged, and unappreciated combatants against a powerful establishment geared to accommodate the needs of exotic, unusual, different, alien, and—most important—"other" Americans.

CHAPTER 2

Politics of Establishment Antipathy

A key aspect needed for the success of demagoguery as a political tool is not only the establishment of in-group and out-group identities but also for a challenge or foe to be presented (or created) for men like Wallace to exploit. Wallace well-defined who was in and who was out of the "good" Americans group and the threat the out-group presented, but another key aspect was creating a fierce antipathy of the establishment—all levels of government, the media, education—basically all established elements of society (sans the police or the military). As Patricia Roberts-Miller offers, Wallace's followers were akin to many who fall under the influence of a demagogue—followers who think their leader is "honest [even if sometimes mistaken] well-intentioned, and authentic." Opposing forces are often found to be "lying, malevolent, and manipulative." Wallace understood (or learned) what would be required following his failed 1958 gubernatorial campaign (where he assessed he had been "out-n-----ed" by his opponent). He fit Roberts-Miller's idea that "the underlying narrative is that our political culture has been damaged" by other demagogues who have led people—sometimes referred to as "sheeple"—astray.[1]

From the moment of his 1963 inauguration and his declaration of a "gauntlet" having been thrown down "at the feet of tyranny," Wallace made clear his entire political identity and call was wrapped up in the distinctiveness of small, good Alabamians (and eventually all Americans) unified against powerful, malignant establishment forces. Decades later, Donald Trump was equally open about his wish to be viewed as *the* force to take on the establishment, clarifying that "I'm an outsider. I am a person that used to be establishment when I'd give them hundreds of thousands of dollars. But when I decided to run [for president], I became very anti-establishment because I understand the system better than anybody else."[2]

In the warmup to the 1964 presidential election—eventually carried out in the shadow of the assassination of a president—35 states conducted gubernatorial elections in 1962, but it was clearly Alabama's new governor, George Corley Wallace, who stole the show among that year's class of leaders. As Trump would masterfully do four decades later, Wallace remained adept at keeping the focus on himself even outside of active presidential election cycles. For 1962, while re-elected governors in California (Pat Brown), New York (Nelson Rockefeller), and Oregon (Mark Hatfield) and newly installed governors in Michigan (George Romney), Pennsylvania (William Scranton), and Texas (John Connally) were all better-known "political commodities" than Wallace, it was Wallace who stole the gubernatorial inauguration headlines in January 1963. His "segregation forever" rhetoric stood out among the gentlemanly crowd of governors in America and served notice in Alabama, and far beyond its borders, that Wallace was a coming force to be dealt with.

Just six months into his term as governor, on June 11, 1963, Wallace again grabbed national headlines by attempting to block two African American students (Vivian Malone and James Hood) from enrolling at the University of Alabama. Wallace placed himself in the doorway of a building on the Tuscaloosa campus in an "act of defiance" against a federal court order to desegregate the school. There he intoned that the court's order was "the unwelcomed, unwanted, unwarranted and force-induced intrusion" upon the university and people of Alabama and represented a "frightful example of the oppression of the rights, privileges and sovereignty of this state by officers of the federal government."[3] The battle to keep Black students out of Alabama's universities was quickly lost—President John F. Kennedy signing an order taking over control of the Alabama National Guard in order to enforce the court's order and Wallace stepping aside in defeat. He later claimed a symbolic win, a tool he would use often where he repeatedly claimed victory in situations where most other observers saw loss.

The red-hot, almost martyr-like rhetoric of Wallace was connecting in Alabama and across the South and soon would compel tragic consequences—culminating in an appalling incident on Sunday, September 15, 1963, when a bomb went off at the Sixteenth Street Baptist Church in Birmingham. Killed were four little Black girls in a Sunday school class, and twenty-two other parishioners were injured, many seriously. The Rev. Martin Luther King Jr. responded angrily to the disgusting attack, confronting Wallace directly in a public telegram that declared, "The blood of four little children and others critically injured is on your hands. Your irresponsible and misguided actions have created in Birmingham and Alabama the atmosphere that has induced continued violence and now murder." King proclaimed the bombing "a crime against humanity" and said, "Governor Wallace is largely responsible for these vicious murders."[4] Wallace responded by denouncing the violence and pledging, "We are going to protect the lives and safety of all our people, both white and colored." He said the bombing was "a tragic event which has saddened all Alabamians" and that "the perpetrators of this vicious crime must be brought to justice. I serve notice on those responsible that every law enforcement agency of this state will be used to apprehend them."[5] President Kennedy stopped short of direct blame on Wallace and other segregationist leaders but told the nation:

> It is regrettable that public disparagement of law and order has encouraged violence which has fallen on the innocent. If these cruel and tragic events can only awaken that city and state—if they can only awaken this entire nation— to a realization of the folly of racial injustice and hatred and violence, then it is not too late for all concerned to unite in steps toward peaceful progress before more lives are lost.[6]

Publicly, Wallace said the primary issue at hand had always been states' rights, the right of Alabama (and any other state) to decide to maintain a segregated public school and higher education system that left Blacks and whites separate. The states' rights argument was a well-worn vehicle for talking about maintaining racial segregation while not having to talk directly about race. Wallace's rhetoric on states' rights folded neatly into the well-established "Lost Cause" campaign promoting the Civil War (and the vestiges of its racist past) as something other than an open desire to maintain the enslavement of millions of African Americans. As historian Gary W. Gallagher noted, "white Southerners emerged from the Civil War thoroughly beaten but largely unrepentant" and went forward in the nearly one hundred years that followed until Wallace's time to recast the war and its purposes. States' rights were a key aspect of the Lost Cause, and changing the subject from slavery to one that promoted "a public memory of the Confederacy that placed their wartime sacrifice and shattering defeat in the best possible light . . . [t]hey collectively sought to justify their own actions and allow themselves and other former Confederates to find something positive in all-encompassing failure."[7]

Wallace made his participation in furthering ideas such as the Lost Cause abundantly clear wherever he went in his first years in public life. In remarks before a skeptical audience at Harvard University in November 1963, he apparently felt the need to offer his own version of American history, repositioning the Civil War as a war of occupation of Southern lands by Northern forces and reciting a litany of wrongs the North had inflicted against the South since the close of the war and throughout Reconstruction. He offered what could only be described as a questionable, paternal, and patronizing description of "the Negro in the South," distinguishing between "Mulatto" people (created he said by the pairing of Northern occupation forces and Southern Black women, sans apparently any involvement of Southern men). He said "mulattoes" had become "more energetic, educated so-called Negroes," and he noted,

> They are not representative in any true sense of their less capable African half brother. When you speak of the Negro in the North, the image before your eye is probably the Mulatto and he constitutes a very small percent of our population. When we speak of the Negro in the South, the image in our minds is that great residue of easy-going, basically happy, unambitious, incapable of much learning African, who constitutes 40 percent of our population, and the white man of the South, in addition to educating his children, has attempted to educate, to furnish public health services and civic protection [for whites and Blacks].[8]

At the center of Wallace's remarks stood the commitment that southerners—and northerners—should be positioned to decide for themselves broader issues (such as civil rights) that were clearly needing to be elevated to a universal federal standard to which all states would be required to subscribe. Education, energy, air pollution and many other federal mandates would follow as President Lyndon Johnson took on the greatest postwar expansion of the role of the federal government since the New Deal. Wallace's rhetoric was designed to create feelings of insecurity and even helplessness against powerful federal forces but differs from contemporary examples of similar rhetoric from Donald Trump in that Wallace argued the establishment wanted to change the South, whereas Trump argued the values once buttressed by a majority-white establishment are being "destroyed or vanquished" and must be restored. Both men relied then (and now) upon key elements of demagoguery explicated by Paul Elliott Johnson, such as "felt powerlessness as a sign of agency, democracy as danger, [and] raced and gendered-hostility toward otherness. . . ."[9]

1964: Developing the "Road Show"

As 1963 gave way to 1964, Wallace clearly reveled in the national spotlight he had successfully drawn to himself, and following an impressive and comprehensive "speaking tour" of northern and western locales, announced he would pose primary challenges to President Johnson for the Democratic nomination in

1964. Wallace's team quickly identified Wisconsin, Indiana, and Maryland as states not only possibly open to Wallace's message of states' rights and battling the federal government in the advancement of civil rights and education and also noted that each of the three states had relatively simple requirements to gain ballot access. In all three states, the Johnson campaign was relying on "stand-in" or "favorite son" candidates to collect nomination delegates for the president who had come to the office less than six months earlier upon the assassination of JFK. While most "establishment Democrats"—particularly in Wisconsin and Indiana—refused to engage Wallace one-on-one on his agenda related to opposing passage of the landmark 1964 Civil Rights Act—in Maryland he found a willing combatant from the establishment and took full advantage. Coming off impressive showings in Wisconsin and Indiana, where he had pulled nearly a third of all Democratic primary ballots cast, Maryland Democrats decided to take on Wallace directly. Daniel Brewster, Maryland's junior US Senator elected to his first (and only) term in 1962, agreed to appear one-on-one with Governor Wallace in a "polite but tense encounter" taped by ABC News for its national program *Issues and Answers*.[10]

Brewster opened his remarks in the exchange by inviting Wallace to withdraw from the Maryland primary and saying that if he did, Brewster would withdraw as well. Wallace refused the "offer" and said he was "running against the President of the United States, the established [civil rights] policy of our government, and in both parties, and I do not believe this will be acceptable to the vast majority of the people of Maryland." Wallace said he did not have "one chance in a million, not the chance my little son would have, if he were running against Lyndon Johnson," but that the issue of states' rights was too important to leave unchallenged. Brewster strongly rebutted Wallace's claims that the civil rights bill would eliminate personal property rights and expressly said Wallace's assertion that the bill would force busing of school children in Maryland was false. He also denied the governor's claims that union rights would be stripped by the bill. At one point, Brewster looked at Wallace directly and said, "Governor, I am afraid either you don't understand the bill, or you misconstrue it on purpose." Brewster said understanding the civil rights bill was easy: "Simply the bill does this: it guarantees to every American the right to vote, to every traveler on the highways of America the right to buy a meal, the right of everyone to a job for which he is qualified without someone telling him 'You can't have it because we don't like your color.'"[11] Wallace was prepared for Brewster's attacks on voting rights and other racial issues in Alabama, and he quickly recounted simmering racial tensions in Maryland. "Well, Senator, let me tell you this . . . everything must not be exactly like you want it to be because

actually you have had more trouble in Maryland than we had in Alabama
. . . you have further to go than we have in Alabama."[12]

The exchange between Wallace and Brewster before a national audience
differed sharply from what Wallace had experienced in the two earlier primaries. In Indiana, the state's gentlemanly governor, Matthew Welsh, standing in
for LBJ, was uncharacteristically sharp in his response to Wallace's arrival in
the state calling him "the man who stood by while dogs were set upon human
beings and fire hoses were turned on groups of peaceful demonstrators." Welsh
described Wallace as "the mortal enemy of President John F. Kennedy. This is
the man whose beliefs were responsible for the deaths of innocent children
in the bombing of a Sunday school class [in Birmingham]." Reporters later
queried Wallace about Welsh's raising of the church bombing but found the
Alabamian judicious in his reply, saying that the bombing "was a dastardly
crime which we hope to solve."[13] Welsh also called to the attention of Indiana
audiences another, lesser-known act of violence that had erupted in Alabama
as Wallace was campaigning in Wisconsin and Indiana. On April 18, 1964, an
arson fire destroyed Macon County High School in Notasulga, Alabama, just as
the school was to be integrated by court order. "The blaze sent flames shooting
in the air, visible for miles around, and left the student body of only six Negroes
temporarily without a school to attend," the Associated Press reported. "It was
up to county school authorities to determine whether to transfer the Negroes
to another desegregated school at nearby Shorter [Alabama]. No white pupils
have attended the [Macon County] high school since the Negroes were enrolled
Feb. 19 under a federal court order."[14]

Welsh said, "There are at least two George Wallaces. There is the campaigner
who dashes about the state of Indiana, posing as a great emancipator, a man
of great tolerance and kindness." He contrasted that with Wallace's published
remarks calling a federal judge who ordered the integration of Alabama schools
as "an integrating, carpet-bagging, race-mixing, bald-faced liar." Welsh warned
Indiana voters, "While the 'second' George Wallace was running around Indiana
last week, he got some help in defying a federal court order that put six little
Negro children into a school. The school was burned to the ground. The 'second' George Wallace was too busy spreading his distorted version of the civil
rights bill in Indiana to take a hand in stopping such flagrant attacks."[15] Welsh
took his frontal assaults on Wallace directly to the home of a large African-
American population, Gary, Indiana, and reminded voters there that Wallace's
Alabama operated "as a police state where scores of thousands of colored voters
are denied their most precious right."[16] Welsh's assessment offered of Alabama
under Wallace meant "On the one hand we're told the Negro schools down
there [in Alabama] are excellent and in the same breath we are told that thou-

sands of Negro graduates of those same schools are illiterate and cannot be allowed to vote." Welsh said the actual truth was that under Wallace, Alabama had become "a police state ruled by the iron fist of would-be dictators whose greatest fear is that their lust for power will be checked by other members of the federal union."[17] Comparing conditions for Blacks in Alabama to those of people in Soviet-controlled East Germany and Czechoslovakia who flee seeking freedom, Welsh said,

> so too are thousands of Negro and white families moving North to escape this modern tyranny. They are not fleeing the good life. They are seeking the good life and we welcome them to Indiana where they may secure their rights and pursue their fortune without fear.[18]

It was clear the establishment, as represented in Governor Welsh of Indiana, was determined to strike back at Wallace and tamp out any embers of doubt he hoped to fan into full flames. In addition, Indiana's Democratic Party machine kicked into high gear and attempted to overwhelm the media coverage Wallace was counting on for his visit to the state's largest university, Indiana University. As Wallace did battle with heckling students in Bloomington, Governor Welsh and President Johnson upstaged him with a full-day visit to South Bend, where the president highlighted federal job training and employment efforts to assist the thousands of Studebaker workers who had lost their jobs when the historic automaker shuttered its doors for good in November 1963. President Johnson's hastily planned visit, announced at the last minute, included a tour of a job training center set up to assist more than 6,500 Studebaker Corporation workers whose jobs had come to an end. Welsh relished the chance to stand next to the president and emphasize the support the administration was trying to give to a still shell-shocked South Bend community. *South Bend Tribune* political reporter Lewis S. Haber wrote that Johnson "dropped onto the Indiana political scene at an opportune time" and that "while the official purpose of his visit here was to observe and comment on manpower retraining, it also could be construed as a boost for the proposed civil rights program and for Indiana Governor Matthew E. Welsh." Haber noted that Welsh remained "at the president's elbow during the entire visit." Haber analyzed, "The message was clear, President Johnson is lending his prestige to Governor Welsh in a trying primary in an effort to keep voters from being sidetracked by Governor Wallace's efforts to capitalize on what Wallace calls his 'states' rights' stand."[19]

Beyond the presence of the president himself, the Welsh campaign benefitted from two other "heavy hitters" who dipped into the state in April 1964—Secretary of State Dean Rusk and Supreme Court Chief Justice Earl Warren both participated in a dedication ceremony for the Valparaiso University School of Law. A crowd estimated at 3,000 showed up to hear the two powerful men speak. While not addressing specific political issues at hand, both Rusk and Warren spoke on themes beneficial to Welsh's effort on behalf of Johnson and the civil rights movement.[20] Welsh told his fellow Hoosiers, "The Governor of Alabama is a master of the art of argument, but he apparently knows very little about our Indiana way of life. If he would lift his eyes above his own ambition, he could look into our eyes and see what we have in our hearts. We believe in tolerance and brotherhood."[21]

Welsh's campaign continued to draw impressive help from across the nation, including an appearance by Senator Edward M. "Teddy" Kennedy of Massachusetts at the annual Jefferson-Jackson Day Dinner sponsored by the Indiana Democratic Party. Governor Wallace skipped the event, claiming a schedule conflict, although it was not clear he was ever invited to attend. Arriving in Indianapolis, Senator Kennedy told reporters, "I am confident the people of Indiana will give endorsement to the programs of President Johnson and President Kennedy."[22] During his speech before an excited crowd of more than 3,000 Indiana Democrats, the youngest Kennedy brother urged each of them to work hard "to show the nation that Indiana is not a stronghold of reaction, but of progress; that Indiana has come a long way since the days of hatred and violence" and asked all those present "who believed in my brother" to back Governor Welsh and President Johnson. He said he and the entire Kennedy family were pledged "to the continuation of the principles and the programs for which the president lived and to the end of the hatred and extremism that took him away."[23]

Wallace seemed unmoved by the establishment pushback from Welsh and Johnson, but he reacted more strongly to an organized response to his candidacy from religious leaders across the state. A group of fifteen Indiana churches, organized by the Indiana Council of Churches, issued a statement "to set the record straight and to apply a Christian perspective to the unsound arguments of Governor Wallace." The letter asserted that "Governor Wallace does not stand basically for the legitimate rights of the states, but for the maintenance of segregation and discrimination which deprive citizens of opportunity."[24] Bishop Richard C. Raines of the United Methodist Church in Indiana issued his own statement to the more than 1,300 Methodist congregations in Indiana, urging them to reject Wallace's candidacy. The *Criterion*, the official newspaper of the Indianapolis Catholic Archdiocese, took an unusual step and published a front-page editorial in which it declared Wallace's "philosophy is evil." The editorial accused Wallace of engaging in "half-truths and distortions" and added, "Governor Wallace is proving himself an apt student of Nazi technique."[25] Finally, the Christian Church (Disciples of Christ)—with its national headquarters located in Indianapolis and hundreds of congregations across the state— made an appeal on behalf of one of its members, Governor Welsh. The Christian Church accused Wallace of using "half-truths to appeal to the worst prejudices of some unthinking Hoosier citizens." The Christian Church urged its members "to think about the real moral issue. . . . from the standpoint of the Christian faith and American constitutional principles, and not to be misled by Governor Wallace's appeal to prejudices and false political issues."[26]

To top off the "establishment" response to Wallace in Indiana, Welsh offered newspaper, radio, and television advertising under the theme "A Solemn Appeal to Decency." Indiana Democrats embraced the emerging television medium and purchased fifteen-minute blocks on sixteen television stations across the state to allow Welsh to make his appeal directly.

As the primary campaign moved on from Indiana to Maryland, "initial pessimism among Maryland Democrats seems to be ebbing as Senator Brewster, on advice from Indiana Democrats, has toughened his stump speeches for direct attacks on the Alabaman." Brewster, for example, openly called Wallace "a bigot and a rabble rouser" and called on Marylanders "to help the president and to help the cause of justice and God."[27] In a radio interview, Senator Brewster was even more candid, saying that Maryland voters "will never turn to the advocates of intolerance and bigotry and bias and all the things that this guy Wallace stands for." He acknowledged Wallace would get many votes in the state, but he added, "Any nut, a real simpleton, can file and get a certain percent of the votes in a primary."[28] As he had in Indiana, President Johnson found a reason to be in Maryland prior to the state's primary. Exercising the power of the incumbency, Johnson opened a thirty-hour tour of Appalachia to promote his "War on Poverty," including a stop in Cumberland, Maryland, with Senator Brewster at his side (as well as the state's senior senator, Senator James Glenn Beall, a Republican). At Cumberland, a crowd of 8,000 filled the Fort Hill Stadium to hear the president offer his support for the proposed Bloomington Dam for Maryland."[29] Johnson and Senator Brewster also appeared before as many as 10,000 supporters for a rally at the Cumberland City Hall Plaza. While there, LBJ read portions of a letter from former President Franklin D. Roosevelt referring to Maryland's "noble tradition in the cause of religious tradition." LBJ continued,

[President Roosevelt] wrote that letter because he knew that this was a state which has always fought for the rights of man. And if that battle takes place on a different front today than it did 300 years ago, Maryland and Marylanders must help to win it. Because that same spirit still lives in Maryland today, I come here to ask your help in carrying forward the American Revolution.[30]

The establishment forces Wallace sought to battle had done their best—but still could not prevent Wallace from drawing off a significant portion of Democratic primary votes and kept alive lingering doubts about the level of support for Johnson's progressive agenda. Wallace claimed victory just as he had in the June 1963 schoolhouse standoff in Alabama. It did not matter to Wallace or his fervent supporters that he had not stopped Johnson from rolling to the Democratic nomination. As Roberts-Miller notes, such deliberation about winners and losers, or even consideration of flaws in policies, plans or statements, "are all kinds of insubordination, rebellion and disloyalty"—qualities not tolerated among demagogic followers. Roberts-Miller highlights researcher George Lakoff's ideas about "the strict father" role of certain demagogic and authoritative forces over people and that strict binary choices push followers toward obedience. The choices are stark: control or chaos, domination or submission, punishment or reward. "There is no pause for self-reflective critical thinking," she wrote, "and questioning authority is seen as rebellion. In this world, obedience to authority is always a good thing."[31] Roberts-Miller's analysis gains in credibility when considering the deadly and inexplicable seizing of the nation's Capitol on January 6, 2021, by Trump supporters who obeyed orders to violently oppose any effort to certify Trump's loss of the 2020 presidential election.

After the dust had settled on the Democratic presidential nomination in 1964 decidedly in Johnson's favor, Wallace seemed happy to grasp a victory out of the mouth of defeat. He eagerly accepted an invitation from Indiana supporters to revive his act in September 1964 as the fall campaign between President Johnson and his Republican challenger, Senator Barry Goldwater, got underway. Wallace focused in on Lake and Porter Counties of Northwest Indiana, two counties he won in the May 1964 Democratic presidential primary, and two counties residing in the shadow of the large Chicago media market. An ad-hoc group based in Hammond, Indiana, calling themselves The Society for the Preservation of Every American's Right made the invitation to Wallace.[32] Once in Indiana, Wallace was in regular form, blaming "left wing beatniks" for trying to take over the Democratic Party and proclaiming again that his effort had "shaken the eyeteeth of the liberals"—underlining what he believed had been a successful challenge to establishment forces. While sixty noisy protestors picketed outside the hall, Wallace told those inside, "People all over the nation are asking how a section like Lake County can vote for the Governor of Alabama. It's because they're tired of being pushed around by big government. This vote [in Lake County] has done a lot to make people think that we had better concern ourselves with the feelings of these people."[33]

Back in Alabama, Wallace remained governor, although some complained he spent more time outside of the state than he did tending to his duties in

Montgomery. As 1965 began, political events in Alabama were taking another troubling turn as a planned civil rights march from Selma to Montgomery was being met with resistance. Wallace told reporters that such a march "cannot and will not be tolerated," citing the need to protect marchers from possible danger from traffic, or counterprotestors. "There will be no march between Selma, Alabama and Montgomery, Alabama," Wallace told reporters, "and I have so instructed the Department of Public Safety."[34] No one seemed to question that in this scenario it was Wallace who represented the establishment—not some malevolent "other." Demagoguery did not require consistency of thinking or action. While it was fully appropriate for Wallace to make open challenges to establishment forces seeking to enforce policy or law, it was an afront to allow a challenge to the authority he held as governor of Alabama.

Wallace's authoritative orders, meant to crush at-home opposition to a "universalized nostalgia" for how things used to be from a mythologized past, were ones he would soon regret. Alabama law enforcement officials—acting on his order—moved with tear gas and billy clubs to violently put down the march as it reached the Edmund Pettus Bridge in Selma on Sunday, March 7, 1965. The brutal police response—earning the day the name "Bloody Sunday"—left 17 marchers hospitalized, and another 50 injured. National media coverage of the smashing of the protest by police made for ugly images carried on television, described by the Associated Press as "an eruption of bloody racial violence." Wire reports indicated, "About 100 troopers stopped the march under direct orders from Governor Wallace."[35] Showing he was angered—and perhaps worried about how the scene played out—Wallace was terse and short with reporters, offering only: "Those folks in Selma made this a seven-day-a-week job. But we can't give an inch. We're going to have to enforce state laws."[36]

The 54-mile Selma-to-Montgomery march eventually occurred on March 25, 1965—including the participation of Dr. King—and involved no violence as seen on "Bloody Sunday" two weeks earlier. As King and the marchers reached the State Capitol, Wallace sat growling at his desk, within earshot of the thousands of civil rights protestors who made it to Montgomery, and ignored their pleas. Wallace had lost again, a massive civil rights march had finally taken place against his wishes, but he and his supporters remained satisfied, even in defeat. Roberts-Miller suggests this is an outgrowth of the phenomenon that it is better to lose than to compromise on some middle positions. "What will you tell your base now that you have to persuade them to accept a [compromise] position you previously insisted was not nearly enough?" Roberts-Miller asks. Demagogues insist that "compromise is suicidal" and that if followers perceive a speaker's hyperbole as cunning, or strategic, they can risk authenticity. For Wallace, he'd rather face defeat than be viewed as inauthentic or uncommitted to the in-group identity. Once a demagogue, such as Wallace, has convinced their audience it is "kill or be killed, any policy short of complete purification makes no sense.... Extraordinary action is called for, you cannot compromise about your own extermination."[37]

The Wallace rhetoric was having influence beyond his own failed ambitions in the Democratic Party. A careful examination of an October 27, 1964, speech by Hollywood film and television actor Ronald Reagan on behalf of the GOP's presidential nominee, Barry Goldwater, reflects conservatives in both parties were adopting anti-establishment positions. Reagan, a former Democrat who had just completed a ten-year run as host of the primetime CBS anthology series, *General Electric Theater*, had decided to back Goldwater for president. Reagan's speech, titled "A Time for Choosing," was broadcast on television and catapulted Reagan into the hearts of Republicans far and wide and easily surpassed any speech Goldwater could give. In his speech, Reagan offered words remarkably similar to the states' rights issues Wallace had been talking about for a long time:

> This is the issue of this election: Whether we believe in our capacity for self government or whether we abandon the American revolution and confess that a little intellectual elite in a far-distant capital can plan our lives for us better than we can plan them ourselves.... Private property rights [are] so diluted that public interest is almost anything government planners decide it should be.... Our national, unalienable rights are now considered to be a dispensation of government, and freedom has never been so fragile, so close to slipping from our grasp as it is at this moment.[38]

Before decisions could be made about whether Wallace would make another run at the presidency in 1968, important issues back home in Alabama had to be resolved. Top of the list was the state's ban on allowing governors to succeed themselves in office. Surprisingly, Wallace lost a protracted legislative battle in the spring of 1966 to change the rules that would allow him to run for a second term. In the end, however, he succeeded in keeping his grip on the governor's office by installing his personal "vessel" in the campaign—his wife, Lurleen, was successfully elected the 46th governor of Alabama in his stead. With Governor Lurleen Wallace handling things at home, George Wallace quickly turned his attention to a coming 1968 candidacy for president. Associated Press reporter Arthur Edson reported from Montgomery in 1967 about how primed Wallace appeared to be for a run. Edson quoted a Wallace friend who recalled the governor's past as a fierce 135-pound boxer and an even more tireless political campaigner: "Oh, he really poured it on. George did. He just kept moving in all the time." This same friend said Wallace retained a simple strategy from his ring days—"attack, attack, attack, and somebody is bound to be hit—and hurt." Edson noted that Wallace stood as a problem for both the Democratic and Republican parties, "though no one seems sure whether the Democrats or the Republicans would suffer more." Wallace, a big cigar dangling at a "rakish angle" from his mouth, was sly when reporters would ask about his specific plans for 1968: "I think I'll hurt the Republicans in the South and the Democrats in the North. [Overall] I think I'll hurt the Democratic Party more."[39]

1968: Perfecting the Message

Key rhetorical themes Wallace had perfected in 1964 were on tap for 1968. Retained was a strong vein of "anti-intellectualism" throughout Wallace's remarks to potential voters. Edson wrote, "Few politicians have approached [the] theme [of anti-intellectualism] as eagerly as Wallace. In almost every speech or news conference, he works in a denunciation of those who he thinks are thinkers and, therefore intellectual morons." The words served an important purpose—framing his campaign and issues as a direct assault on and challenge to establishment forces. As such, Edson wrote, Wallace caused worry among the nation's political leaders looking at 1968, "With his cocky swagger, perhaps he is compensating for being only 5 feet 7—with his impudent grin, Wallace, the spoiler, thrives on the discomfiture of others."[40]

Returning from a 12-state tour in the last half of 1967, Wallace said he was encouraged by the level of support that existed for his planned independent candidacy. Wallace said his campaign was aimed directly at "the little man" who faced an increasing number of "guidelines" pushed by the federal government dominated by "liberal thinkers of the Eastern establishment" who he said controlled both the Democratic and Republican parties. As evidence of his bona fides for "the little man," Wallace offered,

> I used to be a cab driver. I find today that they know more about why we're in Vietnam than some of those Yale professors. They knew by instinct that Castro was a Communist when *The New York Times* was calling him the Robin Hood of the Caribbean. The average man in the street knows what's going on and he's getting mighty sick and tired of having the intellectual giants laying down guidelines for everything he does.[41]

Wallace further defined the establishment forces, however, beyond those in the Johnson White House and the Pentagon orchestrating US involvement in

Vietnam. For Wallace, "establishment forces" included antiwar dissenters whom he deemed traitors and "intellectual incompetents who say the right of dissent gives you the right to give aid and comfort to our enemy in Vietnam." *New York Times* correspondent Donald Janson reported that Wallace drew his strongest response from audiences across his multistate tour when he thrust his fist into the air and declared he would take his campaign "to the length and breadth of the land to give the people a choice in 1968."[42] His emphasis on giving voters a choice fit well with his anti-establishment message that "there's not a dime's worth of difference between the Democratic and Republican parties."[43]

The Wallace campaign was quickly understood to be more than just the now-former governor's rhetoric. Campaign fundraising had gone well, and a full-time campaign headquarters in Montgomery continued to add staff and professionals. Among the staff were attorneys who guided Wallace in gaining ballot access in all 50 states. Meeting the statutory requirements of gaining access to the California ballot were some of the most difficult but provided Wallace a chance to prove his support was widespread—and again not limited to Deep South states. But ballot access was anything but simple. For 1968, the state of California required any qualifying political party to collect 66,059 signatures (or one percent of the 1964 presidential vote in the state) for a candidate to be listed on the statewide ballot. The effort for Wallace was completely wrapped up in the fortunes of the American Independent Party, Wallace's latest "vessel" to obtain his political goals.

To put George Wallace in front of as many potential supporters—and ballot petition signers—as possible, an ambitious schedule was developed for the former governor. From late summer until December 1967, Wallace appeared in more than one hundred California communities.[44] As *New York Times* columnist Tom Wicker put it, "The loquacious and tireless Wallace could easily make 10 speeches a day, and would like nothing better, but since he must speak at each rally to draw a crowd, and since re-registration takes time, only three or four rallies a day can be held." Wicker noted, "George Wallace and the men around him are shrewd and able political operators, and Wallace himself has a singular ability to touch the hearts of a certain kind of people of whom there may be a great many in America."[45] Wicker shared that Wallace was almost always running late, meaning crowds were gathered long before he arrived—but his tardiness was something the campaign tried to maximize. Wallace's late arrival "gives registrars time to get lines formed and their work in hand before Wallace absorbs everyone's attention. Meanwhile, country music performers entertain the crowd; 'Out here,' a Wallace man remarks, 'we use the band to hold, not to draw.'"[46] For those paying attention, even the process to get Wallace on the ballot was an anti-establishment, grassroots effort far from any party or government election infrastructure. To join the American Independent Party and support Wallace in California, a registered voter had to sign a form leaving their current party (Republican or Democratic), and change their registration outright.

The push for ballot access in California came as a new December 1967 Gallup Poll showed Wallace far back in third place in a three-candidate race for president in 1968. Undoubtedly the forces behind former vice president Nixon were paying close attention—most of Wallace's support in California appeared to be coming from conservative Republicans. Speaking to an audience of about 250 supporters at the Lido Lanes bowling alley in Newark—an Alameda County community north of San Jose—Wallace said most of his support in California was coming from Democrats, and he repeated the claim before another friendly audience at a shopping center in Hayward.[47] As the year-end deadline approached to have at least 66,059 certified signatures on hand, the Wallace campaign shifted into a higher gear in California with newspaper and radio advertising undertaken in twelve targeted counties of the state. In addition, time was purchased for half-hour television speeches and presentations from Wallace on stations in Bakersfield, Fresno, Los Angeles, Sacramento, San Diego, and San Francisco—reaching millions of California voters. Further, Wallace himself risked exhaustion with seventeen separate rallies over five days between December 13 and December 17, hitting Sunnyvale, San Francisco, and Salinas the first day; Oakland, Hayward, Newark, and Pleasanton the second day; Hawthorne, Torrance, Los Angeles, and North Hollywood the third day; Maywood, Paramount, Le Habra, and LaPuenta the fourth day; and LaCanada and Lancaster on the last day.[48] For the effort in Salinas (Monterey County), a newspaper ad attempted to draw an audience to the Masonic Temple to hear music and speeches and "to meet George Wallace personally [autographs, handshakes and questions]."[49] In Santa Rosa, San Bruno, San Mateo, and Redwood City, the Wallace advertisements reminded voters, "You must register American Independent Party this month to insure [sic] a choice in 1968."[50] The ads for the event and speeches in San Diego County were more specific and featured a large picture of Wallace superimposed over an American flag image under the phrase, "Stand Up for America." The advertisement for San Diego County voters urged them to "rally 'round and register" and that "Deputy registrars will be on hand to register you as a member of the American Independent Party—the only way to get Wallace on the ballot, the only way to insure [sic] a choice in '68."[51]

Despite his continued progress in California, official forces in both parties were dismissive of the Wallace effort. Democratic and Republican party officials continued to raise doubt about the signature campaign (even as reports emerged indicating that some defectors were being peeled off by Wallace from both parties). California Governor Ronald Reagan (who harbored ideas about jumping into the Republican presidential contest), skipped Wallace's speech before the Comstock Club of Sacramento, of which Reagan was a member. Speaking at the Capitol, Reagan said he assumed Wallace would get the needed 66,000+ signatures for the California ballot but added a dismissive element: "I think almost anyone can get that many names for almost any cause." Asked whether Wallace was more of a problem for his Republican Party or the Democrats, Reagan said, "He's *their* problem."[52]

A Wallace speech in southern California as the ballot deadline approached captured well the anti-establishment appeal Wallace was perfecting:

> The two parties [in America] are Tweedledum and Tweedledee. Some Republicans say we need a change, but we're taking votes from them. I say, let 'em put up or shut up—let them come up with a platform and a candidate that 62 million people in my section of the country can support, and I won't run.[53]

Beyond inviting voters to join him in challenging both parties, he introduced a finer point on his earlier civil rights concerns from 1964. With civil rights now the law of the land, the Wallace forces focused on the potential impacts of such legislation by addressing voters' fears about the prospect of busing school children to achieve school integration. With a nod toward his earlier states' rights issues, but now dressed up under the concern for school age children, Wallace told one audience,

> I don't care if you folks of Chula Vista want to send your kids on a bus to northern California to go to school. That's your business. But HEW [the Department of Health, Education and Welfare] has a plan to destroy the neighborhood school. We don't need anyone 3,000 miles away to tell us where to go to school.[54]

All the long days and complicated petitions circulated, on January 3, 1968, Wallace strode confidently into the historic Miramar Hotel overlooking the Pacific Ocean in Santa Monica, California, to claim his latest victory—ballot access in California. "George Corley Wallace declared himself all but in the 1968 Presidential race, the only deterrent being the improbable circumstance of a quick endorsement of a Wallace-type platform by one of the major parties," Bob Houser, political editor of the *Long Beach Independent* reported. "Wallace and a claque of some 200 cheering, hooting, applauding supporters crowed gleefully over his success in qualifying the American Independent Party for the California presidential ballot."[55] Wallace thanked the more than 100,000

Californians who had signed up for his effort, declaring "I point out that these people are representative of millions of Americans who are genuinely concerned about the current direction followed by our national leadership."[56]

On February 8, 1968, Wallace went to Washington, DC to declare what everyone already expected—*he would be* a third-party candidate for president of the United States. "I fully think we can win," Wallace declared brushing aside the undistinguished history of third-party candidacies for the presidency. "The odds have not been fully in favor of a new party movement in the past, but the odds will be better as the campaign progresses," he predicted. Speaking before a massive throng of reporters inside the Sheraton Park Hotel, he said his campaign was the answer to a cry from across the nation. "The American people are hungry for a change in the direction of our national government," he said. "They are concerned and disturbed about the trends being followed by our national leadership."[57]

As 1968 opened, most national political polls showed Wallace with an anemic level of support in the range of 10 percent of voters, but those numbers would improve as the year wore on. One "poll" in his favor, the annual Gallup Poll of "Ten Most Admired Men" in the world, placed Wallace on its list for the first time ever—in a seventh-place tie with Richard Nixon. For the first time in two decades, the sitting president (Lyndon B. Johnson) was not the top choice of those polled—former President Dwight D. Eisenhower (who was 77 and in the last year of his life in 1968) placed first. It was the first time Wallace had made the list—and it proved he truly had captured the attention of millions of Americans. The fact that he had given voice to the growing frustrations of many about the speed and level of change meant his rhetoric was connecting with many and ensured he would be a factor in the raucous politics of 1968.[58]

While the "success" of the 1968 Wallace campaign could not be measured in a victory on Election Day, Wallace had successfully poked his finger into the eye of establishment Democrats and Republicans, and done so primarily on the strength of his rhetoric. His words had moved the Nixon campaign further to the right and ultimately decimated the hapless Humphrey campaign straddled by Johnson administration woes. Further, by far exceeding initial expectations of most (but falling short of his own goal to throw the contest into the US House of Representatives)—it was not surprising, then, that Wallace had gained at least a grudging level of respect from establishment forces in the media. Donald Trump would do likewise in 2016, sweeping a field of more mainline Republican primary opponents and implausibly "running the table" by scoring a rare Electoral College victory in November 2016 despite a popular vote loss.

1972: Back in the Democratic Fold

All of these factors meant there was no question Wallace would be back for the 1972 contest. Business back home in Alabama, however, had to be settled first. The 1970 Alabama gubernatorial election proved pivotal to keeping Wallace's hold on power—and attention—and resulted in a race won by Wallace who defeated incumbent governor Albert Brewer (who had been elevated to the office upon the death of Lurleen Wallace) in the Democratic primary and was easily swept back into the governor's office in the fall. Beyond retaining his political power base, Wallace came into 1972 with a new wife (who in turned helped him adopt a new "look"), plenty of money and name recognition, and the baggage of a third-party candidacy behind him. Through will or back-door deals, Wallace was back in the Democratic Party for 1972 but still preaching as many anti-establishment messages as ever before. Helping him in making the point was a crowded field of Washington insiders—congressmen and senators—of most every stripe automatically casting Wallace as the "outside man" to take on the long list of institutional candidates already running on the Democratic side. "I represent the people the establishment wants to get rid of," Wallace said. "It's me against the field."[59]

As part of the upgraded look and approach for 1972, free of any mention of race as an issue, Wallace frequently challenged reporters who wanted to cast his campaign as one about race—instead, Wallace said his effort was about returning to values supported by "regular Americans." The "rules" to capture the Democratic nomination for 1972 had also been updated—22 states offering preferential primaries, and another 11 states holding party caucuses. As the year opened, Wallace was far back in the field, but Gallup polling in the five months between January and May showed Wallace's support growing from 15 percent to 26 percent among party regulars. The primary schedule, and the process by which delegates would be awarded by the Democratic National Committee, provided some significant challenges for Wallace's time, financial resources, and campaign prowess. Interestingly, as the primaries progressed and Wallace continued to enjoy success, racking up delegate counts was proving difficult amidst complicated party rules designed to add parity to the process (rules that either the Wallace campaign did not understand or refused to engage). Six primaries were scheduled over a seven-day period starting May 2 with Indiana, Ohio, and Washington DC; May 4 in Tennessee; May 6 in North Carolina; and May 9 in both Nebraska and West Virginia. These primaries forced the Wallace team to make some tough choices, ultimately scrapping any significant effort in delegate-rich Ohio (140 total delegates), with polling there showing other candidates with much larger support.

The Wallace focus went back to where he had enjoyed success before—Indiana—the second-largest prize on May 2 with 76 delegates. There, Senator Hubert Humphrey remained an active candidate with Senator Edmund Muskie having essentially ended his campaign, and Senator George McGovern skipping Indiana altogether. As a result, Indiana would be a head-to-head contest between Wallace and Humphrey, something the Wallace campaign viewed as favorable to highlighting his anti-establishment credentials. Of all the candidates running in 1972, Humphrey was perhaps best known from serving as a senate leader and vice president and being the party's standard-bearer in 1968. Gallup polls showed Humphrey's support always in the range of 30 percent or more nationwide—best in the field. The message of the Humphrey campaign seemed to buttress Wallace's claim on being the outside, anti-establishment candidate with Humphrey openly telling reporters,

> Mr. Wallace is not about to be the nominee of this party. . . . I'm asking Democrats [in Indiana] whether they're going to vote for a man that ran on a third-party ticket in the last election and may very well have cost the Democratic nominee the election. I don't believe the Democratic Party in the state of Indiana wants to go to the Democratic convention knowing that the delegates that it sends there [if they are Wallace delegates] have no chance of selecting the next President of the United States.[60]

The *Washington Post* dispatched George Lardner Jr. to Indiana to cover the Wallace-Humphrey match-up. He quickly picked up that McGovern and Muskie supporters were reluctantly signing up to support Humphrey as the state Democratic Party officially lined up (once again) to oppose Wallace. For his part, Humphrey laid it on the line to Indiana Democrats. Enlisting the help of television actor Lorne Greene (star of the popular NBC drama *Bonanza*), Humphrey talked pleadingly to a crowd of 1,000 gathered on a farm near Zionsville two days before the primary vote: "The test of a man isn't that he says 'send them a message,' but the test of a man is do you stand up and do something about it? Do you have the guts to stand up there and fight for it?" Humphrey appealed to reason by pointing out a demagogic weakness of the Wallace appeal: "It is one thing to talk about our troubles. It is another thing to do something about it. . . . This I know—I have tried. I have not merely talked, I have tried."[61]

Humphrey's last-minute pitches appeared to hold off a dreaded outcome—with Humphrey claiming 47 percent of the vote, just ahead of Wallace's 41 percent. Although Muskie was essentially out of the race, he drew 12 percent of the vote. Speaking in Cleveland, where he claimed a narrow Ohio victory over McGovern 41–39 percent, Humphrey said his Indiana showing was "better than I expected." He added, "If Muskie were off the ballot, we would have the lion's share of the vote. We didn't campaign too much in Indiana. Indiana is a second Alabama to Wallace—he has made this a major campaigning ground."[62]

The Indiana showing was encouraging enough for Wallace to go into Michigan with a strong tailwind. Bolstered by lingering school desegregation battles in Detroit and other urban areas of the state, Michigan looked to be favorable territory for Wallace's message to buck the busing plans to desegregate public schools. Early on it was clear the excitement and energy in the race in Michigan was with Wallace, the candidate easily filling venues big and small with loud and enthusiastic (and almost entirely white) audiences. The *Detroit Free Press* reported that Humphrey and McGovern had both turned to TV and radio advertising to reach Michigan Democrats, ones who repeated claims that Wallace had helped elect Richard Nixon in 1968.[63] Television advertisements were on Wallace's mind as he campaigned across Michigan with stops in Lansing, Kalamazoo, and the Detroit suburb of Warren. Despite a light rain, more than 3,000 Wallace supporters braved the elements to hear Wallace blast the ads that essentially blamed him for Nixon's victory in 1968 and underscored in the clearest terms yet that Wallace was running as much *against* the establishment as he was *for* president:

> Many things have been said about George Wallace and many more things will be said between now and Tuesday. Some of it is being paid for by the Democratic committee that is supposed to stay neutral. This scurrilous Democratic committee that's putting out stuff on me, they are just trying to steal your vote. All they care about is what some newspaper editor says or what some pointy head on a campus thinks.[64]

If Democratic Party regulars were concerned that Wallace would draw off nervous white suburban Democrats (especially in heavily Catholic areas) or rank and file union members wanting to send their leaders a message, it didn't show. Humphrey continued to hammer away on the theme he first used in Indiana—proclaiming, "A vote for Wallace is a vote for Nixon!" He said Wallace brags that "he put Nixon in the White House." In candor, Humphrey acknowledged, "Dear friends, it may not have been the worst thing in your mind that I was defeated (in 1968), but let me tell you something, the worst possible thing that could happen to you was that Richard Nixon was elected. And Mr. Wallace admits that he was responsible for it!"[65]

Wallace's calculations about Michigan seemed to stoke at least some of the fears of mainline Democrats as party officials from 15 states staged a hastily called and private "Democratic Midwest Conference" in Detroit on April 15 "to decide what to do about George Wallace," as the Associated Press put it.[66] Reporters seemed to delight in the conflict Wallace created for Michigan Democrats and Democrats at large. Michigan's Democratic Party openly snubbed Wallace by inviting McGovern, Humphrey, Muskie, Senator Henry "Scoop" Jackson and US Representative Shirley Chisholm to their annual Jefferson-Jackson Day Dinner—but not Wallace. State party chair James McNeely defended leaving Wallace out: "We felt no need to show that the Democratic Party accepts or approves of his brand of rhetoric." Wallace already had given the regular Democrats a few lumps in the Midwest with his second-place finishes in Wisconsin, Indiana and Pennsylvania, "and his strategists are confiding hopes of something even better in Michigan," the AP analyzed. "All the ingredients for another Wallace coup are present in Michigan."[67]

As party leaders met across town, Wallace drew reporters to a Detroit news conference and acted as if he didn't care about being excluded from official party functions or questions raised by Humphrey (and others) about whether he was a "real Democrat." Wallace said: "I would say that a good vote for George Wallace (in Michigan) would be a good message to the president and the Congress to take better care and safety of the children in this state and other states."[68] That evening, Wallace beamed before "a cowbell-clanging crowd of 10,000 jammed into the State Fairgrounds" to hear the governor. In downtown Detroit, only 3,000 Democrats paid $50 each to attend the Jefferson-Jackson Day Dinner at Cobo Hall. As the *Detroit Free Press* reported, "Officials had to close the gates at the fairgrounds more than an hour before Wallace began his speech. An estimated 6,500 people were unable to get into the Community Arts Building when Wallace started to speak."[69] His successes in drawing crowds showing, Wallace undertook a 12-city, 10-day swing through Michigan prior to the May 16 primary. Rallies and news conferences were set for Detroit, Saginaw, Flint, Farmington, Lansing, Muskegon, Grand Rapids, Dearborn, Marquette, Escanaba, Cadillac, and Kalamazoo, all drawing crowds that were eluding the other candidates. A *Detroit Free-Press* editorial was almost gloomy in assessing, "the Democrats are still fumbling for a candidate, and that George Wallace, for all his unacceptability to the party, is a genuine force to be reckoned with. How the Democrats propose to cope with that harsh reality we don't know, but it's a sure thing that Mr. Wallace isn't going to help them any."[70] Wallace was correct in predicting Michigan would "be another Florida" for him as he dominated the rest of the field with 51 percent of the vote (with McGovern a distant second at 27 percent). On the same day, Wallace did equally well in Maryland, winning with 39 percent of the vote but doing so while recuperating in a hospital bed after being shot by a would-be assassin the day before the primary vote. Regardless, Wallace's 1972 campaign and its rhetoric was connecting with a large number of voters ended in Maryland. The Democrats ultimately turned to George McGovern as the party shifted sharply to the left, and President Nixon sailed untouched to a second term.

1976: Finishing What He Started

While others may have questioned whether Wallace was now too enfeebled, or "damaged goods" as some rather unkind analyses offered, to make another run in 1976, those around the governor knew he would try again. Privately, Wallace wanted to "finish what he started" four years earlier as his campaign had captured a lot of momentum, only to be ended by the troubled mind of Arthur Bremer. Family and friends quietly admitted that another campaign was perhaps the best mental or psychological "therapy" Wallace could access as he struggled with depression in the aftermath of his paralysis. Political factors were also driving Wallace's decision to run again, as the Republicans were widely expected to be weakened by the Watergate matter, with President Gerald Ford serving as an unelected and untested national candidate. Polling a year out from the 1976 Democratic primaries gave Wallace reason to have optimism. Not only were voters weary with Washington politics as the Watergate scandal ground on for years until the August 1974 resignation of President Nixon, but a major Democratic player for the nomination was sitting out the race. Senator Edward Kennedy, the top choice of Democrats polled by Gallup at 36 percent, decided in 1976 (as he had in 1972) he would not run for president in the aftermath of his actions following a fatal car accident at Chappaquiddick Island, Massachusetts in 1969. In the same poll, Wallace was second at 15 percent, and overall was the top choice out of those who said they would run (with Kennedy's name removed). Gallup asked an interesting question about what names respondents had ever heard of—with Kennedy, Wallace, Humphrey, McGovern, and Muskie known to more than 90 percent of the respondents. Interestingly, mixed into a long list of "other Democrats"—former Georgia Governor Jimmy Carter's name was recognized by only 26 percent of those polled.[71] A poll by Knight-Ridder Newspapers found Wallace had made progress in overcoming "his long-standing reputation as a racist." The nationwide survey of more than 1,100 voting-age adults showed that two-thirds believed Wallace was a racist in the past but was no longer so—indicating his shift in rhetoric in the 1968 and 1972 campaigns had made an impact. Still, 28 percent of those polled viewed Wallace's political views as racist. Another issue was Wallace's quadriplegic condition, with the same poll showing that "most voters saying that Wallace's confinement to a wheelchair makes no difference in their evaluation of him." Regardless of that view, however, Knight-Ridder noted that only 18 percent of voters said they found Wallace "appealing" as compared to much higher numbers for Humphrey, President Ford, and former California governor Ronald Reagan.[72]

The 1976 field of Democrats was as diverse—and large—as the 1972 lineup had been. Inspired by the sagging hopes of Republicans in the wake of Watergate, any Democrat who had ever considered running for president was likely to at least test the waters for 1976. The candidates included Senator Birch Bayh of Indiana, Senator Lloyd Bentsen of Texas, California governor Jerry Brown, Senator Robert Byrd of West Virginia, former Georgia governor Jimmy Carter, Senator Frank Church of Idaho, delegate Walter Fauntroy of Washington, DC, former senator Fred Harris of Oklahoma, Senator Henry "Scoop" Jackson of Washington, anti-abortionist activist Ellen McCormack of New York, Senator Walter Mondale of Minnesota, former governor Terry Sanford of North Carolina, Governor Milton Shapp of Pennsylvania, former ambassador Sargent Shriver of Maryland, US Representative Morris "Mo" Udall of Arizona, *and* George Wallace. Wallace, Carter, Church, Jackson, and Bentsen were viewed as the center and right wings of the casting call, while Bayh, Brown, Udall, Harris, and Shriver were considered the left wing. Waiting in the "will call" wing was Senator Humphrey, who had formed no formal campaign for 1976, but made it clear he was available as a compromise candidate (despite having run and lost twice before).

While Wallace still desired to keep his anti-establishment identity intact for 1976, it was getting harder for him to make that case seriously. Just re-elected to a third term as governor of Alabama in 1974, Wallace was embarking on his fourth straight presidential campaign *and* leading the Democratic field in drawing down federal matching funds for his campaign. Always a successful fundraiser from literally thousands of small donors across the nation, on the eve of the Massachusetts primary, the Federal Election Commission reported its largest ever (to date) payout to a candidate—Wallace. Because of his fundraising success and federal matching rules for any donations of $250 or less, Wallace had drawn down $2.2 million in federal funds. The "establishment Democrats" who had long been the target of Wallace's bombast were taking notice of "the outsider's" fundraising success. Enlisting the help of direct-mail expert Richard Viguerie, a Republican, the Wallace campaign quickly figured out how to translate the millions of votes and letters of support he had received over the years into cash donations. Viguerie was sought by campaigns right and left, but in Wallace found a client of like mind. Viguerie proclaimed to *New York Magazine* in the lead-up to the 1976 campaign:

I'm realizing as each day goes by that George Wallace and I have more in common than I thought. . . . We agree on busing, law and order, crime, parental control in public schools, attacking immorality in public life, movies and television. . . . I'm with Wallace on anti-pornography. I've raised millions to fight it. These are the concerns of the client, George Wallace, and we incorporate them in every mailing piece, and we don't miss national defense, either.[73]

Viguerie's theory was a simple and accurate one. "You see, in an ideological cause like this, people give money not to win friends, but to defeat enemies. You can think all day long how you would like to change human nature, if you can—but people are more strongly motivated by negative issues than positives."[74] When he started work for Wallace, Viguerie said the Alabama governor's campaign apparatus had fewer than 75,000 contributors but mailing lists numbering in the hundreds of thousands. A lingering $250,000 campaign debt was quickly retired, and Wallace went into 1976 with what was estimated to be more than $12 million available to make what was expected to be his last chance to get the Democratic presidential nomination. And although Wallace's campaign fundraising appeared to indicate he was a serious contender in 1976, reporters also unearthed details that he had raised and burned through millions of dollars on his campaign by the time the May 1976 primaries arrived, including the federal matching funds. Federal records show the Wallace campaign spent freely on jet airplanes, credit card bills for hotels and other expenses, advertising and printing, and other unspecified expenses. While he had started with more than $12 million in hand, at the end of April, Wallace had only $423,000 left to spend.[75]

As he had in 1972, Wallace poured his strongest effort in 1976 into Florida, where he hoped to repeat his surprise performance there four years earlier. Statewide advertising from the Wallace campaign declared, "Only George Wallace stands with the people of Florida on the most important issues"—including inflation "caused by runaway government spending"; the role of federal courts who sought to "make laws that destroy the happiness of millions of our families"; big government that "must get out of the lives and happiness of our people"; "forced busing" that must be stopped "as we return local control of schools without discrimination of any type and freedom of choice"; welfare reform "to get the lazy and greedy off the welfare rolls"; repeal of abortion rights "to protect the lives of unborn children and nullify the Supreme Court decisions on abortion"; foreign aid "discontinued that is not in our national interest"; law and order "to control crime by changing the attitudes of courts and judges who ignore justice for victims"; and opposition to gun control advocates that want "to take the guns away from law-abiding citizens." Direct mail pieces sent to

Florida voters proclaimed that Wallace's "words are his own. He touches the real thoughts of the people on issues.... Only George Wallace tells it like it is. He has no ties to selfish interests, no obligations to any pressure groups or the leftwing as other candidates have, and makes no promises to the favored few as others are doing."[76]

In his personal appearances across Florida, Wallace revived his familiar theme that other candidates were stealing his issues, inspired by his success in poking a finger into the chest of Washington insiders. He added Republican Ronald Reagan to the list of "thieves" of his previously articulated ideas.[77] *Los Angeles Times* writer Ernest Conine took up the issue of whether other candidates had, in fact, appropriated Wallace's messages. He noted, "If you listen closely, you'll notice the other presidential candidates sound remarkably like Wallace as they lambast big government and unresponsive bureaucrats and talk about things like busing and law and order." Conine took note that Jimmy Carter seemed to express himself in many of the same ways as Wallace but "in easier-going terms" and with a better "understanding of grass-root concerns because he has not been contaminated by years of service in Washington." Was *how* Wallace spoke a factor as well? "Wallace had an accent that grated on Northern ears," Conine wrote, adding:

> He didn't come across, even to Southerners, as a man of truly presidential timber. But to millions of traditional Democrats . . . voting for Wallace seemed the only way of expressing their burning resentments. . . . His large national constituency did not wither away after he was confined to a wheelchair. . . . His physical ability no doubt hurt him. Carter emerged as a candidate who could attract southern black votes while giving whites a southerner for whom they could vote without embarrassment—and who might actually make it to Washington.[78]

As the March 9 Florida primary approached, Carter kept the pressure on Wallace—his campaign seeing it as imperative to defeat Wallace in Florida to demonstrate that he, not Wallace, spoke for the New South. Carter aide Patrick Anderson said Carter often spoke of Wallace in Florida, "Playing off the Wallace campaign slogan, Carter would say: 'Let's not send them a message, let's send them a president.'" The elbows thrown could get sharp. Carter was quoted in one appearance as referring to Wallace as "a perennial candidate" and adding, "I suspect he'll still be running in 1988, *if he's able*." Anderson noted Carter seemed to know immediately the "if he's able" portion of his remark was out of bounds, and quickly added, "and I assume he will be."[79] Carter's approach won the day and essentially was the beginning of the end of Wallace's place on the national stage. Taking a narrow 34–26 percent victory over Wallace,

Carter's win in Florida (and again later in North Carolina) was devastating to Wallace's hopes and message.

As the last of the 1976 Democratic primaries wrapped up in California, New Jersey, and Ohio, Wallace was having trouble getting to sleep inside the Governor's Mansion in Montgomery. About 135 miles directly east in tiny Plains, Georgia, a former governor, Jimmy Carter, was also up late on June 9, 1976. Around 2:15 a.m. Wallace telephoned Carter, and the two men talked and ended their rivalry once and for all. During the call, Wallace said he would urge all 168 of his earned delegates to cast their votes for Carter at the upcoming Democratic National Convention. The new pact between Wallace and Carter was not one of affection—but one of political reality that Wallace could not win, and he at least wanted to be on board with helping elect the first southerner to the presidency since Reconstruction. Publicly Wallace said, "I feel that [Carter] is entitled to the nomination. I respectfully request all of the delegates pledged to George Wallace to cast their ballots for Carter on the first ballot." Wallace said he asked only one "agreement" from Carter: "All I would ask of him was his promise that if elected he would use all of his resources to try to make himself one of the finest presidents we have ever had."[80]

On Saturday, June 12, Carter traveled to Montgomery to meet with Wallace in person at the Governor's Mansion. *Montgomery Advertiser* reporter Marcia Kunstel described the cordial meeting that drew the serious national spotlight on Wallace for perhaps the last time:

> The American and Alabama flags gently wafted over the massive white columns of the Governor's Mansion in the sultry Alabama air. Below, two men used to the heat of both the southern sun and southern politics sealed a new alliance with a handshake and an exhortation that national Democrats unite to send a southerner to the White House. . . . The two met Saturday on the mansion's south porch, chatting in 90 degree heat beyond earshot of the surging mass of reporters and dozens of observers lining the iron fence, laughing and shaking hands twice before moving from the shade to the front of the antebellum-styled structure.[81]

Reporters quickly noted the meeting likely symbolized the "changing of the guard" from the Old South to the New South as the more progressive Carter stood poised to go where Wallace had tried desperately to reach for a dozen years. In his formal remarks, Carter was graceful and polite, saying he was happy to come to Alabama to personally thank Governor Wallace for his support and pledge of delegates. Calling Wallace "a very good candidate" and "a formidable opponent," Carter said, "His idea and mine is to pull the party together in the most harmonious way possible." For his part, Wallace said, "I look forward to seeing the November election over and you elected president." Carter answered with words that likely pleased Wallace, acknowledging that his campaign had helped make possible the rise of a southern nominee for the Democratic Party. "One of the things demonstrated this year has been the lack of sectionalism," Carter added. "Division by region is a thing of the past."[82]

Carter's 1976 running mate, Senator Walter Mondale of Minnesota, was named to the ticket after the Wallace confab, but he was well familiar with the governor. "George Wallace, equipped with his racist views and his antagonism toward the North, pounded on northern politicians like Hubert Humphrey (also from Minnesota)," Mondale said. Wallace found success, Mondale believes,

> because his spiel resonated largely in the South, but he was also able to connect with white working union men, [a key part of] Humphrey's base [in 1968] and shrink his vote. He couldn't win overall in the North but he could take votes away from the liberal base. I think it was a real shock to Hubert.[83]

Governor Wallace kept his word and accepted invitations to campaign on behalf of Jimmy Carter in the fall campaign, with Wallace making two campaign appearances for Carter in the panhandle of Florida and one in Mississippi (both states carried by Carter over President Ford).[84] Ultimately, Mondale believes Wallace was of little influence in the 1976 Democratic Party platform or in the successful Carter-Mondale campaign at all. "I think one of [Jimmy] Carter's greatest contributions to America was his ability to clip Wallace's wings in the South," Mondale said. The 1976 effort to control or contain Wallace once and for all as a force in the Democratic Party was real:

> We were trying to limit Wallace's appeal by appeasing him with a speaking slot at our convention and by meeting with him, and trying to co-opt some of his staff [in the South]. Honestly, we also openly commiserated with him about the tragic consequences of the attempted assassination assault upon him. . . . We tried to be kind to him.[85]

Mondale followed Carter's suit—but with much less media attention—and paid a 1976 visit to Wallace later in the year as part of an Alabama campaign swing. "I visited with him in Alabama and I also sat with him at the convention that year," Mondale said. "I believe the growing national revulsion against old-fashioned racism, and Wallace's lifetime connection with it, hurt him a lot."[86] Mondale, along with most every Democrat or any political poll, could see Wallace's political future on the national stage was over, ending as it began, in defeat. It wasn't as if Wallace hadn't poured every ounce of himself into the process—rising from a district judge in a rural Alabama county to being a four-time candidate for president of the United States. He had done so with an unmatched instinct for how to inspire critical feelings of victimhood in the voters he sought, constructed feelings of peril or risk that were key to drawing Americans to his campaign—his crusade.

CHAPTER 3

Politics of Victimhood and Privilege

Beyond identifying the risks "in-group" people face, and the required battle against establishment forces, the rhetoric of George Wallace required his supporters to understand themselves as victims in a system that actually privileges them. They uniformly reject claims of privilege, either muddling the issue of what privilege means or changing the subject to expand upon ideas of victimization. Victimhood, according to Patricia Roberts-Miller, is a "striking characteristic" of demagoguery and is manifested by statements that emphasize "*We* are being victimized by the situation . . . and we have so far responded to this victimization with extraordinary patience and kindness."[1]

Further, even the proposed solutions to problems can be rhetorically twisted to further feelings of victimhood among privileged portions of society who are needed to engage in change. Murray Edelman noted that problems and "troubling conditions" have always existed, but some politicians seem remotely focused on addressing these problems, let alone solving them. Instead, the problems and the proposed responses are used to further division. A classic example in Wallace's era can be found in the growing demands of Blacks (and women and homosexuals to follow) for a greater share of economic, social, and political power. Ignoring the baseline assumption that such minority groups are inferior to the privileged majority, Wallace's rhetoric often attacked the solutions instead and those offering them. Advocates for equality were easily cast as "cranks" making "exotic" demands, and *they* (the advocates) were the problem, not the original discrimination they were seeking to address. Any "gestures" or solutions offered to address discrimination can actually fuel more feelings of "victimhood" because, as Edelman noted, "Legal language and directives to administrative agencies to correct inequities reassure people who worry about fairness, especially those who do not themselves suffer from bias." As a result, any effort to expand such efforts beyond the basic or initial "gesture" of addressing inequity causes majority cultures to reel into claims of a new unfairness they are suffering—emerging with paradoxical ideas such as "reverse discrimination," which fueled vitriolic opposition to approaches such as affirmative action in the Wallace era (and likewise strong reactions against immigration and trade deals in the Trump era).[2]

Ideas about victimhood could be found often in Wallace's rhetoric, his attacks on the US Supreme Court as example, accusing the nation's high court of "cow-towing to the anarchists." He said, "I'm tired of the liberal left-wing element blaming all of you for the breakdown in law and order when it's a small minority of communists and anarchists who are doing this. This situation has been created by the bureaucrats of the Supreme Court."[3] He would go further in articulating what he believed was the victimization of the white majority in America—in pursuit of placating minority groups—than any other modern-day politician. To a group of St. Louis business leaders, Wallace shared,

> The man on the street is listening. The taxi driver is listening. Their *fierce contact with life* has given them some wisdom. We're going to stop some of this pseudo intellectual government imposed upon us by an elite cult. . . . These same pseudo intellectuals explain away crime as a failure of society, their theory being that if a youth turns to crime it may be because his papa didn't take him to see the St. Louis Cardinals play when he was a little boy.[4]

At the basis of the victimhood Wallace was articulating was his idea that working Americans had, in his words, a "fierce contact with life" that grew out of hard work, sacrifice, and delayed gratification. His viewpoint assumed only he and others like him had known such work and life experiences and challenges. Victimization of "real Americans" started with southerners, in Wallace's view, but it was not limited to that. He told 15,000 supporters back home in Alabama in 1968,

> For year's they've been calling us rednecks, hillbillies and peapickers and come November 5, they're going to find out there are a lot of rednecks in this country. . . . Both of the other candidates now say "we've got to have law and order," and they ought to say it, they're the ones that took it away from us. They've created a Frankenstein monster and now the chickens have come home to roost.[5]

Wallace aimed his attack at both the Republicans and Democrats who he said had "succumbed to anarchists" and victimized Americans by "ramming things down our throats" until "there's nothing left to ram." He promised his supporters would rise on Election Day in 1968 and "we're going to have a good throat-clearing."[6] It was colorful and gruff language that always drew applause—and a few rebel yells—but was part and parcel of the larger point of how "victimized" Americans could and should ascend to Wallace's call. Wallace, by design or luck, had colorfully laid out the status many Americans felt themselves in, and by doing so, he created an army of fellow victims. Doing so, however, required that they not be left feeling fearful and powerless. "Fearmongering can work only if the in-group perceives it's in danger of extermination," Roberts-Miller wrote, "but demagoguery typically also includes claims that our triumph is predestined."[7]

In contemporary times, former president Trump used the victimization of Americans as a centerpiece of his argument, but also his *own* so-called victimization, frequently calling out opponents, the media, and others as "unfair" or engaged in "witch-hunts" against him. It's an ironic claim given the wealth and power (privilege) his life had always afforded him. Trump started his campaign on nothing less than the point that America had fallen victim to "open borders" and out-of-control immigration:

> The U.S. has become a dumping ground for everybody else's problems. . . . When Mexico sends its people, they're not sending their best. . . . They're sending people that have lots of problems, and they're bringing those problems [to] us. They're bringing drugs. They're bringing crime. They're rapists. And some, I assume, are good people.[8]

Again, just as Wallace had anarchists and touted "I-told-you-so" language by declaring that "a Frankenstein monster" had been created, he would lay claim to recognizing the victimhood of Americans before anyone else: "The chickens have come home to roost." Trump had equally effective words. Common among Trump's rhetoric have been provocative words such as "rapists," "vermin," "disease," "queerness," "monstrosity," "disorder," "lack of control," and "femininity." As scholar Jennifer Wingard notes, language such as this is used to "isolate particular, non-white, non-male populations as 'problem' groups as existential threats to the U.S. as a whole."[9] Ample evidence of this "othering" process is found throughout all four of Wallace's presidential campaigns and in Trump's 2016 and 2020 campaigns and his one four-year term in the White House.

1964: Tapping into the Unrest

The political landscape leading up to the 1964 election did little to discount "us-vs.-them" feelings. The startling murder of President Kennedy on a street in Dallas and the simmering boil of civil rights activities throughout the South clearly signaled the nation was not at rest politically (or otherwise), and many critical concerns remained unresolved. For Wallace, in the weeks following his failed effort to stop the racial integration of the University of Alabama, he did as he normally did, ignored or refused to acknowledge defeat and instead claimed victory and went back on the road seeking to expand his audience and political stature and did so firmly embracing a message of victimology. Speaking before a gathering of South Carolina broadcasters in July 1963, Wallace broadly linked the civil rights movement to communists and said the movement promoted violence across the nation. "I am weary, and many Americans are, of these actions which endanger the safety of our wives and children," Wallace intoned.[10] His shrewd reference to the phrase "wives and children" was likely once again an "open code" phrase for southerners who had long posited the perceived "danger" of the Black male as sexual predator. Part of the message was the portrayal of a mythical life that was at risk via threats that impacted not only whites, but Blacks as well. He noted without a moment of irony: "The Negro has been treated well in the South, where a good heart has helped him more than all the evil political heads in this nation can ever accomplish." His suggestion that southern Blacks had enjoyed "the good heart" of the white majority helped construct the bigger idea that enough accommodations had occurred and that going further only served to victimize whites. He argued that northern liberals had tried the path of accommodating minorities to a large extent, and it was a failure:

> The northern liberals invited the Negroes to come north to a land of milk and honey. They accepted the proposition, but instead of finding this Utopia, they have found unemployment. They have been stacked in ghettos on top of one another, to become a part of every city's Harlem. Social and economic problems have been compounded. The end result is that this gross hypocrisy has brought guerilla warfare and insurrection to every large city in the United States. . . . Because of this hypocritical spectacle, the Negro no longer wants mere equal treatment, he expects and apparently intends to bludgeon the majority of this country's citizens into giving him preferential treatment. . . . by flaunting law and order.[11]

Wallace advanced his rhetoric in July 1963 by trying to steal headlines at the summer meeting of the National Governors Association in Miami. Once there, he openly attacked one of the nation's last "liberal" Republicans, New York governor Nelson Rockefeller, for allegedly "bankrolling" the efforts of Dr. King.[12] Wallace extended his "road show" up until just days before the assassination of President Kennedy. As 1964 opened, Wallace continued to be a focal point for forces opposing civil rights and not surprisingly he continued to receive speaking engagements across the nation (usually financed by the taxpayers of Alabama who paid for flights and security costs). Invited to speak before a forum in Minneapolis in February 1964, Wallace cast all of American society as a potential victim of the level of change underway in the nation, most especially the push for passage of the civil rights bill: "Misunderstanding and deliberate misrepresentation fostered by those who would *subvert* our heritage and our entire system of government have brought forth an era in American life which *threatens* to divide our people and *destroy* western civilization's greatest dreams and achievements"[13] [emphasis added]. His Minnesota speech was just a warm-up for what he had planned in next-door Wisconsin, as he entered that state's Democratic presidential primary to further expose weakness in support for the civil rights agenda of the Kennedy-Johnson administrations. At Whitewater State College in Wisconsin, Wallace claimed the mantle of being a picked-on victim by his opponents whom he accused of calling him "foul names."[14]

In the same period, during a speech at the University of Washington at Seattle, Wallace was interrupted by laughter and hecklers when he insisted, "I'm not anti-Negro, segregation is not synonymous of hatred."[15] He later complained to reporters that he was not being shown the courtesy he granted to others, an important part of reminding his supporters that to express your concerns about civil rights quickly meant you were victimized by opponents. It is a rhetorical tool that has lasted for decades, with Wallace and his supporters claiming victimization for being accused of being racists—a claim alive and well in the twenty-first century with Trump and supporters wincing when others so labeled them. A prime example was an October 2016 campaign speech by Trump in Colorado: "If you discuss crime in America's cities, they say bad things about you. They call you a racist."[16] Scholar Patricia Davis noted that a basic incongruity exists with those who would claim that being called a racist is the same type of victimization as faced by a person (a minority) who is impacted by racist language or behavior. In other words, new victims are created who assert "claims of racism, rather than racism itself . . . inflict injury upon those who are accused of racist behavior."[17]

As it was by Trump in 2016, the label of being a "racist" was turned on its head by Wallace to further the idea that challenges to his positions were unfair and victimizing. In an April 2 appearance before 200 members of the Madison Exchange Club in Wisconsin, Wallace held out special criticism for some members of the media in the state for allegedly being liberals who were biased against him. He said the state's two largest newspapers, the *Milwaukee Journal* and the *Milwaukee Sentinel,* refused to run an advertisement he attempted to place attacking the civil rights bill.[18] Earlier in the day, he appeared before the City Club of Milwaukee at its weekly meeting at the historic Pfister Hotel, where he was able to make the claims the rejected newspaper ads tried to do: "The civil rights bill is a cloak, and uncontrolled executive control in the body of the bill," Wallace said.[19] Beyond media rejections of his message, Wallace said an organized effort was underway to target him and his campaign by religious leaders. The governor's concern was well placed given that Wisconsin governor John W. Reynolds had taken the unusual step of enlisting the support of religious and denominational leaders across the state to try to sideline Wallace's campaign. Episcopal Bishop Donald H. V. Hallock responded that the church "wouldn't dare tell people how to vote" but quickly added, "But this is more than that, when you've got a real racist coming in on racist grounds."[20] A week later, three Roman Catholic diocese newspapers carried front-page articles warning Wisconsin Catholics that "voting for a racist means cooperating in their evil." The article, written by Father John T. O'Connor, a professor of moral theology from Hales Corners, Wisconsin, did not mention Wallace by name. The *Milwaukee Herald Citizen*, the Catholic newspaper in the state's largest community, noted, "Moral evil is invading Wisconsin. Governor Wallace has come to our state. He is publicly known for promoting that type of racism which has been specifically condemned by Pope Pius XI."[21] The Wisconsin Council of Rabbis acted in like manner and released a resolution denouncing the Wallace campaign. While noting they were reluctant to enter the political process, the resolution said they objected to

> Governor Wallace's opposition to civil rights legislation and his ardent championship of segregation. . . . [His views are] a threat to the moral quality of our nation and to the basic freedoms which every American is entitled to enjoy. . . . We feel morally obliged as religious teachers to declare that the positions taken by Governor Wallace encourage evil race prejudice and constitute an assault upon human dignity. They therefore ought to be decisively repudiated.[22]

To counter the message reaching voters about Wallace and his views and emphasize the "unfairness" of the "attacks" on him by religious leaders, his campaign placed newspaper advertisements under the title, "Religious Leaders *Who Know* Governor George C. Wallace Say This About Him . . . " featuring four quotes from Alabama clergymen.[23] Wallace seemed particularly taken back and surprised by the criticism from religious leaders and told reporters that he regularly prayed to God "to bless all people" and that "racism is evil." He explained, "There is a difference between a racist and a segregationist. Racism is disliking God's handiwork because a person is another color. I am a segregationist. This is in the best interest of the state—for Black and white."[24] Wallace said the only moral issue he saw at play in the Wisconsin campaign

was whether the federal government should take away the rights of any individual state. Wisconsin historian Robert Booth Fowler analyzed that the 1964
campaign revealed that Wallace was able to "hit emotional chords with some
voters, evoking deep hopes and winning some voters but also drawing intense
hostility from many others." Fowler said Wallace had correctly assessed that
"plenty of racial turmoil" existed in white and European ethnic working-class
neighborhoods of Milwaukee and other parts of the state and that "his populist
message would be well-received."[25]

Moving on to Indiana from Wisconsin, Wallace permitted Associated Press
national correspondent Jules Loh, a Georgia native, unusual access to his campaign. Loh apparently had used his southern charm and grace to ingratiate
himself to Wallace, and from that Loh wrote revealing dispatches about Wallace,
his campaign, and the fears and ambitions it inspired every step of the way.
Riding along with Wallace on a car trip from Indianapolis to Terre Haute, a
distance of some 75 miles, Loh exposed that some of the lock-jaw confidence
Wallace seemed to exude in public appearances was tempered with real trepi-
dation about the vitriol he seemed to inspire. Loh wrote,

> The placards jutting above the crowd in front of the hotel waved in threatening
> airs, and even with the car windows rolled up, the hoots and jeers were audible
> half a block away. George C. Wallace leaned forward, clutched the back rest and
> peered across the front seat through the windshield. His right hand reached
> over and pressed the door lock button, but it was already down. He had locked it
> when the three-car motorcade slowed at the edge of town and entered the Terre
> Haute traffic. . . . After six weeks of campaigning in Wisconsin and Indiana, the
> governor of Alabama can recognize from a distance the tenor of his "reception
> committee," as he calls them. So can the two plainclothesmen who ride in the
> front seat of the rented sedan. . . . "Oh my Lord," Wallace said as the car wheeled
> around the corner and the surging, shouting crowd came into view. "Are we going
> to get hurt here?" [Wallace asked.] "No sir," said the driver, Sgt. Lloyd Jemison of
> the Alabama State Police. "Just let [Corporal E. C.] Dothard get out first and open
> your door."[26]

Wallace seemed buoyed by the protests and tumult, even if the demonstrations
got carried away. Four nights earlier, both Jemison and Wallace were struck by
sticks and placards brandished by angry protestors in Kenosha, Wisconsin. At
Terre Haute, Dothard and Jemison successfully navigated Wallace through the
crowd of about one hundred—a mix of protestors and supporters—hurriedly
finding a dining room set up for a news conference. Loh noted that Wallace
seemed nervous until he reached the lectern, wiped his brow, took a sip of water,

and began with irony, "I'm glad to see everybody's in a good humor," drawing a subdued chuckle from the audience.[27] "On a speaker's platform, Wallace is in his element," Loh reported. "He can assess an audience quickly, and has an uncanny knack of putting an unfriendly group somewhat on the defensive." Although some of his audiences could prove a challenge, Loh noted that Wallace was effective at moving the debate—and related questions—to topics he wanted to discuss to demonstrate the victimization that he said was in full swing in America. Loh noted, for example, that the governor often inserted the word "hypocritical" into a discussion of the civil rights bill, invariably inviting a question from the audience about what was hypocritical about it. His reply echoed the one offered at numerous stops in Indiana: "When people lie down in the streets of Alabama, it's described as folks fighting for their rights. When they threatened to stall their cars on the streets of New York, it suddenly becomes disorderly conduct."[28]

Loh observed that Wallace found few converts among his audiences, with hundreds of people walking out of his appearances at both South Bend and Richmond. In Indiana, Wallace "has no state political organization, and his small staff tries to get him before the public by scheduling news conferences in various cities and hoping for invitations from civic groups and colleges," Loh reported. "It isn't always easy and his schedule seems to change from day to day"—as in Evansville where the location of a news conference had to be changed four times when local hotel managers were unwilling to take the risk and refused to rent a room to the Wallace team. There were no illusions of inroads being made that would allow him to actually win the primary, but Wallace was convinced making a point was worth it. Wallace admitted to Loh during one of their car rides across Indiana, "I know there are no votes on a college campus, but it gives me a forum and I do think I get the kids thinking a little bit."[29] Loh decided that Wallace was connecting with some appeal to northern voters because "he doesn't come off as expected." Wallace reminded voters and reporters that he had been stereotyped as an evil man. Loh wrote,

> This is the man many in the North regard as the very embodiment of all that is cruel and ignorant—at least that is the image Wallace believes he has projected, blaming what he calls "the left wing press" for popularizing it. When he turns out to be articulate, genial and very clever indeed, the discovery is often disarming to would-be hecklers.[30]

At the end of a long day of campaigning, Loh sat in the car with Wallace as he relaxed a bit for the hour-long drive from Terre Haute back to Indianapolis. There he noted,

Wallace leaned back in the darkness of his car, took three long draws of a cigar, and said, "You know what I'd like to do someday? I'd like to go into one of these places and tell them what they expect to hear—just how they expect to hear— just to see how they'd react. . . . They expect me to amble out on the stage and say: Hi, y'all! Sho good to see y'all! I'm jes an ign'rant 'ol hookwormy redneck from Alabama come up to visit y'all. Ain't had no education and didn't wear no shoes 'til I was 30, but I come to ask for y'all's vote." Wallace thought about it a while, and chuckled.[31]

Loh's account, which allowed Wallace to affirm what many southerners felt— judgment or ridicule from almost every aspect of American culture that fit well with the generational chip imbedded in their shoulders since 1865. It's no accident newspapers such as the *Tuscaloosa News* ran Loh's dispatches from Indiana on its front pages, likely a story greeted with many nodding heads from its Alabama readers.

As he continued to campaign across Indiana, Wallace accepted an invitation from a conservative students' group at Ball State Teachers College in Muncie where he shared that the increasing critical rhetoric from his "favorite son" opponent, Indiana Governor Matthew Welsh, was further evidence he was put upon. He reminded his audience that Welsh had refused to debate prior to the primary.[32] The personal nature of the protest at Ball State (which included a mock funeral for the four girls killed in a Birmingham church bombing) may have affected Wallace. In his remarks he said,

> You know, we hear all these left-wingers, and picketers with their signs and all, and people have a right to picket, I have no objection to peaceful picketing, that is a part of the American heritage and the American system. But you know, when they talk about human rights over property rights, well, that sounds good . . . but the only country in the world where anyone has any human rights is where own- ership of property is sacred under the law, such as in this country.[33]

In his final primary challenge in 1964, Wallace focused on racially torn Cam- bridge, Maryland. There he went ahead with a rally despite requests that he call it off. He understood the divided nature of Cambridge and offered one of his best-received lines of the night to his all-white audience: "I am not, and I know you are not, a racist or a bigot. We believe in individual American freedom. Never have I made an utterance which would reflect on a man because of his race, creed or color."[34]

Wallace wrapped up his delusional challenge to President Johnson just as newspaper headlines and television news across the nation carried disturbing

news of the continued search for three civil rights workers who went missing June 21, 1964, after being detained by police in Philadelphia, Mississippi.
Four days later, Wallace went stumping for support before an overflow crowd
of 10,000 supporters who packed the State Coliseum in Jackson on June 25.
Wallace was joined by Mississippi governor Paul Johnson in addressing civil
rights and the rise of southern political power. Governor Johnson had suffered
the embarrassment earlier in the day of learning after the fact that President
Johnson had ordered 200 troops, helicopter support, and the FBI into the state
to help search for the missing men—James Chaney, 21; Andrew Goodman, 20;
and Michael Schwerner, 24. All three men, who were attempting to register
Black voters in the state, were later found murdered. When it came his time to
speak (as federal investigators swarmed elsewhere across the state to find the
missing men), Wallace pretended he remained an active candidate for president,
despite having lost the three Democratic primaries he had entered. Wallace and
Governor Johnson urged Mississippians to join with all southerners to vote as
a block to take control of the presidential election. Mississippi residents gave
their neighboring governor a grand welcome, with a band and singers offering "When Wallace Goes Marching In" and a group of "high stepper" dancers
from Hinds Junior College wearing sweaters with individual letters spelling
out, W-A-L-L-A-C-E. It was a garish show of celebratory spirit in a state where
abduction and murder (carried out with the assistance and blessing of local
law enforcement) had become the latest response to the civil rights struggle.[35]

Amazingly, Wallace demonstrated little pause in going forward with "victim-
based" rhetoric that many believed was furthering violence and hatred between
white and Black citizens South and North. Wallace offered fiery rhetoric,
interrupted dozens of times by loud applause, referring to his just-completed
political forays into Wisconsin, Indiana, and Maryland and other speeches
and appearances across the North. Wallace tried to assure his Mississippi
neighbors, "If nothing more, my campaigns in the North have convinced
me that there are southerners in every state of the Union." He recalled with
delight a rally in a south side Milwaukee neighborhood "as one of the greatest political rallies I have ever witnessed." Wallace said he represented for the
nation a southern philosophy that was being embraced across all regions—"a
clear choice between our philosophy and the liberal, left-wing dogma which
now threatens to engulf every man, woman and child in the United States."[36]
Flashing the familiar donkey stubbornness that often was a trademark of the
Confederate past, Wallace declared: "I say to you, let it be known that we came
to win; that our mission is to lead; that we will have nothing less than victory;
and that victory will save our divinely inspired system of individual freedoms."
Reminders of how his audience should feel victimized were key to Wallace's

remarks, declaring that "we have been pushed around long enough" and "we are fed up" and building to a climax, "I'll tell you this: We are going to read the Bible in our Alabama schools. We don't care what the Supreme Court says." Frighteningly in a state where local law enforcement had often been used to inflict violence and suppression upon Blacks and northern whites attempting to advance rights in Mississippi, Wallace had no pause in adding,

> Let it be known that we will no longer tolerate the boot of tyranny. . . . We must destroy the power to dictate, to forbid, to require, to demand, to distribute, to edict, and to judge what is best and enforce that will of judgment upon free citizens. . . . Let's stand up for America! Let's save our country![37]

The messages Wallace delivered on that warm night in Mississippi contrasted dramatically with the formality of July 2, 1964, for a crowded and elaborate bill signing ceremony (broadcast live nationally on television and radio) in the East Room of the White House. There, President Johnson signed the Civil Rights Act of 1964 into law, ending the Wallace challenge. Johnson understood the landmark nature of the legislation and spoke in somber terms,

> We believe that all men are created equal. Yet many are denied equal treatment. We believe that all men are entitled to the blessings of liberty. Yet millions are deprived of those blessings—not because of their own failures, but because of the color of their skin. The reasons are deeply imbedded in our history and tradition and the nature of man. We can understand—without rancor or hatred—how this all happened. But it cannot continue. Our Constitution, the foundation of our Republic, forbids it. The principles of freedom forbid it. Morality forbids it. And the law I sign tonight forbids it.[38]

Two days later, Governor Wallace got his say at a July 4 Rally at the Southeastern-Lakewood Park Fairgrounds in Atlanta. Advertised as "The greatest patriotic rally in southern history and one of the greatest in American history"—Wallace was the primary speaker along with former Mississippi governor Ross Barnett, a die-hard segregationist who had just completed his term of office in January 1964. While far less than the 100,000 advertised as expected to attend, as many as 10,000 southerners braved hot and humid weather to hear Wallace and Barnett. Not everyone was in the mood for listening, however, as the *Anniston Star* reported to its readers back in Alabama. "Three civil rights workers were mobbed and beaten [in Atlanta] Saturday after they entered a states' rights rally," the newspaper reported. "Walking directly into the middle of a large grandstand of more than 10,000 persons present, the Negroes were immediately pummeled and beaten to the cement steps with fold-up metal chairs and fists."[39] An Associated Press account noted, "Several white spectators caught one of the Negro men in the stands and hurled him onto the concrete steps, raining blow after blow upon him, while other white persons chased the other two Negro men to a wire fence at the front of the stands."[40] The melee, eventually broken up by police, occurred during the speech of Governor Barnett and before Wallace had taken the podium. "Several white spectators said the Negroes booed Barnett. A chorus of boos and catcalls from the whites was directed at the Negroes, interrupting Barnett's speech," United Press International reported.[41] Once order was restored and the protestors removed, Wallace spoke noting that it was ironic that he was speaking on Independence Day, just days after "the president of the United States signed into law the most monstrous piece of legislation ever enacted by the United States Congress. It is a fraud, a sham, and a hoax." As expected, his remarks drew a deafening roar from the audience. Understanding he was speaking before an audience hungry for the opposing view to that expressed by LBJ, Wallace said the bill dishonored the nation's heroes for freedom was an act of tyranny and "is the assassin's knife stuck in the back of liberty. With this assassin's knife and a blackjack in the hands of the federal force-cult, the left-wing liberals will try to force us back into bondage—bondage to tyranny."[42]

While Wallace had lost the fight for passage of the Civil Rights Act, it didn't mean he meant to stop fighting. Just as he did when he lost the effort to stop the integration of the University of Alabama, he simply changed the subject and refused to acknowledge defeat. His campaign efforts for 1964 had done little to meet any of his goals—he wasn't the Democratic Party's nominee for president and he had not stopped passage of the Civil Rights Act—but he *had* raised his own profile considerably. On July 19, 1964, the producers of the CBS Sunday news program *Face the Nation* invited Wallace to be their guest interviewed on air by Paul Niven and Dan Rather of CBS News and Ben A. Franklin of the *New York Times*. Understanding his efforts had not met his stated, larger goals, Wallace changed the goals starting off from the top answering a question from Niven by saying his purpose was "to help conservatize both national parties" and to send a message to party leaders to embrace states' rights and local government control, and "bring a halt to this destruction of individual liberty and freedom." Wallace told his interviewers that he was "the instrument through which this message was sent to the high councils of both major political parties" and predicted that this message "will be heeded. My mission has been accomplished."[43] His remarks would set the framework for which he would continue to work as "an instrument" of southern political interests for years to come, expressing the frustrations of his "victimized" followers, whether he actually accomplished anything or not. The mantle he attempted to claim had a familiar sound to it. It was clear, Wallace was, at least for now, comfortable being an "instrument" that played music and songs only some knew or would follow, and worried not that the opposing chorus would grow. Compromise was not possible within the resentful rhetoric of victimhood. It was the fight that drew him more than anything else—winning had become secondary, or was just delayed. "The people of the South are going to wipe the smiles off some of the liberals' faces in the country, and the South is going to be the balance of power in the presidential election," Wallace told his CBS interrogators.[44] He couldn't have been more wrong. The South was no factor at all in deciding the election of 1964 (Barry Goldwater ultimately carrying only his home state of Arizona and five former Confederate states, Alabama, Georgia, Louisiana, Mississippi, and South Carolina), as Johnson rolled to an historic landslide victory.

1968: Offering an Alternative Choice

The scorn of being called a racist was still very much in place as Wallace entered the 1968 presidential gambit, this time as an independent candidate taking on both the Democrats and the Republicans. Presidential scholar Theodore White, writing after the 1968 campaign was completed, assessed Wallace an unrepentant, open racist, but distinguished that Wallace likely did not personally hate Black people—he had known them all his life—as one Alabama reporter advised White: "He's a segregationist, not a lyncher."[45] Because Wallace had enjoyed friendly relationships with many Blacks—although through the filter of a segregated South—he would frequently lay claim to the idea that if Black voters would try to understand his views, they would more openly support him:

> If they believe the things that have been said about us, I can understand their reluctance to vote for us. But we did have Negro citizens working for us in California to get us on the ballot. We had them in Texas. If Negro citizens understand what we are talking about and can get an objective viewpoint of the people of my region and also my viewpoint, I believe that I will get Negro support in the country . . . As time goes by, I believe I am going to get Negro support.[46]

The start of Wallace's 1968 campaign continued to be delayed by events outside of his control between April and June. In April, Martin Luther King Jr. was killed in Memphis; in May, Wallace's wife, Lurleen, succumbed to her battle with cancer; and in June, Senator Robert Kennedy was slain in Los Angeles.

As he took initial steps to get back on the campaign trail, reporters quizzed Wallace about whether the shooting deaths of King and Kennedy had caused him to change how he campaigned: "I haven't thought about that," he said. "We haven't even discussed that yet."[47] Asked directly whether he feared for his own life in the current political atmosphere, Wallace said, "As you know, I've been in many spots. We've had assaults four or five years ago. Some people didn't pay much attention to it then, but it was there."[48] It was a rare moment where Wallace was not openly claiming to be a victim—instead letting reporters make the suggestion that his life could be in jeopardy in the sometimes violent, and always unpredictable nature of 1968 politics. The US Secret Service did confirm it had assigned a security detail to Wallace and his family (consisting of 20 men) three days after RFK was killed. The detail was provided at the direction of President Johnson, and Wallace was free to determine how he would use their services. Further, Wallace campaign events did change somewhat, with the Associated Press showing nationwide photos of a young girl having her binocular case inspected by a federal agent as she and her family entered a Wallace event in Atlanta.[49]

On June 11, 1968, five days after Robert Kennedy's burial, Wallace started an eleven-day "Southern tour" with stops in friendly Memphis and Chattanooga, Tennessee. If anyone had doubted whether events in his personal life (such as the death of his wife) had softened his edge, those ideas were erased with the return of his fiery rhetoric, telling a loud Memphis crowd estimated at 10,000: "I'm tired of folks saying we're sick in this country. I'll tell you who's sick, it's some of the leadership of this country" who had helped "bring about the breakdown of law and order."[50] It was classic fire-and-brimstone victim language that Wallace was perfecting better than most. Leaving his young family behind in Alabama in the care of relatives, Wallace seemed to pour himself into his presidential campaign—some surmising that it was his own brand of grief therapy. Wallace worked day and night to gain ballot access in all 50 states—including an elaborate statewide campaign to gain qualifying signatures for the California ballot—his campaign sidestepping earned media for their own version of "the George Wallace story." A 1967–68 campaign film distributed widely featured long clips of Wallace speaking before audiences in hotel conference rooms and elsewhere under the banner "Stand Up for America." The speech excerpts used included his familiar refrains about law and order, the overreach of federal courts into the lives of regular Americans, school busing to achieve desegregation, and Vietnam. The bottom-line theme: Americans were being victimized by social experimenters in Washington, and it was time to stand up against such oppression. He customized one of his regular lines specifically for his California audience (and drew audience laughter and applause) when speaking at a gathering in Torrance when he said,

> You've read about it, you've seen it. They turn someone loose who is a proven mur-
> derer of five or more people, then some pseudo-intellectual tells us that, "Really,
> he's not to blame, society is to blame because his Papa didn't carry him to see the
> Los Angeles Rams play when he was a little boy"—and he's mad because of it.[51]

Such direct speech was a key part of the Wallace appeal, confirmed by a 1968 Harris Poll that found the strength of Wallace's appeal was strongest among voters for "saying it like it is" and speaking bluntly and plainly about the issues facing the nation. The poll also noted Wallace doing well among military vet- erans and families with ties to law enforcement. Many voters found his tough talk about law and order appealing and believed he may be best suited to bring things together. The Harris Poll would foreshadow trouble to come, however. By the end of September (as the presidential race was just engaging), the number of voters seeing Wallace as their "law and order candidate" began to shrink from a high of 53 percent to just 21 percent by late October. Theodore White analyzed that while voters may have been amused, or even reassured by the straight talk that sounded like it was coming from a friend over the back fence or a guy at the end of the bar, many may have wondered if Wallace was, in fact, presidential timber. White believed that "as media made clear the cold Wallace message, stripping any 'folksiness' from him, those who could not accept the label 'racist' for themselves grew"—and as a result, the number of voters who thought Wallace was a racist continued to climb.[52] Wallace was always ready on the defense against claims he was a racist, whether or not they reassured independent and wayward Republican voters who might have considered him:

> They say it is racist to oppose these federal guidelines that would tell us how to
> run our lives. Well, when you can't talk about upholding the constitution without
> being called a racist, this country has come to a sad day. They say it's racist what
> I say, but they're really using this as an excuse to defend their effort to get control
> of your heart and mind.[53]

In October 1968, during a fiery speech before an all-white audience in Cicero, Illinois, Wallace attacked the Johnson administration-commissioned report on racial disorder. Calling the report "asinine and ludicrous," he warned his audi- ence that the authors of the document "would blame you, the good people of Cicero, for the breakdown of law and order. Those same people would double the taxes on the working man to pay people, not only just for not working, but not to destroy the country."[54]

His crowd warming up, Wallace drew his heaviest applause by noting, "Not one nickel of federal money will be spent to bus any child where he doesn't want to be bused. No one will tell the people of Cicero how to run their schools, and neither will a federal judge 1,000 miles away, when I'm elected president."[55] In one paragraph, Wallace had summarized his message and his appeal—outside threats from Washington bureaucrats sought to impose their will upon people in suburban towns like Cicero. In doing so, he reminded them, they were victimized. It was Wallace, if elected president, who could stand against such powerful forces. Scholar Anna M. Young attributes such an approach to the historic role of populists, with language from Wallace (and later Trump) providing "cover for white nationalism" and that the "bombast, speaking off the cuff, the channeling of 'every man' . . . all of these features enable a performance of a sort of parrhesias [or boldness of speech], someone speaking difficult truths to power."[56]

Perhaps encouraged by the response his remarks about school desegregation received in Illinois, Wallace moved on to Michigan and in Grand Rapids made the idea of busing students to achieve racial balance in Michigan schools the centerpiece of his remarks. Wallace openly sought to tap into the fears of many white parents, and in one flight of fantasy suggested suburban white families in Michigan were victims of "social experimenters" in Washington DC who wanted to put white children in Grand Rapids on school buses and ship them off 160 miles (one way) to predominantly Black, inner-city schools in Detroit.[57] Looking past the logistical ridiculousness of Wallace's claim of Grand Rapids kids being "shipped off" to Detroit, his claim was cynical and cunning at the same time. He spoke just over a year after deadly racially charged riots rocked the Motor City, leaving 43 people dead, more than 300 injured, and 1,400 buildings burned or damaged. He understood white parents in his Grand Rapids audience harbored fears in the backs of their mind that their children would be part of a social experiment to integrate Detroit schools. On the same campaign swing, before a loud and supportive crowd in working-class Flint, Michigan, Wallace accused Nixon and Humphrey of having "succumbed to the blackmail of a few anarchists in the street and passed a law telling you what to do with your property." His take on housing was a direct appeal to the fears the city's white residents felt, months earlier voters having narrowly approved one of the nation's first referendums supporting an "open housing" policy.[58] Wallace found working-class Flint in a major state of transition. In 1966, voters installed the city's first Black mayor, Floyd J. McCree, but the city council refused to pass a nondiscrimination housing ordinance. McCree later pushed a first-of-its-kind housing ordinance that prohibited "red-lining" against Blacks in home purchases or rentals. The initiative was narrowly approved in a public referendum vote in February 1968.[59]

The Wallace rhetoric based in victimhood remained the same, whether the governor was speaking before northern or southern audiences. In Chattanooga, Wallace told supporters that Republicans and Democrats wanted to pass laws to incarcerate homeowners who refused to sell or lease their home to any person. He called such ideas "sick" and declared, "Let's put both of those parties out!"[60] Riffs such as this were met with reminders that the opposition standing in the way were "guideline writers" or "some fellow with a pointed head who can't even park a bicycle." He said as president he would listen "to what the cab driver thinks" and "the man on the street."[61] Strong "in-group" and "out-group" language permeated every aspect of Wallace's remarks. As he told a cheering crowd at Hammond, Indiana, "*Your* day is coming, and *their* day is over."[62]

1972: Sanding Down the Rough Edges

By 1972, Wallace was back inside the Democratic fold, and the rhetoric had been tuned up a bit—some of the sharper edges from the prior eight years gone. Reporters and other observers attributed the change to the influence of his new wife, Cornelia, whom he married in December 1970 just before starting a new term as governor of Alabama. The daughter of another Alabama political family and former beauty queen, Cornelia was not just a cosmetic addition; she had political ideas and ambitions and made those known. In addition, Wallace's team of advisers seemed to be gaining in their political and public relations sophistication as 1972 approached. National news wires picked up the story that George and Cornelia had welcomed the children of Alabama servicemembers held as prisoners of war in Vietnam for a Governor's Mansion Christmas party. Among the gifts given to the POW family members by Governor Wallace (who dressed as Santa Claus for the occasion) were commemorative "George Wallace wristwatches," the Associated Press reported.[63] Despite such improvement, many of Wallace's closest advisers (including his new wife Cornelia) were of the opinion that he needed a new team of captains to run his next campaign for president. Wallace backer and national columnist John J. Synon declared Wallace "indubitably the best political mind now functioning in the interests of this country" but told his readers Wallace could be "his own worst political enemy" because "he does not have now, and he has never had, political lieutenants of stature—and you can't win the presidency without them."[64] Cornelia Wallace agreed, recalling that as she traveled with George frequently as he tested the waters for a 1972 run for the White House, she came away unimpressed with what remained of his organization. She recalled an early trip to Memphis to meet with Wallace supporters:

> And it was just a very small crowd of men, and they didn't look really bright, or intelligent, or just like nice, happy, ordinary people. When we started on our trip back home, I said, "George, is that all you have to run with on a third party movement? Is that your party and all you have?" And he said, "Yes," and I said, "Well, honey, then you better stay at home because you are not gonna make it with *that* group." I assumed the idea was to get elected president.[65]

"[Cornelia] was a very stylish person," said one of Wallace's most trusted aides, Tom Turnipseed. "She used to kid around and say, 'We're gonna 'couth him up a little bit.'" Among her changes for Wallace were elimination of the heavy hair grease that he had become known for and shedding dark black or navy blue suits for lighter colors.[66] Veteran *Alabama Journal* reporter Ray Jenkins noted that George and Cornelia together made "a very stylish and interesting couple" and "to some extent they sort of became a Southern, dog-patch version of 'Camelot,' of Jack and Jackie [Kennedy], but instead George and Cornelia."[67] Perhaps Wallace was finally going to be able to shed some of his more unlikeable qualities and attract new voters with a more mainstream approach. Wallace historian Dan T. Carter accurately noted Cornelia was not just interested in helping George appear or look better to voters; she wanted to play a role in deciding how he could reach the White House, which created conflict. Long-time Wallace aides harbored hostility toward Cornelia, Carter wrote, describing her as "a shrewd political operator in her own right, and she recognized the dangers posed by the governor's old supporters."[68] Wallace's daughter Peggy took notice that Cornelia had a big personality of her own—her uncle being former governor "Big Jim" Folsom. She recalls a family interview on *The Dick Cavett Show* in which Cornelia openly joked, "I am so powerful they had to put a governor on me." Peggy noted, "Everyone was just stunned out of their minds that she made that comment, but that is how she approached their relationship."[69]

Veteran journalist Dan King Thomasson covered two of Wallace's presidential campaigns and said there was no "science" behind Wallace's appeal to northern blue-collar workers. He covered Wallace campaign swings in Indiana, Michigan, and Maryland in 1972 and noted:

> Maryland and Indiana were copperhead states, so they may not be the best examples, but Michigan is more noteworthy. There is a pattern here in the industrial

rust belt of the Midwest, particularly around the auto industry and steel industry, and others. These industries where you have an apprentice program. . . . I went with Humphrey to Ford's River Rouge Plant in [Flint] Michigan, they had a mile-long assembly line. Humphrey went in there and all the skilled laborers, the tool and die people, all those people had their own separate area to work in. . . . The situation was clearly that apprentice jobs, which were strongly union, did not include a single black face—maybe one out of 150 workers. These jobs were passed down from person-to-person all those years, and they wanted to protect the apprentice system that controlled that. . . . If you went to the assembly line area, though, that was heavily African-American and they were jumping off the line to shake Hubert's hand. It was much the same way with the United Steel Workers' unions in Indiana and elsewhere.[70]

In Florida and other states, the battle for union votes broke into open war-fare between union leadership and its members. In a handful of states, local bargaining units went so far as to defy union leadership and make their own, separate endorsements of Wallace. George Meany, the powerful president of the AFL-CIO made clear his opposition to Wallace—new rhetoric and look or not. "George Wallace is a bigot, a racist, and he's anti-labor down to the soles of his feet." Meany and the AFL-CIO leadership seemed out of step on other issues as well, its national political action committee adopting a position in support of busing to achieve school desegregation—providing Wallace with more fodder to encourage rank-and-file members to rebel against union leader-ship.[71] In Michigan, where unionized auto workers were a major political force, Wallace openly courted their support with victim-like rhetoric: "The average union man is fed up," he said and made the claim that the shunning union leadership was giving him could be a good thing. "I think being ignored by the leadership helps you because the people are rebelling."[72] The "rebellion" Wallace sensed may have been real as the powerful United Auto Workers union took the unusual step of endorsing not one, but two candidates in the Michigan primary—Senators George McGovern *and* Hubert Humphrey. Many believed the move by the UAW reflected conflict in whom it planned to support but left no question that Wallace remained an unacceptable choice for union leaders. Wallace had concluded that the Democratic Party had become hostage to "the eastern intellectual snobbery that look down their noses at every auto worker and every average citizen in this country."[73]

Another issue Wallace attempted to turn toward him was the ongoing war in Vietnam. Throughout the working-class suburban cities and towns sur-rounding Detroit, Wallace hammered away at the length of the war and at his opponents—members of the US Senate—who had supported LBJ's "Gulf of Tonkin" resolution that assured conflict would continue in Southeast Asia indefinitely. Wallace understood that many of the white and Black families from across Michigan communities had sent their sons in answer to the draft, but they were also beginning to form serious questions about the wisdom of continuing the war. "They [McGovern and Humphrey] should get you out of Vietnam," Wallace said, projecting Americans as almost victims of their Congress. "They got you in. If they were going to vote for the Gulf of Tonkin resolution, they should have been willing to win it." It was a classic Wallace take, blaming others for the war, making claims that a resolution to the war was being kept from victimized American troops and their families but offering no specific alternative plan.[74] He was, however, optimistic about ongoing peace talks in Paris brokered by the Nixon administration. In answer to a question to what his first priorities as president would be, Wallace was characteristically vague in what he would do differently than the Johnson and Nixon administrations had done, offering weakly that if the war was not concluded by the time he was inaugurated, "I would take what action I thought was necessary in line with whatever the thinking was in the State Department and the Defense Department—whatever is necessary to wind it down."[75] He did state support for an essential requirement to resolve the release of American POWs and MIAs held by or reported missing in North Vietnam, and then he added: "I said eight or nine years ago that we shouldn't be involved in a land war in Asia." Wallace said from his personal visit to Vietnam and from talking to his voters, he knew that morale in Vietnam was low. "The morale is bad because you just can't fight a war on your own territory for 20 years and have your morale boosted," he said. "They go to sleep in North Vietnam and don't worry about their throats being cut at night."[76]

With impressive wins in Florida and North Carolina, Wallace went into familiar states such as Wisconsin and Indiana with high hopes of adding to his delegate count. In Indiana, the race was shaping up very much to his satisfaction with the field cleared of everyone except him and Humphrey. Senator Humphrey was a ready-made target as Wallace offered up some of his favorite rhetorical tropes for a large Indianapolis audience, reminding voters that Humphrey had been in the Senate or the White House for decades, decades of continued growth in welfare, taxes, and other oppressions against working people. He attacked "lazy welfare loafers," "an absurd no-win war in Vietnam," "busing little children to kingdom come," and "thugs who have taken over the streets" and told Hoosiers: "The best way to send them a message from Indiana is to vote for George Wallace!"[77] During the same visit to Indianapolis, the Wallace campaign attempted to raise funds in a more traditional manner by staging a paid luncheon at the Hilton Hotel. The event was lightly attended by only 150 supporters. William M. Chaney, grand dragon of the state's Ku Klux Klan, attended the luncheon to express his support for Wallace but was confronted by a group of women who supported Wallace and objected to the Klan leader's presence.[78] Wallace, when told by reporters that Chaney was present said, "Well, I don't know anything about it. I've never belonged to the Klan, never been to one of their rallies." He emphasized that he was introduced at the luncheon by Norman E. Jones, described by the *Franklin Daily Journal* as a "portly and balding man" who stood at the famous bullet-proof Wallace podium and declared to the all-white audience: "I'm not like ya'all, I'm black. And just to show you that I am, this here is my soul sister," as he pointed to a reticent young Black woman who stood beside him wearing a Wallace hat. "We're here for Mr. Wallace because he goes along with a program for the working man and we are the working man," Jones said.[79] The exchange between the openly racist supporters of Wallace—and more proper supporters who eschewed any suggestion they held racist sentiments reflected the paradox that was the Wallace campaign always. Racist themes were always just under the surface of the governor's message, one meant to inspire a "victim-like" attitude among white supporters and causing them to rush to a champion who would fight for them. It was clear Wallace couldn't have it both ways. New suits and haircuts, a traditional political wife at his side, and more sophisticated campaigning all around could not completely wash Wallace clean of the murkier elements of his past campaigns and his former and current bombast. The "almost there" nature of Wallace's 1972 campaign emphasized that while the message or issues Wallace articulated were connecting, it would take better packaging, better branding, to get those issues home to a working majority of voters. History would show Wallace had laid important groundwork for such future success, but it would be others (such as Nixon, Reagan, and even Carter) who would cross the finish line, not Wallace.

1976: New Challenges

For the 1976 campaign, Wallace not only had to contend with a younger and more jovial southern governor in the race (Carter), he had a direct competitor for the more conservative wing of the Democratic Party in Senator Henry "Scoop" Jackson of Washington. As national columnists Rowland Evans and Robert Novak noted, "the angry despair of low-income whites" were not inspired by Jackson's moderate take, and he was no match for Wallace. This was particularly so when both Wallace and Jackson toured South Boston communities looking for votes for the Massachusetts Democratic primary. Jackson was booed by

Wallace supporters in the Charlestown section of Boston, described by reporters as "an anti-busing hotbed" in the city. Evans and Novak noted, "One perceptive South Boston politician believes voters there, *confronting the loss of their school system and indeed their way of life*, view George Wallace as their only protector [emphasis added]. . . . Jackson came over as cool and self-controlled, but also, as a supporter of busing. No such identity problem is encountered by Wallace."[80] Wallace aides had been advised that busing remained such a volatile issue in Boston that the city was best described as a "powder keg." To that, Wallace told a gathering at a Lithuanian Club that "you can win this battle at the ballot box and peacefully" and reminded them he was with them in their fight for their schools—and their way of life. "When they [the national Democrats] said busing, I said no!" Evans and Novak concluded: "George Wallace has a monopoly on primary voters who feel betrayed and persecuted by busing."[81] And while Boston's busing battles had been famously violent—forever immortalized in Stanley Forman's Pulitzer Prize–winning photograph depicting a white man "stabbing" a Black man with an American flag on a pole. Violence is not just a means to an end for Wallace, Joseph E. Lowndes contends, but was "constitutive of Wallace's politics itself and a key ingredient of his appeal. The combative position of Wallace and his supporters performed over the course of his career helped define his political influence"[82] and accompanied his challenge to mainstream politics evoking both the "unchecked violence that threatened the American people" and "threatened violence on behalf of that same people."[83]

As the Wisconsin and Indiana primaries approached in May, Wallace pivoted from the busing issue that was not as "hot" there as in Massachusetts and elsewhere. The pivot didn't work, however, as it appeared he was going through the motions conducting a maudlin repeat of his campaign four years earlier. While in Maryland for quick—and awkward—visits to the state where his life almost ended in a Laurel parking lot, he took up a favorite complaint casting himself as a victim of "ideological theft" from the rest of the field of Democrats. Wallace accused the other Democrats in the race of "drinking out of the same dipper" he had been using for years. "While most people are drinking out of the dipper, some dip in a little bit on one side and then dip a little bit on the other side. People like Carter should quit riding both sides and let us know where they stand. At least I stand on one side." The only major campaign event in Maryland was promoted as a chance for Wallace to greet and thank faithful campaign volunteers. Once at the event, reporters noted Wallace barely mentioned the campaign workers in a tiny office where only a handful could fit. An Associated Press dispatch indicated Wallace was "heavily guarded" by Secret Service officers "who quickly wheeled him past outstretched hands to a podium in the small storefront headquarters. Instead of meeting supporters outside, Wallace spoke via loudspeakers from inside the room and answered reporters' questions."[84] The reporting was sad and overcame any message Wallace wanted to convey—typifying his last and failed run for the White House. Either there weren't enough victims left to exploit, or the messenger himself had been rendered more ineffective than he knew. Something even greater may have been eluding Wallace in 1976—before and after—that he didn't seem to understand. Wallace contemporaries like Jimmy Carter, with a message of honest leadership that "will never tell a lie," and Ronald Reagan, with a smooth delivery and stronger connection to "real Americans" who felt left behind via words spoken in a folksy, friendly manner minus Wallace's stored resentment, were passing him by. While Wallace had remained committed to what scholar Paul Elliott Johnson described as a "focus on the *felt* precarity" of his supporters' existence (rather than their shared connections with others), he sought to keep backers in the camp of people who self-identify as victimized, "encouraging the well-off and privileged to adopt the mantle of victimhood at the expense of those who occupy more objectively fraught positions."[85] It was a message that had worked before, but by 1976, when spoken by Wallace, the message was as flaccid as Wallace's damaged body sitting in a wheelchair. A key aspect of Johnson's posit is that the victims, the subjects of the demagoguery, include "the well-off and privileged" and despite their standing, adopt the persona of a victim. Did George Wallace ever attract a "well-off" or "privileged" following beyond race? Lower- and middle-class whites were on board often with Wallace, but the changing demographic of the nation, including professional women and minorities in the workforce, independent voters open to either party, and college-educated voters could find no attraction to Wallace's bitter messages. In other words, he could no longer connect. It would take another personality, Donald Trump, who exuded wealth and success far beyond what most voters ever can visualize for themselves, that could draw in the "well-off and privileged" voters that eluded Wallace (and all the requisite power and agency they bring to the political process).

President John F. Kennedy and Governor George C. Wallace at the thirtieth anniversary celebration of the Tennessee Valley Authority at Muscle Shoals, Alabama, May 18, 1963. *Alabama Department of Archives and History.*

Governor Wallace's famous "stand in the schoolhouse door" in Tuscaloosa, Alabama outside Foster Auditorium at the University of Alabama, June 11, 1963. *Alabama Department of Archives and History.*

Protestors were on hand for many of Governor Wallace's stops as part of a 1963 speaking tour at universities across the northeast. *Alabama Department of Archives and History.*

Governor Wallace talks to reporters upon arrival in Indiana, one of three Democratic presidential primaries he entered in 1964. *Alabama Department of Archives and History.*

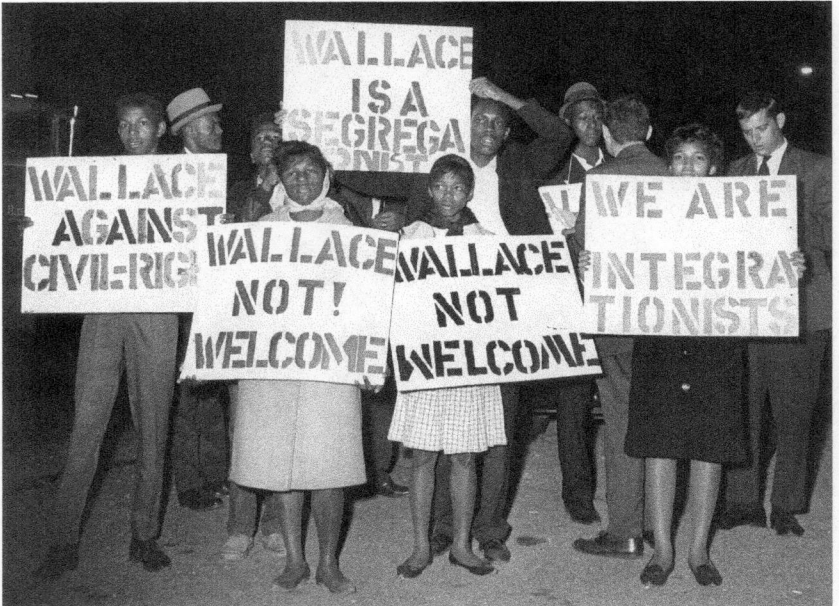

A group of African-American protestors "welcomed" Governor Wallace to Gary, Indiana for his 1964 entry into the Indiana Democratic primary. *Alabama Department of Archives and History.*

Governor Wallace met with President Lyndon B. Johnson on March 13, 1965 to discuss ongoing struggles with the civil rights march from Selma to Montgomery. *Alabama Department of Archives and History.*

Governor Wallace, constitutionally prevented from seeking a second term, speaks on behalf of his wife, Lurleen Wallace (holding her daughter Leigh) who ran in his stead for governor of Alabama in 1966. *Alabama Department of Archives and History*.

George Wallace speaks at a victory celebration for his wife, Lurleen (at right), who was elected Alabama's 46th governor on November 8, 1966. *Alabama Department of Archives and History*.

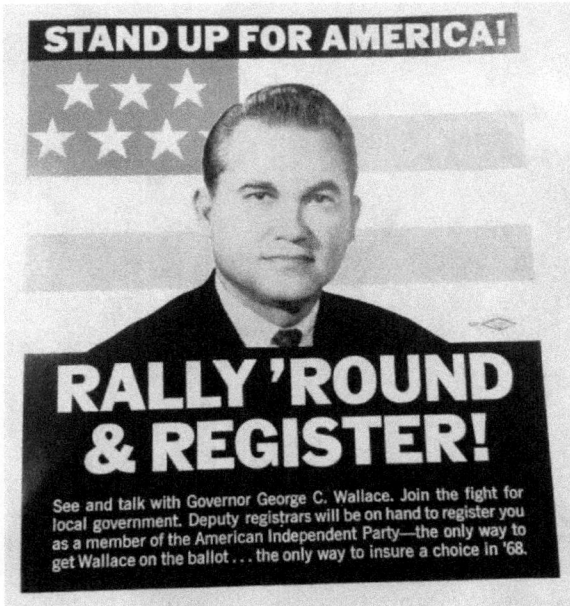

A Wallace campaign poster used in the fall of 1967 to register thousands of California residents for the American Independent Party in order for the governor to gain access to the 1968 presidential ballot in that state. *Photo by Andrew Stoner, files of Alabama Department of Archives and History.*

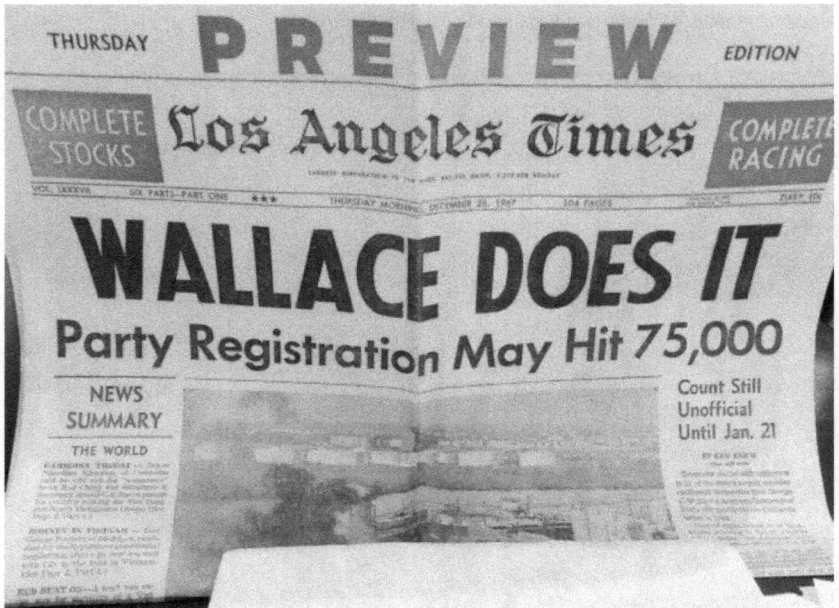

A December 28, 1967 edition of *The Los Angeles Times* declares Wallace's success in gaining access to California's 1968 presidential ballot. *Photo by Andrew Stoner, files of Alabama Department of Archives and History.*

Wallace, who had put his 1968 presidential campaign on hold numerous times, stood as witness on May 7, 1968, for the swearing in of Albert P. Brewer as governor to succeed Governor Lurleen Wallace, who died earlier that day. *Alabama Department of Archives and History.*

"The Wallace Girls" were a standard feature of Wallace's four campaigns for president—the young women charged with circulating buckets throughout rally audiences to collect cash donations. *Alabama Department of Archives and History.*

Wallace's 1968 third-party Presidential campaign sparked a variety of grassroots responses, including this "campaign headquarters" erected in a former gas station. *Alabama Department of Archives and History.*

Governor Wallace and General Curtis LeMay (immediately over Wallace's left shoulder) make their first campaign rally appearance together at Monument Circle in Indianapolis, October 1868. Indiana University Archives.

Wallace's 1972 Democratic presidential primary campaign was drawing large crowds, such as this one in Michigan. Party officials openly worried that he might actually have enough support to win the Democratic nomination. *Alabama Department of Archives and History.*

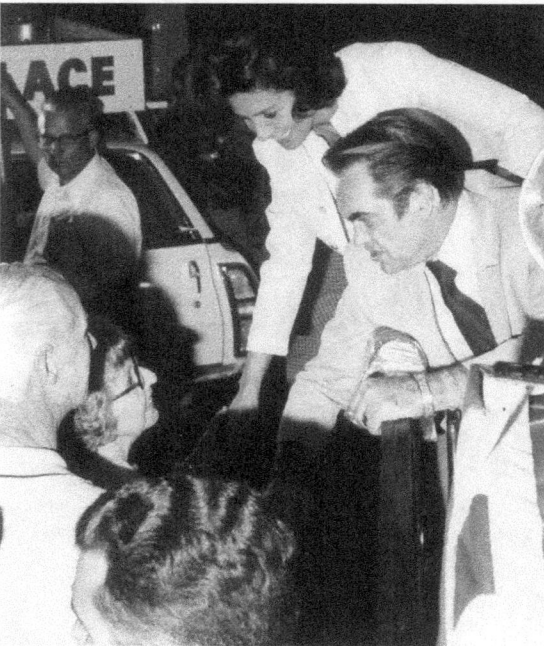

Cornelia Wallace, over the governor's shoulder, campaigned often with her husband during the spring 1972 Democratic primaries. *Alabama Department of Archives and History.*

Cornelia and George Wallace at a 1972 "Stand Up for America" Wallace rally. One political pundit describing them as "a sort of a Southern, dog-patch version of 'Camelot,' of Jack and Jackie Kennedy." *Alabama Department of Archives and History.*

Southern support remained a key component to Wallace's strategy—the "stars and bars" Confederate flag often prominently featured as here in Baton Rouge, Louisiana, in 1972. *Alabama Department of Archives and History.*

Wallace getting up-close with voters at Leesburg, Florida in 1972. Wallace grabbed 42 percent of the Florida vote in a crowded Democratic primary, and carried each of the state's 67 counties. *Alabama Department of Archives and History.*

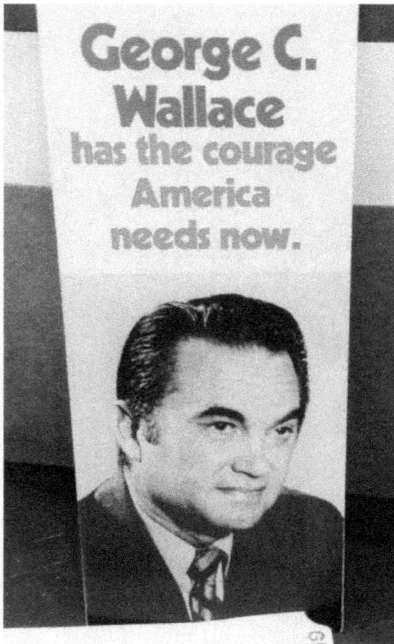

A 1972 Wallace campaign flyer shows the more sophisticated campaign he had learned to run in this third try for the presidency. *Photo by Andrew Stoner, files of Alabama Department of Archives and History.*

Amidst the large crowd on hand at the Laurel Shopping Center in Laurel, Maryland, on May 15, 1972, was a would-be Wallace assassin, Arthur Bremer. Wallace was shot and mortally wounded at the conclusion of this rally, suffering five gunshot wounds. *Alabama Department of Archives and History.*

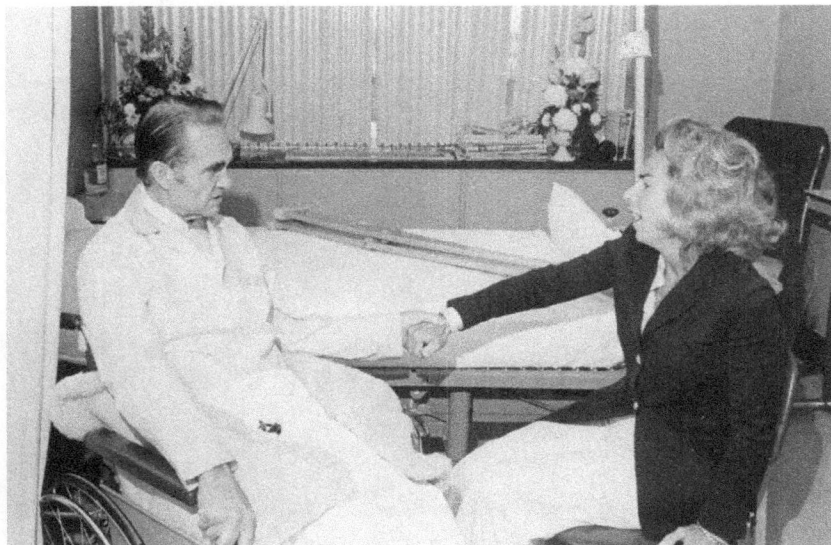

Among those visiting George Wallace as he recuperated in May 1972 at a Maryland hospital was Ethel Kennedy, widow of the late Robert F. Kennedy, cut down by an assassin's bullet in June 1968. *Alabama Department of Archives and History.*

Just fifty-three days after he was shot five times by a would-be assassin, a now wheelchair-bound Wallace returned to Montgomery, Alabama where a throng of more than 5,000 waited at Donnelly Air Force Base to hear him thank them for their prayers and support. *Alabama Department of Archives and History.*

Wallace insisted upon speaking to the 1972 Democratic National Convention in Miami, Florida in July 1972. Making history as the first candidate to address a convention from a wheelchair, Wallace later told reporters, "My campaign ended informally in Laurel (where he was shot). It ended formally tonight in Miami." *Alabama Department of Archives and History.*

A politically-weakened President Richard M. Nixon visited Alabama in February 1974 for a contrived "Honor America Day" celebration, privately seeking Governor Wallace's support amidst growing Watergate concerns. *Alabama Department of Archives and History.*

His final presidential campaign, Wallace is introduced to a campaign rally crowd in 1976. *Alabama Department of Archives and History.*

CHAPTER 4

Politics of Spectacle

George Wallace's ascension to the national political stage coincided with interesting new ideas about the role spectacle plays in the interactions between human beings. French Marxian scholar Guy Louis Debord advanced such ideas in the late 1960s with his commentary on the role spectacle plays in the "social relation among people" and its reliance upon "media images"—images so influential as to create a spectacle that impacts human interactions and relationships. It's unlikely, however, that Wallace spent much time studying or even being aware of Debord and his ideas in the same era. Wallace was, after all, a highly instinctual politician who "governs himself as he would govern others: not by intellect, but by instinct. His 'juices' tell him what to do."[1] Debord's ideas are instructive, nonetheless, to understanding the increasing role the creation of spectacle (and the attention it demands) has played in an ever-increasingly mediated society. In Wallace's era, television was the burgeoning new medium that not only brought the battles for civil rights and the Vietnam War into the living rooms of millions of Americans, but it also served as a helpful tool to introducing men like Wallace to voters outside of the South. The need for controversy—and its ubiquitous theatrical performance—around political issues is essential to maintaining support for some candidates (or their policies). "The absence of controversy . . . leaves room for disinterest, apathy, or only intermittent attention to them," political scientist Murray Edelman posited. "To the advocate of strong measures to counter subversive activities, by contrast, apathy becomes evidence of softness toward enemies; moral passion is inflamed against people who deny a problem exists or refuse to see it as threatening."[2] Taking such stances—we are strong, they are weak—furthers the ingroup/outgroup dichotomy and advances the loyalty/devotion Wallace (and later Trump) were seeking.

Fast forward to the early twenty-first century, and Donald Trump (as Wallace did) harnessed the emerging media of his time—social media—to dominate the public marketplace with his own brand of spectacle. Researcher and author Douglas Kellner offers that "We now live in an era where the digitally mediated spectacle has contributed to right-wing authoritarian populist Donald Trump becoming US President, and Debord's concept of spectacle is now more relevant than ever to interpreting contemporary culture, society, and politics."[3]

Author Heather E. Yates noted that spectacle, as demonstrated in the Trump campaigns (and arguably decades earlier in the Wallace campaigns), is used to force attention upon a campaign, and its performance by the candidate, more so than on its issues. This becomes increasingly important in an era with "low-information voters" dominating the process, voters who can scarcely articulate policy or program positions of their candidate, but can recite chapter and verse one-liners, putdowns and scenes played out at campaign rallies. Yates said "presidential candidates deliberately employ emotional rhetoric over analytical rhetoric, thus cueing emotional responses toward typically noncontroversial issues." While Wallace focused on controversial issues—such as race relations, desegregation, local control of government, the role of the courts, and so on— every issue was constructed into a crisis to help draw an audience. Edelman offered, "News about politics encourages a focus upon leaders, enemies and problems as sources of hope and of fear" and obscures the reality that such news is regular democratic discourse or discussion of varied ideologies. "The effects of [political spectacle] are powerful because these constructions offer answers to troubling questions," Edelman said, illustrating what Wallace was attempting to do, although the emphasis remains on "what conditions are healthy or threatening" and "who is responsible for success and misfortune" were the central point, with little actual effort or thinking expended on answers to such concerns.[4] Further explicating the concept of political spectacle, Yates noted, "Reduced to its most essential component, a spectacle is something to look at and observe, where the campaign is about a candidate's performance rather than substantive debate about public policy options. The political campaign employs a variety of rhetorical tools to create an event of interest for spectators. . . . 'political theater.'"[5]

Yates's description captures well the nature of the Wallace campaigns— particularly between 1964 and 1972 (prior to the assassination attempt upon his life). His 1976 campaign also featured a form of "political theater" but for entirely new reasons centered on the focus of a physically disabled candidate unshielded from the nation's view, seeking the highest office in the land. For all four of his presidential campaigns, a Wallace rally typified the elements of "political theater" with music, patriotic decorations, religious overtones through prayer and collection of "tithes and offerings," recital of the Pledge of Allegiance, and group singing of "God Bless America" and the "Star Spangled Banner." A sort of choreography existed around Wallace rallies—more formal than what was employed by Trump in 2016 or 2020—but just as powerful in its draw. The show was by design, whether formally understood or not, to "displace public and scholarly attention" from actual political problems (along with their causes, consequences, elements, targets, allies, and antagonists) and in some sense may have existed, as Edelman suggested, to create "bemusement" and "oblivious-ness" to underlying issues.[6] A large portion of Wallace audiences showed up for "the show," to hear and see what would happen (and less so out of any long-standing or deep-seeded commitment to the Wallace candidacy). And while many might complain about the disruption of hecklers and protestors, for a long while the loyal Wallace opposition served as a useful tool to creating the spectacle needed. Wallace's out-sized media coverage—equal to or exceeding that for his Democratic and Republican rivals in 1968—is testament to the value of the spectacle in putting his name before voters far outside the boundaries of the state of Alabama. The value (to journalists, advertisers and others) of the political theater candidates like Wallace and Trump could bring is an open secret. Edelman observed that political news coverage has always worked to keep the public "continuously anxious and constantly hopeful" and that "expo-sure to the news involves the public in a world of surprises and drama, defeats and triumphs, unexpected threats and glorifying victories, fears of prolonged changes in well-being, and hopes for the end of worrisome problems [which] makes news reports intriguing for some and the future uncertain for all."[7]

While such analysis of political theater and its requisite role for the news media were little analyzed in Wallace's era, the curtain was completely pulled back in considering the meteoric rise of Trump in the 2016 presidential election cycle. In the weeks following Trump's surprise election to the nation's highest office in November 2016, Jeff Zucker, CNN's former head, told an audience at the Harvard Kennedy School he thought his news network let too many Trump rallies run without interruption on his network, but added, "Listen, because you never knew what he would say, there was an attraction to put those on the air."[8] Another network executive, the since deposed CBS chairman Leslie Moonves, raised eyebrows with a similar claim when he noted, "[Trump] may not be good for America, but [he's] damn good for CBS. The money's rolling in and this is fun. It's a terrible thing to say. But bring it on, Donald. Keep going."[9]

Keeping the momentum going was at the center of everything Wallace said or did politically between 1963 (when he became governor of Alabama) and

1965 (when civil rights marchers attempted to walk from Selma to Montgomery. His controversial inaugural speech, his defiant "stand in the schoolhouse
door" behind him, Wallace set to keep the spectacle going as 1963 concluded.
In October of that year, Wallace's office announced he had accepted speaking
engagements at colleges and universities in the northeast, including Harvard
and Brown Universities, and Dartmouth and Smith Colleges. As expected, the
speeches not only would provide Wallace an elevated platform from which
to promote his views but also would offer journalists irresistible conflict and
controversy for their stories.[10]

At Harvard, Wallace's speech was sponsored by the Harvard-Radcliffe Young
Democrats Club and was restricted to an audience of students and faculty.[11]
Aware that he was not always welcomed in the North but no doubt hopeful about
the media attention such tension could arouse, Wallace's traveling entourage
included twenty-one separate security and policy aides who traveled with him
from Alabama on three separate planes (each one screened for bombs).[12] His
very arrival in a community could prompt protests, as Black students affiliated
with the Congress of Racial Equality (CORE) staged a traffic-stopping protest
in New Haven, Connecticut, the day of Wallace's arrival. Tempers flared as fifty
police officers were called in to break up the demonstration. Six arrests were
made, and two police officers were reported injured.[13]

An overflow audience met Wallace at the Sanders Theatre on the Harvard
campus despite protests that started before his arrival and continued throughout
his speech. The protests, sponsored by a group called the Boston Friends of
the Student Non-Violent Coordinating Committee, walked around the theater
during the speech and sang protest songs. "The marchers distributed a statement
charging Wallace and his administration with being 'directly responsible for
creating an atmosphere of terror and intimidation in Alabama which made the
murder of four Birmingham children inevitable,'" the *Boston Globe* reported.[14]
Inside the theater, a brief moment of tension arose as Wallace "was rushed by
about 200 jeering persons who were held back by police." Outside, protestors
successfully surrounded Wallace's car and let the air out of two of the tires on
the car before police could stop them.[15] Wallace said he sought to speak to his
Harvard audience "with your kind attention" and to "give you, without regard
to whether it is pleasing to you or to me, the law and the facts with regard to
segregation of the races in the South."[16] As the Wallace entourage moved on
to Hanover, New Hampshire, for his scheduled speech at Dartmouth College,
Wallace played with reporters about the idea of entering that state's first-in-the-
nation primary in early 1964. In addition, he repeated claims that he would lead
an effort to leave "uncommitted" a block of southern votes in the Democratic
primary expected to nominate President Kennedy for a second term.

His speech at Dartmouth, sponsored by the student Undergraduate Council, drew a larger audience than at Harvard (with an estimated 3,800 in attendance). Wallace again provided a lengthy history lesson on segregation and court-related cases. He repeated his indictment of the US Supreme Court and its rulings and accused the NAACP of engaging in fraud before the nation's high court. The most poorly accepted portion of Wallace's speech was again his reference to the fact that southerners "do not object to what is being done for the Negro. Our position does not embody hatred," a remark that drew laughter from some audience members.[17] The audience's response seemed to affect Governor Wallace, as he told them, "I don't understand. You laugh when I don't think you will, and you don't laugh when I think you will."[18]

The next day, Wallace was back in Massachusetts at North Hampton for a speech to students from Amherst, Smith, and Mt. Holyoke Colleges. As always, eager to talk to reporters, Wallace said, "I promised John Kennedy support in 1960, but Kennedy won't carry the South now. We are tired of being whipping boys for national politicians."[19] Even before Wallace arrived on the Smith College campus, his "welcome" appeared to be less than complete. Nancy J. Weiss, editor-in-chief of the *Sophian*, the student newspaper at Smith, wrote an editorial that urged that an address by Wallace "would provide, if nothing else, a close-up for an intriguing character study" and could "give us a much more concrete idea of the kind of irrational authority we have to contend with in the civil rights struggle.[20] Although referring to Wallace as "irrational," Weiss's editorial said that his campus visit "points up the whole problem of free inquiry and its limits." (Weiss became Nancy Weiss Malkiel, a Princeton professor and author on American political history.)[21] Smith College President Thomas C. Mendenhall introduced Wallace by noting that "the college officially dissents from the governor's position . . . however, he was invited by a responsible student group, he is here, and he should be heard."[22] An Associated Press dispatch noted students laughed at some of Wallace's jokes, applauded some of his ideas, while hissing others.[23] He drew his highest scorn with a poorly worded comparison of Washington, DC schools as "a jungle school system" and adding, "I believe it is in the interest of Negroes and whites to have separate schools. I don't admit that Negro and white education is unequal at all."[24]

Wallace concluded his speaking tour on November 7, 1963, in Providence, Rhode Island, at Brown University, where he took up the troubling nature of protests occurring in Alabama and in northern cities. He also addressed formally the deadly bombing of the Sixteenth Street Baptist Church. "Bombings have occurred in the state of Alabama as they have in many northern states," Wallace said, amazingly attempting to place the ugly and unprecedented events in his own state into some sort of comparative context to what was happening

elsewhere. "These were dastardly acts, abhorred by all citizens of our state."[25]
Rather than leave his remarks at that, Wallace added further explanation that
weakened his sentiments:

> I would point out to you that although the full efforts of the Federal Bureau of
> Investigation have been placed behind solving these occurrences, together with
> state, county and municipal investigative forces, to date no arrests have been
> made. National news media have indicted, tried and convicted a whole people.
> This conviction cannot be substantiated and this fact should be fully understood
> by you.[26]

It was a curious and ultimately unsuccessful tact to take—rather than to
properly ascribe responsibility for not only the act of murder of the four girls
via bombing, but also the shared responsibility to solve the crime, Wallace
sought division. The news media and the Washington establishment served as
a familiar and reliable foe. Interestingly, Wallace made a distinction between
"riots" in Alabama and those in the North, declaring, "There have been no race
riots in the State of Alabama" but rather "demonstrations led by agitators from
without our state." He added to a spattering of laughter in the audience, "In
no instance were white citizens engaged in any form of physical contact with
Negro citizens"—apparently forgetting that white police officers had beaten
and put dogs on Black demonstrators, while white firefighters had painfully
sprayed Black protestors with powerful water hoses.[27]

While the Wallace campus speeches had drawn the expected ire and controversy (and requisite media coverage), they also highlighted one of the advantages
the once-regional candidate brought to the national stage. As Rohler posited,

> Wallace's achievements as a public speaker were considerable. In an era when
> political messages were increasingly mass mediated and staged either as intimate
> programs or attack advertisements, George Wallace demonstrated that a political
> leader with a powerful message could through public speaking build mass fol-
> lowing. His speeches were neither elegantly written nor powerfully argued. None
> would be considered outstanding examples of effective organization. Yet all of
> them did what effective mimetic oratory does best. They reflected back to his fol-
> lowers their own feelings that they were victims of forces beyond their control.[28]

In Wallace's wake, Ronald Reagan's rising star added elegant and refined oratory, the kind of delivery mastered through years of acting in major motion
pictures and television. Reagan's much-lauded October 1964 speech, "A Time
for Choosing," offered in support of the Goldwater campaign, demonstrated a

finesse that took essential aspects of Wallace's message much further than the 'lil fighin' governor from Alabama could ever do.

Governor Wallace's northeastern speaking tour ended just fifteen days before President Kennedy was assassinated in Dallas, and the political world was turned on its head. Wallace was among a small group of governors who flew to Washington to file through the East Room of the White House on November 23, 1963, a day after JFK was slain, to view the president's body lying in state. As he arrived by plane in Washington, DC, a reporter shouted a grotesque question demonstrative of how divisive a figure Wallace had become for some journalists and many Americans: "Are you glad now that you have a southern president?" Wallace frowned and replied, "This transcends any political questions."[29]

The dust had hardly settled on the Kennedy assassination when Wallace announced he would open the first few weeks of 1964 with a "western swing" that included two stops at the University of Denver and at Colorado State University in Fort Collins. Wallace told 2,000 gathered at Fort Collins that "leftists in Latin America" were behind efforts to create racial and societal strife in the United States, a "back door entrance to the United States."[30] While Wallace's reception in Fort Collins was described by some as more cordial than he had experienced elsewhere, protestors and pickets were back for his speech the next day at the University of Denver. There, a large number of Black students had organized a protest, even though 3,000 showed up to hear his speech at the Student Union Building. "The pickets braved 15-degree weather to appear at the student union," the Associated Press reported. "Observers said 10 percent of the marchers were Negroes. They included college students, men in suits, and men in work clothes. Wallace was ushered into the union by a rear entrance. He was not seen by—nor did he see—the pickets."[31]

Following the two speeches in Colorado, Wallace flew on to the warmer climate of Tucson, Arizona, for two speeches, one before the Tucson Press Club and another at the University of Arizona. Following Arizona, Wallace arrived in Los Angeles, California, with a full head of steam of publicity from his previous stops, and as usual, inspired protests and pickets before and during his scheduled remarks at the University of California-Los Angeles (UCLA). Dr. Charles E. Young, UCLA's vice chancellor, introduced and welcomed Wallace, but he made clear he did not personally agree with the governor's views on race and integration. Young said, "I would like to introduce a man most of you disagree with, as I do myself" and received loud applause.[32] Wallace was met by a small audience of 1,800 "who responded with some laughter and a few hisses," the Los Angeles Times reported. "Otherwise, there was no disorder although campus police were augmented by a dozen Los Angeles plain-clothes officers." As was the case elsewhere, once his remarks were completed, Wallace was "hustled out the rear" and down a private elevator away from protestors, "as a precaution."[33]

Wallace moved on to Oregon, where he said he was there to "emancipate the people of Oregon from the distorted views of the national press and radio and television." He said he had received as many as 2,000 letters of support from Oregon residents in recent months for his positions on civil rights.[34] Journalists observing Wallace's eight-day swing through the West were quick to note that Oregon provided the largest audience of his trip with more than 8,900 students and others jamming the University of Oregon's basketball fieldhouse to hear his remarks.[35] Of Wallace's Oregon stop, the Capital Journal's Douglas Seymour described Wallace's presence as "smooth" as he successfully papered over his record as "a militant segregationist" who had shed his previously perceived "belligerent, frustrated and at times confused" prior public appearances.[36]

Governor Wallace even seemed to handle smoothly a young woman who asked several designed-to-be-embarrassing questions of the visiting governor. Seymour wrote, "'Now honey,' the fast-talking southerner would begin sweetly, and then he'd proceed to turn the question to his own ends."[37] The questions intended to embarrass Wallace focused on the use of fire hoses and police dogs on protestors in Alabama. "Wallace explained the use of the dogs was humanitarian," Seymour wrote. "He declared that if the Birmingham police hadn't used the dogs and fire hoses, many more demonstrators would have been hurt." Wallace declared, "Not a single person was bitten by the dogs. They are trained to grab clothing, not to bite."[38] He said that "only 22 Negroes were hurt during the 45 days of demonstrations, and none seriously" and attacked the "liberal media" for providing "a slanted account" of the events in his state. Wallace drew unexpected laughter from his audience when he offered that Eugene "Bull" O'Connor, the uncompromising Birmingham police commissioner, was a compassionate man. "Eugene O'Connor doesn't have a mean bone in his body," Wallace said.[39] Wallace brushed aside another question about whether Blacks were denied the right to register to vote in Alabama, saying none had ever been so denied, but that widespread illiteracy among the state's "Negro population" means they are not qualified to vote. "There are dropouts by the droves in the Negro school system," he said.[40]

At the University of Washington in Seattle, Wallace spoke as the invited guest of the University Political Union. The Montgomery Advertiser, who dispatched reporter Ramona Martin to accompany Wallace's travels, reported Wallace's Seattle appearance had drawn a larger audience than had shown up for Crown Prince Harold of Norway who had recently spoke on campus.[41] Wallace's reception at Washington was more courteous than at other campuses, reporters noted, with laughter and cheers greeting his speech. About two dozen picketers did show up, but they were greatly out numbered. "The South's segregation leader asked an integrated audience for attention yesterday in Meany Hall," wrote Phil Kipper, a student reporter for the campus newspaper, the *Washington Daily*. "Governor George Wallace of Alabama stood uneasily in front of the packed auditorium . . . selling Alabama's way to social peace and order. He was selling segregation." Wallace said a "misunderstanding" existed between his positions and what was reported by the media or understood by some northerners. "Wallace's brand of salesmanship dwelt on unselling the US Civil Rights bill and selling himself," Kipper reported. "The governor leaned forward on the rostrum, poked his finger at the audience, and smiled and smiled."[42]

Seattle was the last stop of Wallace's tour, and he assessed his endeavors as "a tremendous success" and added, "The liberals would have been astounded and surprised" at the turnout he was receiving along the way. "You would have thought I was back in the South," Wallace said. "Why, when I said the Confederate flag would fly again, they cheered just like in Alabama."[43] Before he headed home, Wallace accepted a last-minute invitation to address students at Victoria University in Victoria, British Columbia, Canada. He didn't let the invitation go to waste—challenging Canadian authorities to admit more Negroes to the nation in order to overcome their record of "preaching one system and practicing another." He added apparently without worry of insult, "you don't have any Negroes here because your immigration laws are such. I feel that if any of you people think this is a great moral issue, you should lead a drive to change your laws and bring in more Negroes."[44] While seven hundred students listened politely to the governor, two adults carrying signs that said "Go Home Wallace" got up and left during his remarks. The Royal Canadian Mounted Police said there were no incidents related to Wallace's visit.

Although Minnesota had no Democratic presidential primary in 1964, and Wallace likely had little opportunity to gain much support among progressives who dominated the party there, he accepted a Minneapolis speaking engagement nonetheless. Speaking as part of the "Great Issues in Government" symposium at the University of Minnesota in February 1964, just under 5,000 people filled the Northrop Auditorium. Another 2,000 people were accommodated in nearby lecture halls equipped with speakers so they could hear the audio of Wallace's speech. Students in the audience sported Black armbands to protest Wallace and generally followed advance instructions from student leaders not to applaud or respond to the governor. Reporters noted Wallace did receive applause five times, one time "accompanied by laughter" when he made the claim that "only 22 Negroes" were injured by police officers in recent riots in Birmingham.[45]

1964: An Earnest Effort

Wallace's visits to Minnesota were helpful in keeping attention on him as John Birch Society members and a fervent antitaxation group in Wisconsin worked feverishly to get him on the presidential primary ballot there. While his first forays in Wisconsin seemed to go well, reporters noted Wallace seemed bothered by the cold temperatures greeting him. "Appleton's chilly weather didn't agree with Wallace," the *Appleton Post-Crescent* reported, with daytime highs only reaching into the 20s, Wallace "confined most of his 'campaigning' to the Conway Hotel." Wallace quipped to reporters who seemed to notice he was feeling the effects of the cold, "If the war between the states had been fought in Wisconsin instead of Virginia, it would have been over in a week."[46]

The next day, Wallace moved on to Oshkosh where he was met by a group of student protestors at Oshkosh State College. Inside the student union, a standing-room-only crowd of 2,000—a mix of Wallace supporters, students opposing him, and just curious onlookers—heard him attempt to speak over frequent interruptions. In the audience, protest placards were raised often, blocking the view of supporters at the back of the room.[47] The spectacle Wallace was hoping his campaign would inspire was well in place. Wisconsin historian Richard Haney noted,

> Wallace's campaign quickly developed a recognizable pattern. On college campuses he heckled civil rights pickets at the entrance and received a mixed reaction from his listeners. Because of the need for tight security, he usually entered and left auditoriums in a manner that permitted him to avoid mingling with crowds. His personal bodyguards taped his car hood to detect any foul play.[48]

Wallace also appeared at Whitewater State College and drew a record crowd estimated at more than 2,000 students and citizens. Again, a handful of protestors were present. "But the auditorium was jammed to overflowing with students standing in aisles, along the walls and peering through open fire exit doors and through windows," the Associated Press reported.[49]

Two days later at St. Norbert College, a private Catholic liberal arts school in West De Pere, Wallace was greeted by a chorus of the Negro spiritual, "Swing Low, Sweet Chariot" and chants of "Down with Wallace!" by a well-organized group of protestors. Inside, the school's auditorium "was jammed with students and faculty who listened critically as Wallace spent 45 minutes attacking the civil rights bill," *Milwaukee Sentinel* reporter Robert N. Leipzig relayed.[50] Before Wallace arrived, papers were distributed to everyone in the audience reminding them of two points: "One, if you applaud this man, it means that we as a

Catholic college approve his actions and ideas; and two, if disorderly conduct prevails, we reduce ourselves to his level and successfully feed his campaign machine."[51] The *St. Norbert Times*, the weekly student newspaper at the college, trumpeted the national coverage Wallace's appearance had engendered, quoting a United Press International report that noted, "A coldly silent St. Norbert Catholic College student body greeted Alabama Governor George Wallace's attack on the proposed civil rights bill." The UPI report added, "The governor, who usually seeks out students to shake hands, moved quickly from the auditorium after his speech and walked at a brisk pace to his car. Students stared silently as he passed."[52]

A noteworthy campaign appearance for Wallace was on April 1 before an overflow and raucous crowd at the American Serb Memorial Hall on West Oklahoma Avenue on Milwaukee's south side. The Milwaukee event would turn out to be the biggest spectacle of his entire Wisconsin foray. Reporters described the audience packed into every inch of the hall as "boisterous" and "his most enthusiastic reception in Wisconsin since he started campaigning. The segregationist governor's 40-minute speech was interrupted 30 times by cheering and applause." [53] The pitch of the event was set early by Bronco Gruber, owner of Brownie & Ann's Tavern, who had arranged the Wallace event. Before introducing Wallace, Gruber made a point of singling out two Negro men who had stayed in their seats during the singing of the national anthem. "There are some here tonight who do not have the courtesy to stand up—and they're none other than these two colored gentlemen here," Gruber said, pointing out the men. Boos and catcalls from the crowd followed with several people shouting at the men, "Go back to Africa!"[54] Gruber invited the men to leave, and the crowd cheered wildly as the two men and about a half dozen other Black audience members also left.

Returning to his introduction of Governor Wallace, Gruber emphasized his Serbian heritage and said, "My people fought oppression" and noted he had fought for the United States and allied forces in World War II in the Pacific. One Black man who remained in the hall, the Rev. Leo R. Champion, interrupted Gruber by repeatedly shouting, "Get your dogs out!" One Wallace supporter shoved a sign in the Baptist minister's face every time he spoke up until Gruber had had enough. "Listen, mister," Gruber shouted at Champion, unable to finish his sentence because the audience began to roar in approval. "I'm going to tell you something about your dogs, padre," Gruber said. "I live on Walnut Street and three weeks ago one of my friends was assaulted by three of your countrymen, or whatever you call them." Accompanied by cheers, Gruber lectured the minister by saying, "They beat up old ladies, 83-years-old. They rape our women folk. How long can we tolerate this? I can't tolerate it!

Did I fight at Guadalcanal and come back for this?"[55] Apparently, one white audience member had grown impatient, and shouted at Gruber that Black men had also fought in World War II. Gruber offered lamely, "I never saw a black man at Guadalcanal."[56]

Once Gruber's "performance" was concluded, Wallace's subsequent speech was almost anticlimactic, the governor sticking to his now-familiar themes regarding the civil rights bill. Wallace directly addressed a *London Times* story published hours earlier that claimed he had previously referred to European immigrants as "lesser breeds," by dismissing the report: "They are trying to make me the issue, but I'm not the issue."[57] A standing ovation concluded Wallace's speech, and he remained in the hall for more than an hour, plunging into the crowd to sign autographs and talk personally with hundreds of happy supporters who wanted to shake his hand. Campaign officials said more than 1,000 pieces of Wallace literature were distributed to the audience.

Officials at historic Marquette University, a respected Catholic university located in Milwaukee, announced they had approved one of two student requests to allow Governor Wallace to speak on the campus. An April 3 speech entitled "State's Rights, Civil Rights, and Federal Authority" was subsequently scheduled. As was becoming customary for Wallace's campaign, his Marquette appearance drew a large group of protestors—a mix of Marquette students and Milwaukee community protestors gathered outside the Medical School Auditorium. The crowd outside the facility grew so large, police cordoned off 15th Street and delivered Wallace to the venue via a side door. Milwaukee police eventually took to loudspeakers mounted on patrol cars to appeal to the crowd to clear the area. Before Wallace could speak, Milwaukee Fire Department officials were called to check the building after a bomb threat was called in. As firefighters entered the building, one of them was struck by a can thrown from the crowd. Clods of dirt were also hurled at Wallace's car when it arrived at the auditorium.

As the 1964 Wisconsin campaign drew to a close, protestors and pickets continued to haunt Wallace throughout the state and the response of some of them would overshadow anything he had to say. On April 5, "personal body-guards and Kenosha Police had to protect Governor Wallace from a crush of pickets at Kenosha after he held a press conference at the Dayton Hotel," the *Milwaukee Journal* reported. As Wallace stepped from an elevator inside the hotel, about seventy-five protestors jammed into the lobby shouting a deafening chant: "Wallace, Go Home!"[58] The breathless Milwaukee account continued the focus on the spectacle of Wallace's appearance:

Police opened a path for Wallace. The crowd quickly closed in, however, and pressed against the group protecting Wallace—a uniformed officer holding one of Wallace's arms and a detective the other, with several guards and aides beside and behind them. A reporter near the group reported being struck by fists several times, but was not hurt.[59]

Outside the hotel, despite a cold rain pouring down, one hundred more protestors awaited Wallace and his entourage "as officers rushed Wallace across the street to his car."[60] The *Kenosha News* reported that the protest against Wallace "touched off the loudest demonstration in downtown Kenosha since the end of World War II."[61] One thirty-three-year-old Kenosha man was detained by police after one of his picket signs allegedly struck Governor Wallace on the side of the face, witnesses and police said. Wallace, however, denied he had been struck when asked about it later. His bodyguards, Alabama State Troopers Lloyd Jemison and E. C. Dothard, both reported they were struck by fists. Wallace said the response at Kenosha "does not reflect the attitude of the people of Wisconsin. It is just one of those unfortunate things. We believe in peaceful picketing . . . [and] many of these people [here today] came from outside Kenosha."[62] Following the Kenosha events, Wallace continued on 10 miles north to Racine for another news conference at the Clayton House Motel where another crowd of about 150 protestors jammed the lobby and front entrance. Wallace "winked" at the protestors but did not respond to their jeers.[63]

His expected "nonwinning" victory in Wisconsin completed, the "Wallace Whirlwind" arrived in Indiana for the first time on April 14, 1964—just four weeks before the Indiana primary—the same day his campaign opened a headquarters inside the venerable Claypool Hotel in downtown Indianapolis. Wallace's first stop was a speech scheduled before students at Butler University in Indianapolis. A small group of Butler students planned a protest against Wallace, clarifying that they did not object to him being allowed to speak on campus, but they objected to his "attempt to introduce racism into Indiana."[64] About 100 Butler students showed up for the protest, while another 500 took seats inside Jordan Hall to hear Wallace speak about his campaign. "I am campaigning for states' rights and local government control," Wallace said. "If you in Indiana want civil rights legislation, I say that's fine. But if you want it, do it yourselves. Don't let Washington tell you how to do it."[65] Speaking for about 25 minutes, Wallace asserted that his campaign in Indiana was not about segregation; rather, it was about the civil rights bill, "which will destroy the American concept of government." In these moments, Wallace demonstrated his ability to reinforce "dominant ideology" to achieve, as Edelman said, the effect of "diverting attention from historical knowledge [or] social and economic analysis" rendering context as meaningless.[66] Trying to relate his concerns to college students, Wallace said, "The government has enough to do without picking out pledges for a fraternity or a sorority," drawing applause from the students. While Wallace seemed to connect with his audience, the expected or desired "spectacle" did not ensue, at least not on the Butler campus.[67] One student asked Wallace if he actually expected to win in Indiana, and he seemed to indicate that he did not, offering: "If I get any votes at all [it's a victory]. If I get significant votes in this state, we're going to have them jumping at both national conventions this summer." As he was often called upon to do, Wallace denied he was a racist and as evidence offered, "I am just as interested in the Negro in Alabama as I am the white."[68]

The Wallace campaign took notice of the size and volume of protestors organized outside the Terre Haute House Hotel, where a news conference was scheduled. Set up by the local NAACP chapter, among the protestors was a prominent local Catholic priest, the Rev. Bernard Strange, photographed raising a sign in Wallace's face.[69] It was publicity Wallace valued, especially since a photograph of the confrontation was wired to newspapers across the country.

At Earlham College in Richmond, Wallace "was received coolly but politely by an overflow crowd in a 700-seat auditorium," and a petition calling his policies "inhuman and undemocratic" had been signed by 801 of Earlham's nearly 1,000 students.[70] As had occurred at St. Norbert's College in Wisconsin, the nonresponsive audience was not to Wallace's liking, or at least his aides said that was the case. The "Wallace people" said they welcomed the protests their appearances inspired—mostly because of the intense media coverage it guaranteed—but veteran UPI correspondent Eugene J. Cadou noted that Wallace's "composure frayed a bit amid a raucous, jeering reception" during appearances at Indiana University in Bloomington. Once there, Cadou reported that "the Alabama segregationist met his roughest audience" with "about 200 hissing, cat-calling students," who walked out in the middle of his speech.[71] Wallace feigned, at least, concern: "You fellows are going to wear me out," Wallace said as he struggled to make his points within choruses of boos, guffaws, laughter, and open heckling. More than 7,500 students showed up to hear Wallace make four separate speeches on the campus sponsored by the student-run Conservative League. During the afternoon session, the mostly student audience broke into laughter when the club's president introduced Wallace as "a man who has done much to improve the lot of the Negro in his home state."[72]

During his remarks, Wallace stopped at one point, clearly irritated by the interruptions, and told the hecklers: "You want to make a speech? I suggest you hire a hall. I beg of you to let me proceed."[73] *Indianapolis News* political reporter Edward Ziegner noted Wallace "had a flash of temper when he tangled" with Brandies University student Robert Z. Zellner, a former field secretary in Alabama for the Student Non-Violent Coordinating Committee. Zellner peppered

Wallace with questions about whether Blacks were allowed to openly register and vote in Alabama—bringing a tepid response from Wallace: "There have been times, in past years, when Negroes couldn't vote, and whites couldn't vote either."[74] The response drew laughter and Zellner demanded from the audience that Wallace "answer the question!" Wallace replied that more than 105,000 Negroes were eligible to vote in Alabama (a considerably small portion of the nearly 500,000 total voting age-eligible Blacks in the state in 1964). When Zellner attempted to force Wallace to provide county-by-county statistics on eligible voters, Wallace cut him off angrily.[75] "You're an agitator!" Wallace said. "You've been in and out of more jails in Alabama than anybody."[76]

Following his remarks before the heated evening audience of nearly 3,000 students, Governor Wallace, surrounded by four Alabama state troopers, three staff aides, and two Indiana State Police troopers "was hustled through the side door of the auditorium" for his safety. Outside the hall, another 400 protestors surrounded Wallace's car and security team as he entered and exited the venue, some of them chanting, "Don't sic the dogs on us, George!"[77] The *Indianapolis Recorder* reported on the protests that included brief, minor skirmishes, saying, "One tense moment occurred when two white male students—one wearing a Confederate flag, the other an 'equality' sign—had a short verbal battle. Campus police standing nearby were visibly tense and then relaxed when the flag-wearer moved on." Also spotted in the crowd were a group of young white males wearing yellow tags reading "SPONGE," which they said stood for Society for the Prevention of Negroes Getting Everything.[78] As was the case in the past, the reporting about the response to Wallace's remarks—the spectacle and theater of it—was lengthier than any retelling of what he actually said. Part of this phenomenon may have been that Wallace routinely used the same "stump speech" wherever he went with little variation, and reporters had become bored with the same content. The more exciting aspect of the story, then, was the response the speech generated.

Wallace took his campaign to what was expected to be at least cordial territory, the campus of the University of Notre Dame in South Bend. There, students from both Notre Dame and nearby St. Mary's College pledged to stage a "silent and respectful" protest against Wallace—including urging male students to show up dressed in suit and tie.[79] Despite their efforts, reporters noted that Wallace was met with "a jeering, singing mass of University of Notre Dame students and faculty members, who at one point, almost broke up his speech to the Roman Catholic school's Academy of Political Science."[80] As Wallace spoke inside the Joyce Center, more than 400 pickets, "including a number of priests and nuns, circled the university fieldhouse and heckling by students inside the fieldhouse forced a 15-minute break in the Alabama segregationist's speech about 10 minutes after he began."[81] During the break, Wallace kneeled at the edge of the stage and shook hands with supporters and signed autographs until order was restored. To cap off his South Bend visit, police were unable to prevent one protestor from letting the air out of a tire on Wallace's campaign car. "Jeering students pressed so tightly against Wallace's motorcade that police and deputy sheriffs had to throw shoulder blocks to shove them back," the *South Bend Tribune* reported. "Several times protestors kicked Wallace's car."[82]

The "spectacle nature" of Wallace's Indiana drive continued two days later as he prepared to speak before an overflow crowd at Emens Auditorium at Ball State Teachers College in Muncie. He once again drew a large assemblage of protestors and was escorted into and out of the Ball State campus with much fanfare by Indiana State Police and Delaware County authorities. As he was introduced, a large spattering of boos could be heard in the audience.[83] After another second-place finish (in a two-man race) in Indiana, Wallace moved on to his final primary challenge in Maryland. With him went the spectacle his campaign was engineering across televisions and newspapers everywhere. Even Wallace's attempt to file the paperwork for the primary could be controversial as the *Baltimore Sun* photographed a man identified as "a Prince George's County integrationist" who attempted to block Wallace's car with his body as the governor left the State House in Annapolis.[84] As Wallace opened his Maryland campaign office in Baltimore, the *Baltimore Sun* also focused on the fracas around Wallace's appearance at the Lord Baltimore Hotel, describing his news conference as "turbulent" conducted "in the wake of a noisy, rowdy clash in a hotel lobby between segregationists and civil righters with an American flag as a pawn."[85] It was not surprising, then, that the managers of the Lord Baltimore Hotel eventually asked the Wallace campaign to go elsewhere. As the *Sun* reported,

> The lower hotel lobby outside the lounge [for Wallace's news conference] was jammed by Wallaceites and integrationists alike. Members of each group were so emotionally wrought up that their yelling at each other and their booing and cheering continued for almost 30 minutes after Governor Wallace had left the area.[86]

One of the more troubling dust-ups occurred when a brief struggle ensued over an American flag being brandished by a civil rights protestor calling Wallace "America's Hitler." A Wallace supporter briefly shoved the man in front of news cameras and called him "a filthy Communist." At the conclusion of his news conference, reporters noted that "it took several policemen and a lot of shoving and stepping on toes to clear the way for the Governor and his wife,

Lurleen.... [and] the 'We Want Wallace' chants all but drowned out the boos of the integrationists."[87]

In racially charged Cambridge, Maryland, Wallace accepted the invitation of the Dorchester Business and Citizens Association to speak about his candidacy just eight days before the primary. The Dorchester County group included about 900 citizens who actively opposed the new public accommodations law enacted earlier in Maryland. Wallace's campaign said it considered Maryland a "fertile ground" for its message, and the governor himself told a *Baltimore Sun* reporter, "I'm not coming into Maryland as a segregationist. I want to make that clear. I'm not coming in as a rabble-rouser, either. I'm coming in to campaign on the issue of federal versus states' rights."[88] Wallace said he was aware that Cambridge and other parts of the state's eastern shore communities had been "the scene of recurring racial troubles" but was not concerned about creating further problems. He said, "If I had thought there would be trouble, I would not have decided to come to Maryland. I will not do anything there that could cause trouble." He said ongoing racial strife in the state was "a matter for the good people of Maryland to decide."[89]

At Cambridge, in the hours before Wallace's scheduled speech at the Cambridge Rescue and Fire Company Arena, cars fitted with loudspeakers drove through the city's white neighborhoods inviting folks to come hear Governor Wallace speak. Conversely, peace songs were played over loudspeakers of a Black church in a mostly "Negro neighborhood" of the city. All of the elements for an ugly—perhaps even violent confrontation—were in place at Cambridge. However, Wallace's supporters came, about 1,500 of them, and heard a rather standard stump speech and returned home without incident.[90] That did not save the city from the expected turmoil, however. Reporters noted that Black leaders, particularly young ones, were unhappy with the decision by local civil rights leaders to forgo a formal protest of Wallace. An impromptu march got underway and eventually resulted in a clash with National Guards troops when demonstrators refused to disperse and clear a city street. Fourteen arrests were made within the sprays of tear gas. Five guardsmen and two protestors were reported injured. A small Black child died that evening in a nearby home, with Black leaders insisting he had died as a result of the tear gas sprays. A county coroner, however, ruled the boy died of congenital heart failure.[91] The demonstration was no surprise; the night before a group of about 50 "youthful Negroes paraded singing through the streets of the Negro section, tossing firecrackers and stones in apparent protest to Wallace."[92]

The *Baltimore Sun* and Associated Press circulated alarming photos of National Guardsmen holding rifles and bayonets at the heads of prostrate demonstrators on the ground. *Sun* reporters Charles Whiteford and Douglas

D. Connah Jr. reported "scores were sickened by the tear gas sprayed over the demonstrators who were lying in the street." The report said that "the Guardsmen were wearing gas masks and with bayonets at the ready marched more than three blocks through the Negro section breaking up the crowd."[93] The *Baltimore Afro-American* carried a banner headline the day after the fracas declaring, "Wallace invasion ignites Cambridge riot: 7 hurt." The newspaper reported that although Cambridge had been "at the brink of an explosion several times since last summer's violence," racial tension had been held in check, and the city had been peaceful.[94]After the fact, Wallace told reporters he was saddened by the violence and said he would not have gone forward with his speech at Cambridge except for the fact that assurances were given no demonstrations would take place. It was unclear how sincere anyone took Wallace's remarks given that the coverage of his appearance had once again stolen national headlines.

Wallace kept plugging away in Maryland. On May 9, he gave a 40-minute speech to about 1,200 students and faculty inside Shriver Hall at Johns Hopkins University in Baltimore. Reporters noted that Wallace was "greeted by hearty, and friendly, applause" as he took the stage, but noted the student newspaper had called upon protestors to stage a silent protest. "The plea was obviously ignored and the governor received more applause, and only a scattering of hisses, throughout his speech," *Baltimore Sun* reporter Bruce Winters relayed.[95] The reception seemed to please Wallace as well as he told reporters later that he was impressed with the welcome he had received. "This tops them all," he said. "We had nothing like it at this stage of the campaign in Wisconsin or Indiana."[96] Days later, Wallace drew an impressive crowd of 10,000 to the University of Maryland field house on the College Park campus. While many people in the crowd were either there to protest Wallace or were just there to watch "the show," the attention served its purpose in keeping the focus on Wallace's message, and less on his favorite-son opponent in Maryland, Senator Daniel Brewster. Brewster spoke to an ad-hoc rally in front of the university's library about an hour before Wallace arrived for his speech and drew only about 1,000 observers.

In Maryland, Wallace even used the trouble his campaign faced in finding a "home" as support for his calls for states' rights. When the Lord Baltimore Hotel asked his campaign to find another location for his news conferences and events, saying the picketers he drew were a distraction to other hotel guests, Wallace noted, "They said the pickets were creating a disturbance, and we would have to move." "They had that right. That's my point. They are running a private business and they should be able to serve anyone they please."[97]

The campaigns of Governor Wallace and Senator Brewster came to contrasting ends—Wallace concluding things with a loud rally before a mix of supporters and opponents, and Brewster having a member of the Young Democrats speaking on his behalf at a club meeting. Speaking before an audience of 1,000 at a rally sponsored by the Congress for National Sovereignty at Richard Montgomery High School in Rockford, Wallace was met by a parade of more than 100 Catholic priests carrying signs reading "Civil rights is a moral issue" and "Christians must love all men."[98]

1968: Continuing the Spectacle

Wallace's subsequent 1968 presidential campaign as the nominee of the American Independent Party relied heavily upon political spectacle, all the way up to its bitter ending in defeat. Reporters George Lardner and Jules Loh captured well the spectacle of the latest Wallace effort by noting that 16,000 people paid $10 each to attend an Election Night "victory rally" at Montgomery's Garrett Coliseum only to witness, as Walter Cronkite of CBS News intoned, George Wallace "go down to ignominious defeat." To that point, Wallace had commanded a loyalty from supporters that most politicians would envy. "He was their avenging angel," Lardner and Loh wrote. "George Wallace said out loud what they nervously kept to themselves, articulated their deepest fears, [and] promised revenge." Describing Wallace as the "deftest demagogue" of a generation, Lardner and Loh said the "missionary zeal" in which his followers came to hear him articulate their fears and hates worked because he had "uncovered a fantastic welter of discontent." Key to all of it was the spectacle of the Wallace rally:

> The halls where Wallace spoke were arenas of hate. Magically, the venom dissipated in the crisp breezes of a football stadium or courthouse square. But whenever the roistering maverick brought his road show under one roof, the reverberating chants and counter chants of partisans and hecklers, the sweaty animosities, and the bald-bright lights of the television cameras served as an invitation to violence.[99]

The open conflict at Wallace rallies in 1968—often resulting in violence—was "just part of the show" for many but may have, in the end, turned off as many voters as it caused to pay attention. Gathering attention as a third-party candidate was the name of the game for Wallace, who lacked the resources and the power of an established national party or even an incumbent in the White House. Associated Press reporter Arthur Edson was among those who seemed to understand what the Wallace "effect" was all about. He wrote, "Few politicians create excitement. They may be well known and well informed—but well ignored. The picketing, the shouting, the rocking of his car generate interest and guarantee publicity. Wallace loves it." In Wallace's own words, it was as simple as this: "This is a people's movement, and if you don't believe it, you just follow me around the country. I think you're going to see a lot of politicians run over in 1968—and I'm going to help run them over."[100]

Even lower-key events—such as ballot signature drives required in the waning months of 1967 to get Wallace on the California ballot—were pulled off under the light of a spectacle. A "meet the candidate" and "sign the petition" event at the Chula Vista Municipal Golf Course Clubhouse in San Diego County was typical. The event featured entertainment, including acts such as "rockabilly" star Skeets McDonald (best known for a one-hit wonder, "Don't Let the Stars Get in Your Eyes") and gospel singer Wally Fowler and the Sunshine Trio. The *Chula Vista Star-News* reported about 150 people were present for the event (including about 40 members of the Wallace "official entourage"). Outside the venue, an equal number of students from Southwestern Community College (several of them Black students) marched with picket signs opposing Wallace's presence. Interestingly, campaign officials invited some of the students to come inside to hear Wallace speak (and likely to create some fireworks for media coverage), but some of the students declined (others among their number already having infiltrated the audience inside). In the audience was Stephen Cropsy, president of the Campus Action Committee at the community college, who raised his hand to ask a question. Wallace asked him, "Do you want to go to the boys' room, son?" but Cropsy said, "I wish to differ with you." Wallace was having none of it. "Listen son, I hired this hall today, you can hire it tomorrow."[101] Cropsy then led about thirty students in a walk-out—Wallace labeling them "the free speech folks" as they exited. It was as if Cropsy and his followers had read the Wallace script in advance. The walkout, an important symbol to those conducting it, served a dual purpose of also aiding the Wallace campaign. Once having insulted those who left the room, Wallace returned to familiar themes, drawing his longest ovation for his suggestion that as president he would remove a figure familiar to Californians, their former governor and now Chief Justice Earl Warren of the US Supreme Court.

The theatrics were repeated often. At a Wallace event in San Leandro, an outburst occurred when 18-year-old Fred Danbert of Newark, a student at Ohlone Community College, challenged Wallace to prove his statement that many of the marchers at Selma, Alabama, had been out-of-state agitators from Berkeley and elsewhere. "Were you there?" an irritated Wallace asked Danbert. "Don't tell us how to run our state or one day you'll come to Alabama and may not come back."[102] The comment from Wallace was especially poorly considered—given that out-of-state men attempting to register Black voters in Mississippi had disappeared and were later found murdered just two years earlier. At a speech in Santa Barbara, a half-dozen hecklers yelled "Sieg Heil" as Wallace was introduced, but they were drowned out by supporters. During the question-and-answer period that followed, one college-aged young man asked Wallace, "When you become president, Mr. Wallace, how long will some of us have to get out of the country?" Wallace replied tartly to the man, "Let me say to you, ma'am . . . [drawing laughter], I'd let *you* leave the country."[103] As expected, the more liberal or progressive a city, the more likely protestors. As a result, Wallace made little effort in San Francisco proper (although campaign efforts were underway in suburban East and North Bay communities). However, he did draw 1,000 people to a speech at Veterans Auditorium in San Francisco.

The 1968 campaign quickly produced moments of conflict reminiscent of the 1964 effort including at events designed to be friendly and favorable to Wallace. In early March, Wallace flew to Omaha, Nebraska, to attend a special state convention of the American Independent Party needed to nominate him and make him eligible for the ballot there. He told reporters that his plans to visit Vietnam had been delayed by his wife's rapidly declining health, but he added, "We feel good about her at this moment." While supporters provided a brass band and cheers for Wallace in Omaha, as usual, protestors were also present. The Associated Press reported, "Wallace attempted to shake hands with several of the hecklers who shouted, 'Black Power' as they ran toward him asking if he would shake their hands." The "Negro" youth mostly ignored Wallace's gesture; only two of them offering their hand in return.[104] Omaha police moved in to put down a small "riot" that erupted after 50 of the Black protestors were tossed out of the AIP gathering. "Police formed a flying wedge and drove the demonstrators from the auditorium after they began pelting the speaker's platform with sticks, bits of placards, paper drinking cups and stones," AP reported. Police reported 13 persons were injured in the resulting melee and that 10 local businesses were looted or damaged. A shot from a 12-gauge riot gun used by police struck one 16-year-old boy. As he had in California, Wallace commented as the demonstrators were removed from the room, telling his audience, "These are the free speech folks, you know. And these are the kind of folks the people of this country are sick and tired of." He urged the protestors to "go home and watch the news, these cameramen are making you look like hoodlums. You guys are not doing anything to help yourselves."[105]

Peggy Wallace Kennedy, the governor's second child, was an 18-year-old girl planning to go to Mississippi State College for Women in 1968, but she was still eager to help her father's campaign in any way she could. She said she took advantage of the campaign as a chance to spend time with her father, who was away from home often. She made several appearances on stage with her father in Florida, but she recalls most a raucous reception the governor received in Providence, Rhode Island. The Providence rally made headlines—national columnists Evans and Novak describing a heated "white backlash" that the Wallace campaign inspired in the state "even before his rally almost broke up in warfare between an angry platoon of screaming Negro militants and the several thousand Rhode Islanders who had come to hear him speak. The ferocity of that demonstration against Wallace only made the backlash burn brighter."[106] Peggy recalls the day well,

> They told my father backstage [before he went on] that it looks like it was going to be a really, really bad, a rough crowd. But my father wanted to go out and speak anyway. He was really rather fearless. It was a rough crowd and I was on stage and the protestors began to throw things on the stage, and there were fights in the crowd between the Wallace people and the protestors. The police were trying to break those up as my father was trying to give his speech, but the protestors kept interrupting him.[107]

Providence was one of many locations where Wallace used his familiar retorts to protestors, including offering to autograph their sandals after the rally, and pretending to mistake a long-haired male protestor as a female. "He would just love the back and forth of that, and that would really rile the hecklers up even more," Peggy Wallace Kennedy said. "In Providence, that was a very, very bad experience. It was a real ordeal getting us back to the car after the rally."[108] Once back in the car with her father, Peggy noticed that her light-colored dress was marked up with small dark pen marks in several places. Wallace Kennedy explained,

> The security guards told me the protestors had done that—that they were so close they could reach in and mark my dress. In the event that I was ever away from the group, with the markings, they would be able to tell I was with the Wallace group and they would be able to target me. We were able to get away from that crowd, but it was a really, really bad experience.[109]

For Wallace Kennedy, and almost anyone else, such a scene was unsettling and uncomfortable. For Wallace and his campaign hierarchy, it was what they were counting on to keep the attention going. As one top Wallace aid, Tom Turnipseed, acknowledged many years later, the campaign often lacked any organized plan or objective: "We were too busy campaigning" for any serious contemplation about whether the "heat" of the rally spectacles—the violence—could actually backfire and turnoff the voters it had caused to look.[110] Author Heather E. Yates, however, notes that events or circumstances are in place in certain political cycles where spectacle may be more likely than others. She cites the 2016 campaign between Donald Trump and Hillary Clinton as an example—Trump surprising the Republican establishment by easily walking away with their presidential nomination and likewise shocking the nation by winning the Electoral College; all the while the Democratic Party was making history as the first major party to nominate a woman for president. The Wallace, Nixon, and Humphrey 1968 campaigns—in as tumultuous a political year as ever occurred—likewise may have set the stage of a "disruption of the conventional order of the electoral process," and as a result, "the campaign cycle would quickly define itself as an unconventional campaign; a year of radical rhetoric, and the personalization of the campaign through digital media platforms . . . creat[ing] a new form of spectacle in political theater."[111] While the 1968 campaign had no "digital media platforms" to contend with, television was still a new medium being embraced in massive numbers by most Americans.

Where the campaign took its message could be as big a part of the spectacle as anything for Wallace. Following the disastrous Democratic convention in Chicago, both Wallace and Nixon took the cue and quickly made their way to Chicago to campaign as in contrast to the Democrat's show that fell into chaos. A large crowd witnessed Wallace's noonday motorcade along State Street in Chicago—a route many pols favored, but motorcades were a difficult "event" for reporters to cover, according to Dan King Thomasson, a Scripps-Howard reporter. "The motorcade was a string of convertibles set to drive through the Downtown Loop," Thomasson recalled:

> [Reporters] jumped on the back of one of those cars so we could be right in behind Wallace. As we got to the Loop, pretty soon there was a big crush of people on either side of the car. I was joined by four other guys, Teddy White, Joe Alsop, John McLaughlin, and John Farmer and another guy who decided to straddle the hood ornament. Well, this went on for several blocks through the Loop and the crowd, estimated at more than 100,000, just to see this guy. But we didn't stop. They kept driving on to the hotel [once we were out of the downtown parade route]. Instead of stopping and dropping us off, they took off with us on the back of this sedan going very fast. They couldn't have cared less about what happened to us—they were speeding along and we were clinging on for our lives.[112]

Earlier in the month, Richard Nixon drew a Chicago streetside crowd estimated at 400,000. Wallace used the same route employed by Nixon. The *Chicago Tribune* gave Wallace credit for drawing an impressive crowd—estimating it at 100,000 people (above the 50,000 estimate provided by the Chicago Police Department).[113]

From Chicago, Wallace moved on to Cicero, where a rousing crowd of 8,000 showed up to hear him pledge that he would stop America's "kowtowing to every anarchist group that roams the streets."[114] The crowds in Cicero were assisted once again by good timing—the Wallace rally taking place between shift changes at the large Western Electric Plant in the city. Wallace and his handlers didn't pause for a moment in their plans to have a campaign rally in Cicero—a mostly white "sundown town" on the outskirts of Chicago in Cook County. Cicero had a troubled history. Beginning in the Prohibition Era, mobster Al Capone controlled Cicero and passed on the influence of organized crime in the city (and its colorful bars and gambling houses along Cermak Road) to his successors Anthony Accardo and Sam Giancana. As early as July 1951, the city had witnessed ugly race riots as 4,000 white citizens descended upon a West 19th Street apartment house and nearly destroyed it in response to a Black family moving in. Similar violence erupted in the city in September 1966 when 200 members of the Congress of Racial Equality (CORE) attempted to lead a march for fair housing in the city, riot police holding back an estimated 3,000 protestors who showed up for the march. In Cicero, the Wallace audience was almost entirely positive, but clashes still occurred. The *Los Angeles Times* reported that three Black students from the University of Chicago who carried signs that said "Wallace Thrives on Ignorance" were set upon by about twenty young white men. Two of the Black students, identified as Jack Frey and George Coleman, both twenty, fled the rally after their signs were ripped from their hands. However, as they attempted to talk to reporters a few blocks away, "white youths surrounded them and took turns running up and kicking and spitting on them. Two policemen stood nearby watching, making no move to help the students."[115] *Boston Globe* political reporter S. J. Micciche, traveling with the Wallace campaign, reported ugly comments coming from some of the governor's backers in Cicero. A steelworker (who wouldn't give his name) said he supported Wallace "because he's the only one who can keep them N-----s in line." A grandmother in Cicero shared she liked Wallace as "a red-blooded American, an all-American." Her daughter quickly added, "Them Negros want to take over everything."[116]

As the closing month of the campaign opened, Wallace continued his Midwest swing, moving on to Michigan where large audiences turned out for the Wallace bandwagon in Grand Rapids, Kalamazoo, Lansing, and Flint. In Grand Rapids, speaking before an overflow crowd at Houseman Stadium, Wallace thanked hecklers for their loud protestations suggesting,

> I appreciate your activities, because you've gotten me a half million votes today. . . . I want you to get this straight, when I become president and come

to Grand Rapids or Los Angeles or Birmingham or Washington, D.C., and a group of anarchists lie down in front of your president's automobile, they won't lie down in front of anything anymore. And if any of you doubt my statement, you just ask me back to Grand Rapids and try me.[117]

Reporters noted Wallace "found his most responsive crowd" in Flint, a blue-collar city filled with automotive manufacturing workers, many of them migrants from the South. In Flint, more than 11,000 partisans easily shouted down a handful of protestors, with Wallace telling the agitators: "You fellows can't outlast me."[118] *Detroit Free-Press* reporter Barbara Stanton noted Wallace was "almost invisible behind the bunting-bedecked podium."[119]

The Wallace campaign returned again to Michigan in late October for a major rally in Detroit that quickly devolved into the ugliest—and perhaps most widely reported—melee of the 1968 campaign. News accounts and television film of the event focused more on the fighting among protestors and Wallace supporters than on anything the candidate had to say. Although he drew a respectably large crowd to Cobo Hall in downtown Detroit, "at one point near the end of his speech, a free for all broke out near the rear of the auditorium when several Wallace supporters and protestors picked up chairs and hurled them at each other," UPI reported. Wallace noticed the ugly violence unfolding in the massive room—saying into the microphone to little effect: "Let the police handle it." Wire reports indicated the police did rush in and "wrestled two long-haired teenagers to the ground and dragged them from the hall. Wallace backers attempted to hit the two prisoners, and a Wallace supporter was seized by police and taken along."[120] It was the second but most serious fight during the rally. An earlier fistfight just under Wallace's lectern near the front of the rally briefly interrupted the proceedings. During his speech, Wallace reminded his Detroit fans—as he did everywhere—"I can assure you that when I become president, we're going to restore law and order." The Associated Press version of the Wallace story said the candidate had cut his regular speech short because of the melee. "The free-for-all was touched off when a man snatched from another man's head a plastic hat with a Wallace sticker on it, tore it up and threw the pieces in his face."[121] Other reports indicated anti-Wallace protestors sprayed some sort of chemical irritant into the face of some of Wallace's backers and wrestled signs away from them even before the rally started. Wallace seemed to believe the ruckus was benefitting him, shouting to protestors: "You came for trouble and you got it." He followed that with an assurance to his supporters: "If you want to stop all this nonsense, you vote for me November 5th and I'll stop it."[122] In the end, 10 people faced various charges, including inciting a riot, resisting arrest, or criminal assault and battery. One police officer was hospitalized after being struck in the face with an aerosol can that contained a liquid that caused burns.[123]

The media attention on the unruly nature of Wallace's 1968 rallies was, for the most part, appropriate. There was no escaping that George Wallace could provoke strong feelings from voters—and that continued all along the trail. Reporters, however, seemed to relish having a little fun at Wallace's expense (a new kind of spectacle *turned on* the Wallace campaign as opposed to *coming from* the campaign). In September, Wallace and his top staff were angry about a problem that grew out of the rather loose requirements the campaign had for screening volunteers. Given that the American Independent Party had no history, and no hierarchy to navigate in order to gain access to power, it is not altogether surprising that a variety of hangers on emerged—and some of them with interesting back stories. One of those was an Indianapolis divorcee named Ja-Neen Welch, who claimed to be a model and spokeswoman for various automotive companies, including Dodge and Hurst Performance Products. Welch first came to the attention of reporters and others during campaign appearances in Indiana, Illinois, Ohio, and Florida as she emerged from the Wallace campaign plane. In Chicago, she even convinced Wallace to pose for a picture with her, cheek-to-cheek, on the runway at Midway Airport. Reporters quickly noted Welch's attire—short mini-skirts including "a bright gold-colored outfit with a Wallace campaign ribbon" when appearing in Ohio.[124] Others described her as "a platinum blonde" or "a shapely blonde." During a campaign stop in Florida, Welch sat in reserved VIP seats at the Wallace rally decked out in all white, sporting a large white Stetson cowboy hat. In Hammond, Indiana, Welch was introduced as a former TV spokesmodel who had appeared in a series of Dodge Rebellion advertisements. She came on stage before Wallace was introduced "outfitted in skin-fitting silver slacks, jacket and Western boots and hat, she assumed her now famous pose, finger appoint at the crowd, and said, 'The Wallace rebellion wants you!'" Welch offered kisses for every donation over $20 at the rally, while "Wallace girls" passed plastic buckets through the audience for those wanting to make smaller donations "and go unkissed."[125] Welch seemed to enjoy talking to reporters, frequently sharing an undated photograph of herself and Wallace taken at the campaign's headquarters in Montgomery. "Miss Welch claimed she had ESP (extra sensory perception) which enables her to 'prevent' accidents, a capability which she declined to attempt to explain," the *Orlando Sentinel* reported.[126] The question quickly arose of just who she was and what was her actual relationship to Governor Wallace? Campaign spokesman Dick Smith, who refused to allow reporters to speak directly to Wallace about the matter, responded angrily and declared, "That girl's never been close to George Wallace, she's never been within 20 feet of George Wallace."[127] Smith angrily rebutted Welch's prediction that she would be married to Wallace after the election, calling the claim "ridiculous"—though Welch herself was telling reporters, "It wouldn't do him any good for us to announce our plans now. But I will say this much: I wouldn't object to being the next Mrs. Wallace." Wallace aide Vernon Merritt told the *Indianapolis News*, "I can assure you the governor has no plans for getting married. I doubt if he has ever met the girl. I don't know her, but I may have talked to her on the phone. She's a model, isn't she?"[128] A statement from the Wallace campaign in Montgomery said Welch had been "fired" as a campaign volunteer for her "erratic behavior, including her reports of having visions, extrasensory perception and being a seer."[129] Smith said, "She will no longer have anything to do with the campaign. You can bet on that."[130] Wallace himself was in no mood to discuss Welch. When a *Chicago Tribune* reporter asked him about what her role was in the campaign as he arrived for a big October 1 rally, Wallace replied: "Ask me a sensible question and you'll get an answer."[131]

Beyond the JaNeen Welch "affair" dogging Wallace, just the physical act of campaigning was proving difficult. For two days in a row, on October 22 and 23, Wallace was struck by objects hurled from the audience. In Oshkosh, Wisconsin, an apple core struck Wallace on the shoulder, and the next day a penny struck his face during a speech in Youngstown, Ohio. Others in the Ohio audience also tossed a spool of electrician's tape, a rock the size of a mothball, and an egg, which smashed near him. After the items came near him in Youngstown, Wallace pointed to the audience and said, "That's it, throw something. You're quite a fellow, you are. I can take anything you anarchists can dish out, remember that." Wallace later told reporters, "I don't like to get thrown at, but I guess it's all part of the game. This is something new in the campaign. But I've been thrown at before and I'm used to it. I'm certainly not afraid."[132]

A rally at San Diego produced a rare flash of anger from Wallace, who at one point, glared at the protestors and yelled: "Why don't you young punks just get out of the auditorium?"[133] An Associated Press dispatch on the encounter noted, "Normally Wallace is content to taunt hecklers . . . he has rarely, if ever called them punks." This group of hecklers, however, seemed to get under Wallace's skin with a new tactic of holding up Wallace placards and trying to shout him down as he spoke with chants of, 'We Want Wallace!'" Confused by their disruptive yet supportive chants, Wallace stepped away from the podium and whispered to one of his security guards nearby, apparently unsure what the protestors were chanting. Returning to the microphone Wallace said bitterly, "If you're really for me, just sit down and let me finish my speech."[134] To finish, Wallace had to shout the rest of his remarks.

Generally, the Wallace campaign felt safest back home in southern locales, but outbursts could break out most anywhere in 1968. The campaign was caught off guard for what was to be an affable rally in friendly El Paso, Texas, thought to be safely within "Wallace Country." Without question, Texas was friendly turf for Wallace, but little of that was to be found on October 17. Wire reports from Southwest Texas said Wallace's planned speech was ended "in an uproar when he was hooted and jeered from a platform by 250 flannel-lunged hecklers in the El Paso Coliseum. Wallace strained and struggled to be heard over the chants of 'KKK All the Way,' and 'Sieg Heil, Sieg Heil.' After a fruitless half hour, [Wallace] gave up and walked out, droplets of sweat beading on his forehead." While the hecklers were only 250 in an audience estimated to be more than 7,000, they proved effective grouped together on the floor of the coliseum in front of Wallace's bullet-proof podium, "and Wallace was unable to make himself heard over their chanting," United Press International reported. As Wallace supporters chanted, "We want George," in response to the protestors, the tumult was such that Wallace's "words were barely audible over the shouting."[135] More than words were exchanged, with shoving matches breaking out between Wallace supporters and protestors. Wallace himself noticed the skirmishes, asking, "Ladies and gentlemen, I know that some of you are worked up tonight, but let the police handle it." As events took place, Wallace tried his regular tactics of making fun of protestors and even blowing kisses at them with a smile on his face. In the end,

> The rally degenerated into a shouting match between the two groups. Wallace, unable to make himself heard, walked up and down the stage waving to the crowd. "The people of Texas and this nation are tired of subsidizing what you see here tonight," he shouted. When order failed to return, he left the coliseum and returned to his motel.[136]

Wallace had a similarly frustrating experience at Denver, Colorado, when the public address system for his rally continued to fail (and was likely sabotaged), along with hurled tomatoes and "a hippie-type love medallion" reaching Wallace on stage. The Denver audience, a large one of more than 10,000, included mostly supporters but also a large number of "hippies who would not be shouted down. When the microphone system seemed to fade, [Wallace] finally gave up."[137] The medallion thrown missed Wallace, causing him to step from behind his massive bulletproof lectern and dared hecklers "to throw another rock." Veteran journalist Jules Loh reported that several fist fights also broke out during Wallace's speech. The Denver appearance had been hyped by full-page advertisements his campaign placed in the *Rocky Mountain News* showing a school bus rolling down a road. The headline read, "If you're wondering why more and more millions of your fellow Americans are turning to Governor Wallace, follow as your children are bused all across town."[138]

The decided turn in heckling by protestors away from Humphrey and toward Wallace as the 1968 campaign wore on did not go unnoticed. While all three major candidates in 1968 experienced their moments with hecklers, Wallace took the brunt of the abuse, most agreed. Martin Schram, writing for *Newsday*, reported on "The Year of the Heckler" and said Wallace had "been the subject of the campaign's most vitriolic heckling." Schram noted, "At virtually every stop, at least a couple of hecklers are violently manhandled and roughed up by Wallace supporters. . . . And for most of the campaign, Wallace has reveled in their attention. He has never figured on converting his hecklers, so he has used them to solidify his position[s]."[139] Wallace's aides told reporters that the hecklers were actually helping Wallace, getting him more attention and coverage than a third-party candidate might otherwise expect. "They said publicly that they liked having the hecklers along," Schram wrote. "But then something happened. The hecklers started getting smart," creating a strain on Wallace in trying to get his message out. Schram reported that in Denver, the candidate was forced to cut his speech in half when hecklers made it impossible for the audience to hear him. Reporters caught Wallace in an angry, unguarded moment as he whispered to one of his aides that he hoped the hecklers would charge at him and provoke a violent confrontation. "In San Diego, he challenged a heckler to come down and confront him," Schram wrote. "His temper has grown short."[140]

Later in October, as his poll numbers continued to sag from a high of 22 percent a month earlier, Wallace returned to Indiana for a rally at Evansville and drew a respectable crowd—but one that was almost too evenly matched between supporters and protestors. Nick Kotz, a Pulitzer Prize–winning journalist for the *Des Moines Register*, traveled to Indiana for the Wallace stop. He relayed, "If hatred was in the heart of the people who gathered [in Evansville] in front of the county courthouse, it was at least not on their lips *before* George C. Wallace began to speak."[141] A crowd of 5,000 "hollered themselves hoarse with cheers and boos and turned on each other with vulgar profanities and were restrained from physical contact only by the presence of several hundred law enforcement officers," Kotz reported. The hecklers in Evansville "became the embodiment of all evil as he sees it," Kotz wrote. Unlike Nixon or Humphrey rallies, the mix now included supporters and protestors, as well as the curious who came to see the show. The show included the usual country and western band opening, and then, "Wallace, his thin black hair immaculately oiled and combed back in a sizeable pompadour, comes forward to the microphone, half smiles and waves to the crowd. The show is underway."[142] In the Evansville audience were "two clean-cut, well-dressed Negro high school students and a few of their white friends" who came along to boo Wallace. "As always," Kotz wrote, "Wallace's sensitive ears have detected where the most protest is coming from, and, as always, his first move is to go to the edge of the platform near them and blow mock kisses in their direction." His remarks to protestors included regular insults—"There's nothing wrong with you that a good barber couldn't cure," or "You know a lot of four letter words but there's two you don't know anything about—W-O-R-K and S-O-A-P."[143] Kotz observed the youthful Evansville hecklers "were not hippies and had no longer hair than any other student, and looked well-scrubbed and cleanly dressed. But the Wallace lines are the same whether confronted by genuine hippies and revolutionaries or just plain students." Wallace's supporters at Evansville were rough on the Black students present to protest, as Kotz reported:

> The crowd is shouting at the policemen to "show those n-----s where they belong," and Wallace says of all those who are shouting against him: "We're going to drag you *under* a good jail. That's where you belong." His support-ers, the workingmen and shopkeepers and housewives who 20 minutes before engaged in cheerful chit-chat, roar their approval.[144]

The peak of the Wallace campaign rally spectacle was an impressive "show" in the grandest of all venues in the nation—New York's Madison Square Garden on October 24, where an audience of 20,000 showed up—"one of the largest indoor political rallies in New York City since the 1930s," according to historian Dan T. Carter.[145] United Press International made special note that the rally was likely "a dream come true" for Wallace—a former boxer—to be the main event at Madison Square Garden. UPI reported,

> While inside the arena, the screaming, flag-waving crowd gave Wallace a 15 minute ovation when he stepped on the stage. . . . outside the huge arena, police clashed with an anti-Wallace crowd. Screaming "police brutality" and "pig, pig, pig," more than 1,000 persons surged in the streets. The protestors were scattered by nightstick-swinging police, mounted and on foot.[146]

The media reported more on the aftermath than on Wallace's speech. In total, 30 arrests were reported on various charges, such as disorderly conduct and resisting arrest. A handful of minor injuries were also reported. James T. Woo-ten of the *New York Times* covered Wallace's Madison Square Garden rally, dubbing it "a carnival like atmosphere" and added, "None of those who came to hear Mr. Wallace heard anything he has not said before." Wooten picked up on impatience among the Wallace throng, "who had listened to a succes-sion of appeals for money and guitar and singing performances by country musicians."[147] On the floor of the arena, Confederate flags waved in the crowd, laughter came from Wallace's pointed remarks about reporters and protestors, all surrounded by blue-helmeted police and plainclothes security personnel, Wooten reported. Fellow *Times* reporter Homer Bigart described the security outside the arena as "a fortress" where as many as 3,000 New York City Police Department uniformed officers kept more than 1,000 anti-Wallace protestors at least a block away from Madison Square. Bigart offered this account:

> Rocks and soda bottles were thrown at patrolmen . . . Policemen charged a crowd with nightsticks flying and seized a teen-age youth who was led away with blood running down the back of his neck and a welt over one eye. Potentially the tensest moment came before Mr. Wallace arrived at the rally. A surging crowd of anti Wallace youths spilled onto 34th Street near Seventh Avenue. They surrounded a busload of Wallace supporters from the Long Island suburbs, slammed their fists against the windows and shouted obscenities. The police rescued those in the bus, but meanwhile the demonstrators had wrestled Wallace hats and Confederate flags from pedestrians. The rebel flags were raised triumphantly aloft and set afire.[148]

Bigart detailed "the ugliest outbreak" when a group of Wallace supporters "began attacking a small group of Negroes" from the Beulah Baptist Church. "Some of the Negroes were punched or spat upon. 'Hey, n-----s, get out of here!' someone in the Wallace crowd screamed. The police moved the Negroes to a secluded corner where they remained seated under protective custody."[149]

In his remarks, almost reported as an afterthought in media coverage of the event, Wallace fired up his regular tropes about the Supreme Court, about a lack of law and order, and about problematic plans to integrate public schools. The former governor accurately noted that the *New York Times* would likely ignore most of his remarks: "I'm sure *The New York Times* took note of the reception that we've received here in the great city of New York."[150] The New York City rally was a success in terms of crowd size and visuals for Wallace in a convention-like setting, but many political analysts openly questioned whether Wallace had any significant level of support in New York—upstate or downstate. So the question remained, with few days left to convince voters, was Wallace in New York for any other reason than to stroke his own ego?

As the 1968 campaign came to its blistering end, Lardner and Loh stated,

> In the beginning Wallace managed to orchestrate it all into prospective votes. The politics of protest, it seemed, had come full circle. He needed hecklers as foils. But could not be baited with impunity. Their obscenities simply won him more support. . . . The Wallace campaign both enhanced and degraded the art of heckling.

... But in the end, the violence that trailed him served largely to scare the voters away. Tramping through the grapes of wrath is always risky business. If Wallace's campaign was vulgar, intimidating, terrifying, it also was vastly entertaining.[151]

1972: A New Look, a New Threat

For his renovated 1972 campaign fashioned to capture the Democratic Party's nomination, writer Jules Loh discerned, Wallace's new wife Cornelia had "housebroken him" as he returned to the Democratic Party fold and attempted to add credibility and respectability into his campaigns (elements lost during the spectacle of his previous two bids). The result, Loh determined, was that reporting about Wallace's campaign also became more conventional:

> The absence of hecklers in most of his crowds also contributed to the new image—a rather dull new image, considering that in previous campaigns hecklers had been an integral part of a Wallace speech, offered to the public as clear and present examples of the need for more law'norder, somebody handy for the cops to bop right there in the aisles.[152]

One troubling—and nearly deadly—spectacle playing out in the shadows of Wallace's surging 1972 campaign was known only to the lost and troubled mind of a miscreant young man from Milwaukee, Wisconsin—Arthur Bremer, just twenty-one years old. For Wallace, his higher level of respectability and embrace (at least by many of the Democratic Party's voters, but not the party's leaders) played out in a hopeful way that caused Wallace and some of his closest advisers to believe he might finally have broken through. Subsequent investigations would show, however, that the violence Bremer brought to end the Wallace campaign in May 1972 had shadowed Wallace (after attempts to get near President Nixon had failed) throughout his 1972 campaign forays into many states, most noticeably in Michigan and Maryland. There was no evidence uncovered that indicated Bremer was present for Wallace's early big primary victories in both Florida and North Carolina, although FBI officials indicated he may have been near the campaign in both Wisconsin and Indiana.

On May 10, 1972, an overflow crowd of 6,000 supporters filled the Dearborn Youth Center Dome Room to hear Wallace warn Michigan voters that "it was not too late" to stop busing of school children in the state. "I want the press to take notice that the great mass of people in this area are for George Wallace, and they are going to carry the state for us."[153] Wallace was enjoying a good ride in Michigan. Although still loathed by Democratic Party officials as an outsider they wished would go away, he clearly was calling the agenda of the primary as his opponents—all establishment Democratic Senators—chased him on issues such as busing, welfare, taxes, and federal spending. Unknown to Wallace, among those in an overflow crowd crammed into the Dearborn Youth Center that evening was Bremer, who later admitted that he had stalked Wallace to the site in order to shoot him. Bremer wrote about driving across Michigan trying to reach Dearborn in time for the scheduled 8 p.m. rally. Although he arrived at 6:15 p.m., according to his diary, the size of the crowd kept him from getting into the actual room where Wallace spoke. As Wallace entered to make his speech, Bremer *had* managed to get next to a window in an entryway for the building. In his troubling personal diary later seized by federal law enforcement authorities, Bremer wrote, "There were windows on the sides of the hall and some people, the lucky ones, had a view into the hall to see what they could hear." He criticized the Secret Service detail with Wallace for failing to note that two large windowpanes were all that separated Wallace from Bremer's gun. "Somewhat careless, I thought of the [Secret Service]. The thin glass was weakly reinforced with wire mesh. But no trouble for a bullet at all. That was my plan."[154] Bremer wrote, "When Wallace appeared behind the curtain we 'supporters' went wild. . . . [He] came over to wave hello twice. Then [he] came over to ask if we could hear the singers over the speakers. He used sign language." Bremer called the venue "a glorified junior high school auditorium" and said as Wallace took the podium, "We at the window could see him thru [*sic*] a crack in the curtains."[155] As Wallace's speech continued—as Bremer put it, "He talked and talked. The ranks thinned. Not even many at the windows. . . . I wanted him to wave at us and come close as he left." Bremer questioned, "Did the Secret Service men really think a piece of glass was a deterrent [*sic*]? Not to me! I was all set. Jacket opened. . . . Waiting, waiting . . . he's left the podium!"[156] To Bremer's frustration,

[Wallace] took less time to wave goodbye than he did to wave hello. And he didn't come right up to the glass (15 feet instead of five feet away). . . . Two 15 year-old girls had gotten in front of me. Their faces were one inch from the glass. It would shatter with a blunt-nosed bullet. They were sure to be blinded and disfigured. I let Wallace go only to spare these two stupid innocent delighted kids. We pounded on the window together at the governor. There will be other times.[157]

Later, the Wallace campaign moved on to northern Michigan and the upper peninsula of the state, an area unaccustomed to attention from any national political candidates. At Marquette, Wallace spoke to an open-air rally of about 4,000 supporters at the ShopKo Shopping Center. The AP reported, "Although there was bright sunshine, ice still covered Lake Superior and snow lingered on the ground when he landed at the Marquette Airport." During his speech, students from Northern Michigan University attempted to interrupt his remarks, prompting Wallace to say, "This is my show up here. You have your show later."[158] Later at Escanaba, about 2,000 people attended an airport rally. Later, the Wallace campaign flew south for a campaign rally in Cadillac, Michigan—and the troubled Bremer was also on the move in Michigan. Reading in a newspaper article that Wallace was due back in lower Michigan, Bremer drove more than 200 miles from Dearborn to Cadillac to try again to kill Wallace.

In his speech before 2,000 people inside the Cadillac High School gymnasium, Wallace proclaimed, "I believe Michigan has the key to stop busing. In this great state of Michigan, when you put your foot down on the 16th, you'll find the President listening, and the Democrats listening."[159] The *Traverse City Record-Eagle* described Wallace's Cadillac rally as "a hand-clapping, foot-stomping revival that would make any evangelist jealous."[160] Media fixation on the spectacle of the Wallace show seemingly continued. Bremer's diary reflected he arrived early in Cadillac and was questioned by a local police officer as he slept in his car near the high school rally site. The police officer did not search Bremer's car (where a gun was hidden), however, and accepted the young man's answer that he was "just waiting for the governor." The "spectacle" of the Wallace rallies, however, seemed to be lost on Bremer. He described the Cadillac rally with a sense of boredom: "The same singers. The same songs. Two [Secret Service] men flank the stage as 'Wally' talks . . . behind his usual high bullet-proof podium. More agents flank the crowd and the stage entrance. Bored gargoyles, unmoving, unemotional, searching."[161] As in Dearborn, Bremer was unsatisfied with the position he had gained in order to take a shot at Wallace, and deemed he was too far away to actually successfully slay the candidate. Bremer wrote of how he enthusiastically cheered each of the applause lines in Wallace's stump speech—"I want him to feel comfortable" but lamented that he needed to "get closer" in order to fire his gun, and had even tried calling out to Wallace encouraging him to "shake hands, shake hands" after he finished speaking. "At the end of the speech, I try to push the people in front of me and in my row forward out of the way so I can get close. No luck."[162]

Bremer followed Wallace to another rally, this one at the Kalamazoo National Guard Armory, where he went mostly unnoticed in a crowd of 2,300, dressed in a red, white, and blue polyester suit and applauding enthusiastically at the governor's speech. As the *New York Times* reported later, Bremer, outfitted in a garish "red, white and blue outfit," talked up a young woman handing out anti-Wallace leaflets produced by the Young Workers Liberation League, a Communist-oriented organization founded in Chicago in 1970, but no other connection between the Marxist group and Bremer was ever established.[163] The *New York Times* report further indicated Bremer was once again questioned by local police after he was spotted sitting in his car near the rally site hours before the event started. Again, no search was undertaken of Bremer's vehicle, where he had hidden a handgun.[164] Bremer himself wrote in his diary that he chose to attend the 8 p.m. Saturday night rally in Kalamazoo over Wallace's outdoor rally in Warren because "I favored an indoor rally . . . I considered the alternatives carefully" and added, "Kalamazoo inside. I would have to fight all of Detroit to get a good seat in Warren. Kalamazoo wasn't so populated."[165]

Once in Kalamazoo, Bremer picked up a copy of a "Send Them a Message" Wallace campaign sign—his plan: "I'll soon be on the front steps of the Kalamazoo Armory to welcome him. Got a sign from campaign headquarters here to shield the go for the gun. Is there anything else to say? My cry upon firing [at Wallace] will be, 'A penny for your thoughts.'"[166]

For unknown reasons, Bremer once again decided against firing his gun at Wallace in Kalamazoo and instead extended his plan. An FBI investigation would later show that Bremer left Michigan and drove through the night and the next day to New York City, where he took a hotel room and hired a prostitute. Later, he left for Maryland after reading newspaper articles that indicated Wallace would do last-minute campaigning on Monday, May 15, the day before the primary.

Wallace's 1972 Maryland campaign started in earnest on May 7—as Wallace split his time between Maryland and Michigan. As he opened the effort in Maryland, 3,000 supporters jammed the Fifth Regiment Armory in Baltimore, while smaller crowds showed at Hagerstown and Cumberland. At Hagerstown, young Black protestors interrupted the proceedings repeatedly. The *Birmingham News* back in Alabama reported, indicating that while protests had been fewer for Wallace events in 1972, in Maryland he still inspired a vitriolic response:

> About 50 blacks carrying McGovern signs tried at intervals to drown out Wallace. Several persons were seized by police when scuffling broke out between blacks and whites following Wallace's speech. . . . At least three blacks and two whites were handcuffed and loaded into a paddy wagon.[167]

In Cumberland, Wallace opened a full-throated attack on the news media. "The press has twisted and distorted almost everything I've ever said or done," he said. "They've got folks believing now that I'm against certain people just because of who they happen to be." Wallace said a fuller understanding was needed of his "stand in the schoolhouse door" from 1963, terming it a challenge "to a faceless, omnipotent bureaucracy interfering in state business and usurping states' rights." He said in 1972, race was "a passé issue, a moot question."[168] In Frederick, at the Prince George's County Shopping Center, Wallace ducked pennies hurled at him as he tried to speak. Associated Press photographers caught one of Wallace's security aides accidentally striking Wallace in the face with a piece of cardboard as he attempted to shield the pennies from hitting the governor. The AP noted that, Wallace's "appearances at rallies in Frederick and Hagerstown in the western Maryland mountains and in Landover, a Washington suburb, drew protests by blacks and young people who tossed missiles."[169]

An intense FBI investigation showed that the troubled Arthur Bremer was first spotted at a Wallace rally in Milwaukee on April 4, 1972, and again at Wallace events in Michigan. Wallace campaign volunteers in Wisconsin and Michigan would later tell FBI agents that Bremer had come to Wallace headquarters, under the premise of being a supporter and campaign volunteer. As was the case with most every political campaign, volunteers were not particularly screened—most campaigns were happy to take help from anyone who wanted to assist. The *Chicago Daily News* reported the FBI tried to place Bremer at Wallace campaign events in both Indianapolis and Terre Haute, Indiana.[170] What is known that Bremer's diary and news film archives confirm Bremer *was* in attendance at Wallace speeches in Dearborn and Kalamazoo, Michigan. Bremer was not spotted again until Monday, May 15, when he was witnessed and photographed in the audience for two outdoor Wallace rallies, first in Wheaton and then in Laurel, Maryland. As he narrowed in on shooting Wallace, Bremer continued his habit of "wearing eye-catching clothes" and "pushing his way to the front of crowds at political rallies"—yet he still escaped notice of Secret Service agents. One Secret Service source suggested that campaign rallies were filled with people wearing red, white, and blue coats and dresses, and that gaudy campaign garb was not uncommon.[171]

One day before the Maryland primary, Wallace flew from Montgomery, Alabama, to Washington, DC, and immediately was driven 25 miles north to the Wheaton Plaza Shopping Center for a 30-minute rally. At the rally, "Wallace was the target of a tomato and a number of paper airplanes tossed from a crowd of about 1,500, many of whom had come to heckle, rather than to listen," the AP reported.[172] The *Baltimore Sun* reported the Wheaton audience was "hostile" to Wallace where "he was assailed by insults, McGovern and Humphrey signs, symbolically clenched fists and tomatoes. None of their tomatoes hit their mark. One was knocked aside by a Secret Service agent and another flew so wide of the Governor that Mr. Wallace ridiculed the tomato tosser."[173] Two network television reporters were at Wheaton that day, ABC's Steve Bell and David Dick from CBS. As Bell recalled, the protests at Wheaton provided a lot of material for a good story, and both he and Dick had decided that unless the protests continued at Laurel, the day's story was clearly the angry protestors at Wheaton. The Wheaton rally stood out to Bell:

> It was really the only time I saw not only protestors, but people throwing things, like rotten fruit, at Wallace. And [Wallace] loved it. He was taking them on verbally and standing his ground while the Alabama highway patrol [officers] had big pieces of cardboard and they were standing on either side of him, and in front down below, swatting stuff away with the cardboard. This was unlike any event previously that year, in 1972. I am told that this sort of thing was a regular part of the 1968 campaign, but it wasn't in 1972.[174]

As Wallace completed his remarks, a CBS News cameraman later told investigators he overheard Bremer asking a Montgomery County police officer whether he could steer Wallace toward him because he wanted to shake his hand. The police officer reportedly said that the governor made his own choices on where he would go and that he could not assist Bremer in meeting the governor. Frustrated at Wheaton where he couldn't get close to Wallace, Bremer drove on 25 miles north to the Laurel Shopping Center on Fairlawn Avenue in Laurel, where Wallace had a 3 p.m. rally scheduled. Bell recalled he went to Laurel and made a quick observation that the crowd was much more supportive and subdued than the one at Wheaton, and decided to head back to Washington, DC, to process his film and prepare his report for that evening's broadcast of *The ABC Evening News*, anchored by Howard K. Smith and Harry Reasoner.

Once in Laurel, Wallace's rally started about ten minutes late, and the governor spoke for about forty-five minutes before a friendlier crowd than he had encountered earlier at Wheaton. Secret Service records indicate the governor mounted a stage bearing the shopping center's name as Billy Grammer and his band, as usual, opened the rally with a round of country music. The Secret Service record indicated Wallace concluded his remarks at 3:56 p.m. and dismounted the stage to go greet voters. The *Baltimore Sun* reported that the Wallace crowd was "composed largely of middle-aged people. The governor's supporters, many of those wearing Wallace buttons, stood directly in front of the podium while dozens of long-haired youths kept their distance to one side of the shopping center parking lot."[175] Witnesses reported Bremer was present and called out, "Hey George! Come here! George, take my hand!" By then Wallace had shed his jacket and was in short-shirt sleeves and waded into the crowd to greet voters.

Two minutes later, gunshots exploded, five of them striking Wallace.

Lauren Pierce, a cameraman for CBS News, captured the entire shooting on film, showing Bremer extending his arm from in between others in front of him and firing while wearing an odd smile on his face. Pierce said the gun came from "a mass of bodies" near him and that the gun "looked like a cheap .38 special, fired at point blank range."[176] Pierce said he could see people in the crowd shoving Bremer's shooting arm downward after the first shot rang out—"which probably accounted for the abdominal wound" to Wallace. After he was shot, Pierce said, "[Wallace] fell back. I thought he might be dead or dying. But then he opened his eyes after a long while and his wife came running to his side (on the ground) and embraced him. It was total confusion."[177] While Wallace's primary "body men," Alabama State Police captain E. C. Dothard and Secret Service agent Nick Zarvos were down from having been struck by bullets, Wallace supporters began to subdue Bremer and to wrestle the gun from his hand. "Witnesses said they saw people punching the assailant," the *Baltimore Sun* reported. "He had blood coming out of his nose and a cut on the back of his neck," said Fred Knapp, a sixteen-year-old newspaper delivery boy who had stopped to hear Wallace speak.[178] In the chaos that followed, it took several minutes for an ambulance to arrive to transport the critically wounded Wallace to the hospital. Initially, he was loaded into the back of a station wagon as desperate police and Wallace's aides scrambled to get him to the hospital. Eventually reloaded into an ambulance, the trip took fourteen minutes, Wallace arriving at the emergency room of Holy Cross Hospital (thirteen miles southwest of Laurel at Silver Spring, Maryland) at 4:19 p.m.[179] Prince Georges County Police corporal Mike Landrum placed Bremer in a headlock and dragged the young man to a police cruiser nearby.

Years later, Wallace reconstructed the scene from his perspective in a calm manner that reflected the "acceptance" he said he had found in his heart and mind for what had happened to him. While running for a fourth (and final term) as governor of Alabama in 1982, Wallace told a local reporter:

> [After my speech], the Secret Service said, "Let's go to the car," but the crowd felt very friendly [to me]. I said, "I wanna shake hands, shake hands," so I threw my coat over to the Secret Service man and I stepped into the crowd and as soon as I did, I heard what sounded like five firecrackers. I said to myself, "Well, this is it." I didn't feel the bullets in me but I fell to the ground, I knew I was shot. I knew I was paralyzed because one of my friends looked down and said, "It's not bad, governor, it's not that bad," and I said, "Well, you look again, it is bad. I can't move my feet, I'm paralyzed." And after that, of course, I nearly died. I was nearly dead by the time I got to the hospital.[180]

In his 1976 book, *Stand Up for America*, Wallace said he lived in fear of violence on the campaign trail. From the time he began moving across the nation in 1964 he had "lived with the possibility of assassination." He wrote,

I had made enemies, and others had been made for me by people who had consistently and deliberately misrepresented my political and racial philosophies. To say that I was indifferent to the danger would be incorrect. The eternal presence of the Secret Service agents was a constant reminder of what had happened to President Kennedy, Senator Robert Kennedy and Rev. Martin Luther King. But events moved too fast to permit much time for morbid reflections.[181]

Wallace said he was made aware after the fact that Bremer had also been present at Wheaton, and "I probably saw his face from time to time as I glanced out over the crowd, but it meant nothing to me and I have no memory of it." He recalled in the moments he laid on the parking lot pavement, bloodied and wounded, Cornelia threw her body over his and whispered to him: "You're going to be alright, honey. I'm going to get you out of here. I'm going to take you home."[182]

While cameras from ABC and CBS captured the startling events at Laurel, newsmen like Steve Bell were kicking themselves for having broken off from the rally and returned to the news bureau in downtown Washington, DC, to prepare their stories. Bell recalled,

> We thought with all of the protests and stuff being thrown at him at Wheaton that this would be the lead story on the news that night. We were down at the [ABC News] bureau and I can remember walking out of the wire room and hearing a desk assistant shouting, "Wallace has been shot! Wallace has been shot!" I was petrified because I wasn't there. Our crews were still there and got it all on film, but we had to race back to Silver Spring, Maryland, to Holy Cross Hospital where he was taken and we did live reports that evening from there. We basically set up housekeeping for the two months that followed out on the front porch of Holy Cross Hospital.[183]

Not surprisingly, Wallace's shooting was national news and reached Wallace's family members by television and radio reports before any official notifications could be made. Daughter Peggy Wallace Kennedy was walking between classes at college when a friend passed her and remarked, "Well, your dad must be OK then?" Peggy replied, "What do you mean?" and the friend told her about radio reports indicating that George Wallace had been shot in Maryland. "This person thought he must be OK because I was still there at school, but I just hadn't heard the news yet," she said. "They took me to the [college] President's office and they got me to Washington, D.C. For the child of a politician, it was a nightmare, we were always afraid something like that is going to happen."[184] Adding to her concern, Peggy said, was a minor disagreement she had with her father over the breakfast table earlier that morning. "He was very irritated that day, he had a lot of tension," she said, prior to leaving Alabama. "He was mad because Cornelia was running late and he just wanted to get up [to Maryland] and make it a one-day trip and come back." She added,

> He was in an irritable mood and he and I had words, unfortunately, and I left the breakfast table. My apartment door [in the Governor's Mansion] was open and I can vividly remember hearing his footsteps coming down the steps as he was leaving. I recall he stopped and talked to a security officer about wearing a bullet proof vest, but said he did not want to wear it, that it was too heavy and too cumbersome.[185]

Once at the hospital in Maryland, Wallace's son, George Jr., recalled "Cornelia wasn't hysterical, but she was close." Her response was understandable: "She had been with Dad when he was shot, yet it was Dad who consoled Cornelia on the ambulance trip to the hospital. Later, she recovered her composure beautifully before going on television to assure the nation that Dad would recover."[186] As Wallace's children visited with him briefly in an intensive care unit at the hospital—following his emergency surgeries—they were reminded of their mother's dying moments at the Governor's Mansion back in Montgomery four years before. "I recalled that even though he was in terrible pain, he recognized us all and reached out for our hands and said, 'How ya'll?'"[187] Peggy said, "We were just thankful that he had lived, that he was alive."[188] The shooting happened, Peggy believed, because her father could not resist interacting with people:

> He was such a hands-on person, he liked to shake hands with people, especially at a small rally like that one at Laurel. . . . He was really fearless, he never talked about being afraid or talked about being in fear of being shot or killed or anything. He may have said something to Cornelia or others, but he never talked to me about that. I know that as a child of a father who is out in the public like that every day, *I was afraid* and I would hold my breath when he went out and let it out when he came back. . . . You're always afraid that something like that is going to happen.[189]

ABC newsman Steve Bell believed that initial reports about Wallace's condition were "attempting to make his condition sound better than it was, and by the second day, there was talk that his campaign was not over and we were given mostly favorable reports on his condition. . . . I'm sure they were giving us the most positive assessment possible."[190]

Despite his crippling injuries, Wallace scored two primary victories in the aftermath, rolling up an impressive 51 percent of the vote in Michigan (Humphrey finished second back at 27 percent, and McGovern third with 16 percent), and 39 percent of the vote in Maryland (ahead of McGovern at 27 percent and Humphrey at 22 percent). Unable to campaign in subsequent Democratic primaries, Wallace dispatched surrogates to Oregon, Rhode Island, California, and New Mexico, where the Alabamian recorded unimpressive showings against McGovern. While most observers believed the assassination attempt upon Wallace had essentially ended his quest for the Democratic nomination, others analyzed that his own campaign had made that task considerably more difficult even before Arthur Bremer stepped from a rope line of supporters. In the weeks before he was shot, Wallace was saying publicly that he could be a player for the nomination (and also influence the party's platform) by rolling up a large popular vote (despite falling terribly short on actual delegates needed to be nominated).

During the period of Wallace's recuperation, the Harris Poll found that feelings of well-being for Wallace were growing. Harris reported the percentage of people who saw him "as a man of high integrity" rose from 40 to 56 percent, and 75 percent of respondents agreed with the statement that Wallace "is brave to keep running for president after he was shot."[191] While voters polled seemed to warm up to Wallace in the aftermath of his critical injuries, the same poll found no increase in the number of people who wanted to see him elected president. Twenty-four percent of Democrats polled wanted to see Wallace be their party's nominee—the same number as before he was shot. Only 17 percent of all voters—Democrats, Republicans, and independents—wanted to see Wallace run again as a third-party candidate. Pollster Lou Harris noted, "The Democrats have a deep dilemma as they await the possible visit of Governor Wallace to their convention in Miami Beach." Harris said the Democrats would likely do better if Wallace ran as a third-party nominee (drawing more votes from Nixon than McGovern), but, "On the other hand, public sympathy for the Alabama governor runs so strong now that any unfair treatment of Wallace [by the Democrats] could cause deep resentment against Democrats and their ultimate nominee."[192]

The primary season concluded with Wallace still confined to a hospital bed, but his campaign continued to emphasize any positive news about the governor's condition. Despite efforts to put the best face on things, doctors were not prohibited from discussing publicly the challenges he faced related to the bullet lodged next to his spine causing paralysis below the waist. Physical therapy sessions were interspersed with a parade of high-profile visitors, including President and Mrs. Nixon, as well as Senator McGovern and his wife, Eleanor. Senators Humphrey and Jackson and Representative Shirley Chisholm also made lower profile visits, as did Senator Teddy Kennedy and Ethel Kennedy, widow of slain

Senator Robert F. Kennedy. As the July 10 opening of the Democratic National Convention loomed on the horizon, Wallace's backers were eager to get their candidate out of the hospital and to the convention. Whether the move was in Wallace's best health interests appeared unclear (and likely a secondary consideration)—especially amid increasingly optimistic reports on Wallace's health in the weeks following the shooting. As a result, just 53 days after he was shot, Wallace was released from the Maryland hospital and was flown to Montgomery, Alabama, and the spectacle of his campaign continued.

Transported via an air force medical evacuation jet to Donnelly Field in Montgomery, his stop in Alabama was required in order to reclaim his official duties as governor. Because Alabama law required Lt. Governor Jere Beasley to be named "acting governor" of the state because of Wallace's extended absence, returning even momentarily to Alabama territory reinstalled Wallace to the full power of his office. Wallace was only in the state for just over two hours before departing again for Miami and the Democratic convention. Steve Bell and his cameraman from ABC News won the draw to be the network "pool" reporters to go onboard the plane for the flight to Alabama and then on to Florida. "We were all in one area in the plane, I wasn't isolated from George on the flight down," Bell recalled. "Obviously, I wasn't bothering him either, although I am sure that we talked, and I was responsible to provide a pool report after the flight to the other journalists."[193] For his report that aired on July 7, 1972, Bell described Wallace's return to Alabama as "dramatic," but he noted that the governor "appeared to be nervous, even apprehensive about his first big speech, but there was no evidence of that when he began talking."[194] Bell's "pool" report indicated that Wallace was seated in a passenger seat, and not a hospital bed, for the second leg of the trip from Alabama to Miami—signing autographs and talking to crew members. Bell took note that Wallace said he was ready to make a serious run for the Democratic nomination if front-runner George McGovern were to fail on a first ballot. ABC News reported on the same day Wallace arrived in Miami that his would-be assassin, Arthur Bremer, had successfully sought a further delay in his federal trial on multiple charges.

Wallace arrived in Alabama on an air force medical evacuation jet authorized by President Nixon and was the center of all attention to more than 5,000 loyalists who awaited his arrival on a hot airport tarmac. "The crowd was held a good distance from the governor by a cordon of [police]," *Montgomery Advertiser* reporter Don F. Wasson noted. "A platform had been erected which Wallace reached by wheelchair up a long incline." Wasson said the crowd was happy but more subdued than a normal Wallace rally. Even the presence of the Troy State University band failed to whoop up the crowd, most of them who "seemed to want to see for themselves how the governor looked, how his voice sounded and they wanted to hear from his own lips his future plans." In his brief remarks, Wallace appeared "visibly touched and gave the short little salute that has become a campaign trademark."[195] In a voice described as weak, Wallace made brief remarks saying the prayers of his fellow Alabamians had been "an inspiration" to his recovery. He also praised hospital staff in Maryland for their help. "I thank God for having saved my life," he said, but he referred to the shooting as only a sidelining setback.[196]

From Montgomery, the Wallace party continued on for a short flight to Miami, where the Democratic National Convention was about to get underway. Wallace was met again by a large group of reporters curious about his condition, as were the loyalists back in Alabama. "I am still an active and viable candidate even though I was sidelined for a few days," Wallace said. "We're back in the fight." He added, however, "As it stands now, I have no plans to go on the convention floor. I'll have to play it by ear and do whatever is the proper thing to do."[197] Democratic Party officials were careful to appear accommodating, notifying reporters that ramps and other adjustments had been made so Wallace's participation in the convention would be as easy as possible. The accommodations continued as presumptive nominee McGovern agreed to allow Wallace to speak on July 11 from the platform of the convention (interestingly on the same night when Coretta Scott King, the widow of Dr. Martin Luther King Jr. also spoke). UPI reported that "special box seats" and a ramp had been installed in the convention center for Wallace's convenience if he chose to come to the arena. Ultimately, except for his scheduled speech from the platform, Wallace chose to remain in his hotel suite and watched the convention via a special closed-circuit television feed provided by the DNC.[198]

For his speech before delegates, all eyes were nervously focused on Wallace as he was wheeled to the rostrum towering above the convention floor. The spectacle of lifting Wallace into position to speak from high above the convention floor gathered as much attention as did his actual remarks. The spectacle nature of the Wallace campaign had changed forever, moving from the reaction he could generate from his supporters to the rhetoric of resentment he had perfected, to the awkward show now of how an enfeebled and paralyzed gunshot victim could compete on an often-unforgiving political stage. As his chair reached the podium, TV cameras caught Wallace as he quickly pitched his arms forward to grab onto the podium and to get his bearings. Mercilessly, microphones failed to pick up the collective gasps of many watching, worried that Wallace was at risk of falling out of the wheelchair. Photographs in newspapers across the nation the next day juxtaposed Wallace in his wheelchair looking like he was perched on a high ledge. The *New York Times* reported that Wallace made "a wheelchair appearance" before the convention.[199] "Two Secret Service agents and an Alabama state trooper lifted the governor, in his gleaming, chrome wheelchair, to the convention platform," the *Times* noted. A frequent Wallace critic, DNC Chair Lawrence F. O'Brien was there to greet him—apparently trying to put all hard feelings in the past.[200]

While applause for Wallace was polite upon his introduction, a few lingering "boos" could be heard from the floor despite his obviously weakened physical condition. Delegates in the New York and New Jersey delegations remained seated, while other convention delegates stood as they applauded Wallace. He told the delegates, "I am here because I want to help the Democratic Party. I want to help it become what it used to be—the party of the average working man."[201] It was a much smaller (and clearly less-inspiring agenda) than he had promoted throughout the early months of 1972 as he sought to be the party's presidential nominee. The *New York Times* report indicated that although Wallace's voice appeared "noticeably stronger than in his previous public appearances," the content of his remarks was not received as helping coalesce the party around the imminent McGovern nomination. Wallace offered no endorsement of McGovern, but he also appeared to close the door to a third-party campaign that could hurt McGovern (and Nixon).[202]

Speaking for only twelve minutes, reports seemed more focused on his condition—the *Times* report concluding, "The governor was carried from the platform as he arrived, two Secret Servicemen at either side of his wheelchair. They lifted him down off a special wooden platform and then rolled his chair down a wooden ramp that had been assembled and then quickly dismantled in six-foot sections."[203] *Orlando Sentinel* reporter Jack McDavitt reported, "Wallace, his legs crippled by a would-be assassin's bullets, but his voice strong and fiery once more, made a dramatic appearance" and offered a speech interrupted by a mix of cheers and boos. "Wallace is the first wheelchair-bound convention speaker since the late Franklin D. Roosevelt [and] was carried to the podium by Secret Service agents and a husky member of the Alabama State Police."[204] The *Anniston Star* dispatched editor Steve Traylor to Miami who noted that while delegates were polite to Wallace's speech, they voted down every single platform amendment his supporters entered.[205] As *Montgomery Advertiser* reporter Don F. Wasson noted, Wallace's speech took twelve minutes, and the convention took less than five minutes to reject on a voice vote the minority report presented by Wallace regarding the party's platform.[206] Wallace assessed his own speech this way: "It was a relatively short speech, and it was followed by polite applause. . . . My campaign ended informally in Laurel. It ended formally in Miami."[207]

1976: One More Try

Despite the ugly and frightening reality that his life had nearly ended in his pursuit of his political ambitions, Wallace was determined to make one more run for the presidency and entered the 1976 Democratic presidential primary campaign. It was a campaign that would be like none other in modern times, a wheelchair-bound candidate who had survived an assassin's bullets trying once again to defeat the odds. Reporters and political observers were paying attention; it was more of the don't-look-away nature of every Wallace move. Among those interested in how a clearly diminished Wallace would fare this time was trailblazing journalist and columnist Mary McGrory of the *Washington Post* who made a cold February trip north to Boston to sit in on one of George Wallace's rallies. McGrory said she was thinking what many journalists were thinking—was there any life left in a Wallace campaign on the national level? Two years earlier Wallace had won an unprecedented third term as governor of Alabama by rolling up 83 percent of the vote against two opponents in the general election. But it was still a different Wallace than had made three previous presidential runs—Wallace and his family had all but given up hope that he would ever walk again—and he seemed resigned to campaigning from a wheelchair. It would be new territory in American politics—Franklin D. Roosevelt had enjoyed the cooperation of a national news media that rarely, if ever, showed him struggling to walk or stand. Photographs of FDR in a wheelchair didn't emerge until many years after his death in 1945. Wallace, however, lived in a different era, and regardless of the fact he *had* been the victim of a horrible crime when he was shot in May 1972, he didn't inspire sympathy in everyone.

McGrory observed what she assessed a typical Wallace "show" in Boston that day, but at a much smaller venue than what had been the practice in 1968 and 1972—the rally at the Lithuanian Citizens Association Hall in South Boston drawing just 500 people. Wallace's Boston appearance was considered his first major foray as he once again skipped the first-in-the-nation New Hampshire primary a week earlier. McGrory quickly noted Wallace's opening act, Billy Grammar of the Grand Ole Opry, made a point of telling the audience, "We come here to be friendly." She noted that Grammar's failure to answer a song request from a young audience member was the only dust-up in what she described as "a year of rage over school busing" in Massachusetts and elsewhere. Though they didn't expressly say so, the Wallace campaign visit to South Boston was strategically scheduled just days after a violent clash between antibusing protestors and police outside of South Boston High School just a half mile from the Wallace rally site. As the Associated Press reported, the melee at the high school had been ugly:

The crowd hurled tear gas cannisters, bricks, stones and lead pipes as the police broke up a march of men in the neighborhood that has been the core of resistance to court-ordered busing for school desegregation. . . . The clash came against a background of several antibusing incidents here in recent days, including the breaking up of a court-sponsored parents' meeting by a jeering mob.[208]

McGrory wrote, "The Wallace people did the usual thing—sang country-western songs, passed plastic baskets for contributions, handed out packets of confetti." A local priest gave the invocation and "blessed himself and practically everybody in the hall, except for the visiting Protestants on the stage."[209] After Cornelia Wallace was given a bouquet of red roses,

> South Boston's new God was wheeled in. In a storm of confetti and shouts, George Wallace was installed behind his bullet-proof podium. His face was puffy and pasty, but his voice rang strong over his powerful microphone. He could have taken them anywhere he wanted. But he had to be careful. There was blood on the streets of Boston last week and Wallace cannot be the candidate of violence. . . . So he used the word "peacefully" and said it slowly. . . . It was one of the few counsels [the audience] received in quiet.[210]

Wallace still held power over his followers, McGrory wrote, despite the fact they were smaller in number than ever before. He told his followers that the central question facing voters in 1976 was "whether or not the great middle class is going to survive" as the federal government grows, social experiments continue to quash individual rights, welfare cheats steal money from everyone, and the media and "ultra-liberals" tear down traditional American values.[211] The *Lowell Sun's* Statehouse reporter, Loring Swaim, covered another Wallace rally at the National Guard Armory in Norwood in which the governor declared that if Massachusetts Democrats responded, "you'd see a bunch of pointed heads and politicians in Washington looking like cats on a hot tin roof, trying to get their positions in order, all sounding like George Wallace."[212] Attended by 1,000 Wallace loyalists, Swaim noted that the governor didn't need to spend much time convincing anyone of anything. They were there to "go wild over his positions. There was no selling to do; virtually everyone appeared to know why he or she came—and the adulation shook the rafters."[213] While the Wallace rallies still inspired his true believers, it was clear there was fewer of them than ever before. Other things had changed as well, Swaim described:

> The side doors opened, Secret Service squads entered, eyes peering in every direction—and Wallace is wheeled in. Within moments, his wheelchair has been

lifted backwards up the steps and waving his arms, he was wheeled into position into a three-sided protective podium topped by bullet proof glass. A microphone is in place in the center. Wallace likes to rest his arms on the glass at either side. As he moves into his speech, he will raise his arms and fingers, jabbing the air to emphasize a point. There is an affectionate smile in response to his pitch.[214]

The media coverage in Massachusetts was just the first of a series of reports from the 1976 trail that seemed to emphasize how the Wallace rallies looked and felt, rather than what was said. The "spectacle" coverage from the past had turned from reporting on rowdy audiences spoiling for a fight to more tightly drawn analyses of Wallace—most particularly his physical stature.

In Florida, Wallace was determined to repeat his winning performance from four years earlier and made 25 separate campaign appearances across the state. He was on a mission to try to stop the growing momentum for another former southern governor, Jimmy Carter of Georgia. Reporters seemed fixated on whether Wallace thought he could match his performance—42 percent of the vote—from four years earlier. As reporters pressed Wallace on questions regarding his health, the governor ignored their queries to highlight his upcoming appearance as the Grand Marshal of the Daytona 500 stock car race. An unexpected setback occurred during the new struggle to attract votes in Florida, however. On February 2 in Pensacola, an Alabama state trooper helping to lift Wallace's wheelchair into an airplane slipped and dropped Wallace to the ground. Hours later Wallace appeared with a cast on his leg for strained ligaments. Although he went forward with a television interview before seeking treatment for his leg, the accident immediately revived questions about Wallace's physical health. Television and print photographers had not shied away from capturing images of Wallace being loaded into and out of vehicles and his wheelchair—the Roosevelt era tradition of hiding such realities was long gone by 1976. Wallace himself assured that his sprained knee would not stop what reporters were now calling his "wheelchair-bound candidacy," UPI reported. "Wallace's knee was injured when aides dropped his wheelchair as they were lifting him onto an airplane" but that Wallace continued on to a later rally at Panama City Beach, Florida. "I was getting on an airplane and the people lifted me and dropped me," he told the Panama City Beach audience. "I guess I was the victim of a case of 'stumbilitis,' but I'm perfectly all right. The president of the United States doesn't run the country with his feet and legs, he runs it with his head."[215] Later, at Lake Worth (in Palm Beach County), more than 3,500 persons showed up—causing Wallace to make two separate speeches so that he could speak to everyone who attended. However, the next day a full day of campaigning was suspended as Wallace went back to Alabama to consult with his regular physician about his leg injury. His Florida campaign literally crippled by Wallace's injury, he finished second in a devastating loss to Carter.

The road would get rougher. At Wallace's only major speech in Wisconsin for that state's April 1976 primary—before the Madison Optimist's Club—a cruel demonstration occurred in the parking lot outside the speaking venue. While Wallace protestors had always held a lot of venom for the governor, the Madison "protest" in 1976 was particularly distasteful and hurtful. There, a handful of young people donned paper masks made from a photograph of Arthur Bremer's face and rolled around wheelchairs with signs that read "George: Stand up and be counted" (a play off his "Stand Up for America" campaign theme of years past). United Press International reported it this way:

> It was as cruel and insensitive an incident anyone had seen on the campaign trail in a long time, but Alabama Governor George Wallace brushed it off philosophically. . . . "Free Artie Bremer, give him another chance" the students sang. "He should have shot him in the head, instead he shot him in the pants." That wasn't enough . . . one sign read "Wallace doesn't stand for his country."[216]

Wallace saw the demonstration as he arrived. He commented later at Janesville: "I don't pay too much attention to that. We've got a few kooks every place. All those young fellows who do that will grow up, forget all that and become good citizens." Governor Patrick Lucey, who had said Wallace was the only candidate among the Democratic field he could not support, was angered and apologized on behalf of the people of Wisconsin "for the lack of basic human sensitivity shown." Wallace said Governor Lucey had called him personally and said, "The people of this state have been very kind to me over the years." Wallace said apologies weren't necessary—adding: "I don't want any sympathy. I paid a pretty high price for being involved. Nobody should vote for you because you are in a wheelchair. But they should not vote against you because you're in a wheelchair if you are physically or mentally able."[217]

The demonstration organizer, twenty-one-year-old Bennett Masel of Madison, identified himself as an expelled student from the University of Wisconsin and a reporter for the *Yipster Times*, the newspaper of the Youth International Party (Yippies). He was cited earlier by police for a separate incident in which he allegedly spat upon Senator Henry Jackson at the Madison airport. Defending Masel's demonstration was Michel Fellner from *Takeover*, an "underground" Madison newspaper. "We felt that George Wallace was such a grotesque symbol, and a grotesque man, that a tasteless demonstration would be appropriate."[218] The unpleasant display at Madison was just a preview of how bad things would get. On primary night in Wisconsin, there was excitement and tension in the air for everyone but George Wallace. Carter won a razor-thin victory over US Representative Morris K. Udall, 37–36 percent. Wallace drew only 12 percent of the vote, a major disappointment to him and his campaign.

As winter gave way to spring in 1976, it was clear the Wallace campaign was still a spectacle, but this time for different reasons. Gone now were large arenas with loud crowds of supporters doing battle with hecklers. Wallace himself said rallies were no longer effective—blaming the media for focusing on ramps used to get him to the stage or photographs and video of campaign aides lifting his wheelchair to the dais. It was apparent that the spectacle of the Wallace campaign was now one of sadness and defiance. In Michigan, a state Wallace had won going away in 1972, the realities that his campaign was quickly coming to an end were obvious. In Lansing and later at Muskegon, fewer than 100 supporters showed up, prompting obvious contrasts with the large throngs his campaign drew four years earlier. One reporter even took note that as Wallace was wheeled along a rope line at the Lansing airport, a gap in the line of supporters "left Wallace's hand outstretched in greeting with no one there to grasp it."[219] Later, a planned "major" rally for Wallace served up disappointment. He told fewer than 200 supporters that he had stood up for and spoke out for them when no one else would. "When I spoke out about the problem of crime, they made fun of me and said I was a racist. . . . Now most of them [candidates] are saying the same things, but they're saying them a little sweeter."[220]

The sparse crowds for Wallace continued to dominate news coverage of his campaign—a *Detroit Free Press* report indicated only 70 supporters showed up at Saginaw, fewer than 200 in Flint, and just two supporters as he departed the Saginaw airport. "Unlike 1972, when Wallace once filled a hall twice in one night for rallies at the State Fairgrounds in Detroit. . . . In the 1976 campaign, his political strength is all but evaporated." Wallace's parting words took on a melancholy tone about the entire matter, repeating earlier claims that he had stood up for Americans "who think like you and me" when no one else would, and he added, "I want you people in Michigan to know, whether you ever vote for me again, that you did something for me after I got shot. You helped me recover."[221]

The sad tone of the closing message of the Wallace campaign in Michigan reflected the reality—on primary day Carter and Udall staged a fierce battle, with Carter edging Udall 43.4 to 43 percent. Wallace was crushed with just seven percent of the statewide vote. The massive "crossover" vote predicted from Wallace supporters to Republican hopeful Ronald Reagan in Michigan seemed to have little impact—President Ford capturing all but one of the state's 83 counties in the Republican Primary in his home state.

Maryland seemed an appropriate spot for the Wallace spectacle to reach its conclusion—it was after all the place where the bullets from a deranged man's gun had cut down Wallace. In Wheaton, Don Campbell, a Gannett News Service reporter, reported on Wallace's planned appearance there at a campaign headquarters. He noted there was a "small band of loyalists, some of whom had driven long distances, waiting in front of the little storefront headquarters on Georgia Avenue, next door to Abe's Jewish Book Store" to see their man. "They wore Styrofoam hats with banners proclaiming, 'This is Wallace Country.' A woman midget sitting in a wheelchair was parked up front behind the police barrier.... While two doors down Georgia Avenue a crowd of young long-hairs stood in the doorway of a tavern and drank beer and kept asking when Wallace would arrive."[222] Wallace was 45 minutes late for his only Maryland appearance and was heavily guarded even in transport from the airport to the Wheaton office by officers from the Montgomery County Sheriff's Department and the Maryland State Police. Campbell observed,

> The crowd of 200 cheered [as Wallace arrived], and then fell silent, every eye on a Wallace aide who opened the trunk of the car and lifted out a wheelchair, unfolded it, and rolled it around so that Wallace could be lifted out of the car and into it.... Wallace was rolled into the tiny headquarters, stopping long enough for a few questions. Inside, pandemonium reigned as reporters and cameramen fought their way through the crowd to get set for a press conference. Through it all, Wallace sat calmly, occasionally shaking the hand of a newsman and saying, "It's good to be back in Maryland."[223]

Campbell noted that "the feistiness of four years ago was almost gone." He admitted, "Frankly, the health issue has been raised and that hurt," and added many reporters refused to report that he had about 25 percent of the popular vote so far in the 1976 Democratic primaries.[224] Wallace said he did not expect to do well in Maryland—nothing approaching his performance four years earlier. Referring in general to the Laurel shooting, he said: "Had this not happened to me in 1972, not only would I be here as the frontrunner, I'd be here as the President of the United States. I got shot out of the saddle and couldn't run."[225] He emphasized that he held no ill will toward Maryland—

> The people of Maryland had no more to do with the Bremer shooting than the people of Alabama. I came here to let people know I appreciate what they did for me and for my morale after I was shot. It meant so much to me after I was shot— the hospitality to me and my wife were very good in those tragic times.[226]

Scripps-Howard reporter Ted Knap also reported on the Wheaton stop, writing:

> It was not much of a last hurrah for George Wallace in the state where he was
> shot four years ago at the height of his career as a presidential candidate. No
> tears, no farewells, just a news conference during a token campaign appearance
> in a tiny state headquarters that could not afford a telephone. Wallace said he
> wasn't bitter about being shot and permanently crippled. . . . But said the "health
> issue" has been his main problem in the primaries this year. . . . Wallace looked
> tired and older than he had just three months ago when he was packing overflow
> crowds into big halls in and around Boston during the busing-dominated pri-
> mary campaign in Massachusetts.[227]

The final vote tally in Maryland had been as bad as expected—Wallace finishing
last with just 4 percent of the statewide vote in a state that provided a rare late
setback for Carter. California Governor Jerry Brown surprised everyone polling 49 percent to Carter's 37 percent. Despite the setback, the Carter campaign
could not be stopped, and Wallace was forced to face a reality he had seemingly
avoided for more than a decade—he was never going to be president of the
United States, let alone the nominee of the Democratic Party for that office.
While he had moved mountains to become a major contender—especially for
portions of the 1968 and 1972 campaigns—he ultimately lacked the elements
other candidates pulled together to reach the goal. There were many reasons
why Wallace failed, including creating a spectacle that held no meaning—offering a cry to voters to follow but with no knowable direction or policy to be
found. It was ultimately political spectacle without meaning. As scholar Mary
E. Stuckey suggests, spectacle can be used to advance policy or big ideas. She
asks us to picture Ronald Reagan at Normandy recognizing the sacrifices of
the "greatest generation" and the resulting balance of power in the post–World
War II era. Or even Barack Obama at Selma trying to bind up the wounds
of the past and focusing on the work yet to be done. In the end, Wallace and
later Trump simply "confuse and conflate policy with spectacle"—and it's an
empty pursuit.[228]

CHAPTER 5

Politics Mediated

The media was at the center of creating the necessary spectacle for George Wallace. While demagogic language and almost theatric staging of political events is important, scholar Heather E. Yates lists media coverage "that fixates on candidates who create spectacle" and media coverage that "handles political campaigns as adventure and entertainment" as essential. In fact, one of the most frequent complaints of political media coverage is its lack of focus on issues or policy discussions and instead focus on either "horse-race" coverage to determine who is ahead and who is behind or on the spectacle created by one or more candidates. The latter point was one Wallace (and later Trump) placed at the center of the process. As Yates explained, "The politics of political spectacle involves evaluating how politics-as-entertainment may influence voters' appraisals and, ultimately voter choice." But such campaigns run the danger of "increasing feelings of affinity or enthusiasm" but failing to truly engage "fringe or less-engaged voters."[1]

Author Jody Carlson suggested that "the press functioned as Wallace's own public relations mechanism" and that the media not only brought "George Wallace to the attention of the public, they also publicized his issues . . . into millions of living rooms."[2] It was a symbiotic relationship from the start:

> The press saw Wallace as good copy, and played right into his hands. They bought his role and pictured him as an underdog, a pitiful and powerless figure struggling against great odds and the opposition of the federal government, and people could see it on TV. Presented this way, Wallace also appeared, despite his ideological aberrations, as brave and undaunted, a hero.[3]

Carlson goes as far as to suggest, "If Wallace had been ignored by the press and the establishment, few would have paid him any attention" at the ballot box.[4] Wallace historian Dan T. Carter concluded that the former governor was "surprisingly successful at wooing reporters and journalists" when he wanted to. He based his interactions with journalists on "his instinctive grasp of how the system operated. The former Golden Gloves boxing champion understood that the media thrived on confrontation."[5]

Not surprisingly, though, in the aftermath of his losing campaign efforts, Wallace and his compatriots looked for some*one*, or some*thing* to blame. A nearly constant source of blame was the news media. Wallace had lived and died via his relationship with newspaper, radio, and television reporters. While crafting each time a campaign meant to draw the unflinching eye of the media—particularly television cameras in an era when television consumption by Americans was exploding—he nonetheless winced at the type of coverage he would receive. From the beginning, he openly accused reporters of purposefully distorting and misrepresenting his positions on issues or focusing on negative aspects of the campaign and ignoring what he had to say about issues. It was a familiar refrain—many politicians have engaged similar combat with the media. Famously, Richard Nixon had declared the media victors over his vanquished quest to be elected governor of California in 1962. His "concession remarks" that year—after a staggering loss by the nation's former vice president and 1960 Republican presidential nominee to incumbent Governor Pat Brown—Nixon was bitter and apoplectic with reporters. Declaring it his "last press conference" (it wasn't; he staged the ultimate political comeback six years later), Nixon darkly scolded the media:

> I leave you gentlemen now, and you will write it. You will interpret. That's your right. But as I leave you, I want you to know—just think how much you're going to be missing. You won't have Nixon to kick around anymore, because gentlemen, this is my last press conference. . . . I have always respected you. I have sometimes disagreed with you. . . . I hope that what I have said today will make television, radio, and the press, first recognize the great responsibility they have to report all the news, and second, recognize that they have a right and a responsibility, if they're against a candidate, give him the shaft, but also recognize if they give him the shaft, put one lonely reporter on the campaign who will report what the candidates says now and then.[6]

As he stomped off into the darkness beyond the television lights, Nixon personified much of what Wallace and others have often felt about the media. Men like Nixon, Wallace, and Trump wore their "suffering" from the media coverage they inspired on their sleeves and struggled to rise above the fray. Trump famously struggled in his relations with the media, beyond playing them for ready foils at his rallies (as Wallace did). The Committee to Project Journalists, an independent nonprofit organization designed to promote press freedom, offered a revealing study in 2019 by Stephanie Sugars that found since his entry into the 2016 presidential election cycle, Donald Trump had sent more than 5,400 tweets about the media "that were critical, insinuating, condemning, or threatening." Beyond promoting the term "fake news" (first tweeted by Trump in December 2016) to describe any unfavorable coverage of his campaign (or subsequent administration), the CPJ study found "several journalists who say they were harassed or threatened online after being singled out on Twitter by Trump." While Trump attacks on the media were somewhat more frequent during his campaign, after taking office as president, Trump added the phrase "enemy of the people" (first used by Trump in February 2017) to describe the news media, urging his supporters to "do your part to fight back against the media's attacks and deceptions."[7] The hatred Trump feels for the media appears to be felt equally by reporters who cover Trump and find themselves frequently referred to as "losers" and "awful people" who ask "nasty questions." Jack Shafer, a writer for Politico, attributes the mutual antipathy to a vast misunderstanding of demagogic candidates by the media. He posits,

> Demagogues like Donald Trump exhaust the patience of the political press corps because reporters fundamentally misunderstand the candidates' appeal. Report- ers like to think that logic and reason hold sway, so they believe a demagogue can be easily disarmed by exposing his crimes against logic, his pandering to the uninformed, and his manipulative emotionalism.[8]

Scholar Paul J. Achter expands upon that point, declaring that "not since Rea- gan has a president been so associated with television and so understood in terms of television." He argues that Trump perfected the "dramatic potential" of a television character—moving between beloved and respected and hated and reviled—but ever in motion—and ever causing the camera to be pointed in his direction. Adding to the television dominance—and resulting appeal for many—of Trump has been the removal of the Fairness Doctrine that once required broadcasters to offer "equal time" and meet other community service obligations.[9] Irony then resides for Trump—as it did for Wallace—in that he attacks the very news media he must engage as part of his political pursuits. Achter notes the media both "vilifies" Trump all the while "enthralling audiences endlessly"—even those who are not his supporters. "Trump's fascination with television is only surpassed by the industry's fascination with him," Achter said.[10]

The battles George Wallace engaged with the media could be fierce, but there are no known instances where Wallace encouraged violence or action by his supporters against the media. In fact, reporters indicated that they were unsure Wallace actually believed all of his own rhetoric about the media, finding him engaging later in friendly and personal interactions with reporters behind the scenes. Several reporters came to believe that Wallace's verbal assaults upon them—especially in political rally settings—were just "part of the show" and represented no deep personal animus. One reporter even recalled an instance where after Wallace ridiculed media coverage he had received, he encouraged his followers to "leave those fellows" alone—gesturing to the press corps that followed him—and blamed their "pointy-headed, liberal" editors "back East" for the real problems. While Wallace's "attacks on the media" were likely viewed as convenient sources for rhetoric to advance anti-establishment and in-group/out-group ideas, there is scant evidence Wallace understood the media as Trump does. Wallace's era—where newspapers and radio and television stations were all powerful—contrasts dramatically with the more contemporary era in which Trump operated. Social media empowered Trump beyond his own platform to that of the cascading social media platforms of his supporters and surrogates who often command as much attention and "space" in the marketplace of ideas and information as does the "traditional media" that was dominant in the Wallace years. Minus such technology in his time, Wallace became a master of mediated politics as it existed at the time, but fell short, as Yates suggested, by successfully increasing "feelings of affinity or enthusiasm" for his campaign and his long list of wrongs. Absent a cogent, comprehensive policy platform about how to address such concerns, Wallace ultimately failed to engage "fringe or less-engaged voters" and thus lost all four attempts he made for the presidency.

From the beginning, George Wallace was a good story. Starting on his first day in office as governor of Alabama, extending into his first year in office, Wallace unleashed an amazing display of media competence from a determined heretofore small-time politician. Both in his speaking style and in the content of what he said Wallace understood the dramatics of television media and seemed far ahead of others in his era. While governors and mayors in larger states and cities were used to commanding media attention, few other southern figures could eclipse Wallace's consistent ability to be the center of the story. Without much delay, Wallace successfully cast himself as the opposite pole to the Rev. Dr. Martin Luther King Jr. in this era and commanded as much attention and scorn or support as King did. This appeared to be at least a portion of the goal in the weeks following his symbolic "stand in the schoolhouse door" as less than a month later he accepted an out-of-state invitation to address a large meeting of southern television and radio broadcasters meeting at Myrtle Beach, South Carolina, in July 1963. It was likely a friendly audience as Southern journalists had generally been favorable to not only the content of Wallace's message but also the drama it delivered. Privately and sometimes not so privately, many journalists were pleased with the idea that a Southerner might finally break through and be returned to the presidency in the modern era. Cognizant of his friendly reception in Myrtle Beach, Wallace shed his normal disdain for the media, stating instead, "Radio and television are important communications media. Your contributions to civil, political, social and economic life of our nation are many and substantial."[11] Lest he choke on such words of praise for journalists, Wallace quickly moved to co-opting the audience by reminding them of the many shared values and experiences between fellow southerners—what he called "interwoven histories" of all southern states—"not just a geographical designation" but "a philosophy, a way of life that has won friends in every part of this great nation. Southerners, in this definition, are going to save this nation." Wallace described the nation's political landscape as captives in "a sickening spectacle" filled with too many politicians and too few statesmen (the governor no doubt counting himself among the former group). He suggested, "We have had enough of [John F.] Kennedy in Alabama [and] we see no relief in the candidates proposed by the Republican Party."[12] Wallace also took time to attack civil rights demonstrators—challenging the media representatives present to stop referring to them as "demonstrators" while calling those arguing for southern positions as "rioters" or "Southern mobs." He chastised reporters for their coverage of

> these so-called "demonstrators" [who] break laws, destroy property, injure inno-
> cent people and create civil strife and disorder of major proportions. . . . I per-
> sonally resent the actions of the federal government which have created these
> conditions. As a loyal American and as a loyal Southern Governor, who has never
> belonged to or associated with any subversive element, I resent the fawning and
> pawing over such people as Martin Luther King and his pro-Communist friends
> and associates.[13]

Turning on the media outside of the South was becoming a regular feature of Wallace's rhetoric and was clearly in place less than six months later as the governor spoke at Brown University in Providence, Rhode Island. While there, Wallace concluded his remarks by attacking the media—the very media poised to cover his every utterance. He said as a southern governor he could not count on the media to give him a fair reporting. "Every news media of national importance, every powerful national politician, and particularly the political elements of the courts, have fought to avoid having the truth explained. This is a mighty combination," Wallace said. "None of the national news media have found it proper to explain to you that the cause we represent [segregation] is not one of hatred or malice, but one of principle under the Constitution of the United States."[14] His open suspicion that the media sought to misrepresent his position on segregation reflected the uphill fight he was facing in his early years on the national stage. It also reflected the reality that back home in Alabama, racial strife continued to tear at the seams of society all while the governor went far and wide preaching a gospel of "leave us alone" and recommitting himself to a segregated South.

1964: A Double-Edged Sword

By the time he reached Cincinnati, Ohio, in early February 1964—just as he prepared to jump into three Democratic presidential primaries to continue to make his point—Wallace seemed to understand the double-edged sword of the media was helping him in some respect. In Cincinnati, Wallace conducted a news conference and gave two speeches, and Cincinnati Police Department officials confirmed they were braced for possible problems. "Tear gas guns and riot helmets were stacked Monday . . . and other plain clothes officers will be assigned to seven districts to handle any possible school problems," the *Cincinnati Enquirer* reported. The police preparations were prompted as Wallace's Cincinnati visit coincided with a just-launched boycott of the city's public schools by Black citizens. None of that slowed Wallace down as he told reporters that "the racial problem is infinitely greater in Cincinnati and Cleveland than it is in Alabama." It was no accident that he jumped into the powder keg in the city. He had no other reason to be in Ohio except to exploit the troubles simmering under the surface there. Even in his interactions with reporters, Wallace could create a form of spectacle in how he responded to the media. While refraining from calling reporters names (as Trump has sunk to), he would often challenge reporters and question the motives for their queries. In an exchange at Cincinnati that many reporters noticed, Wallace seemed interested in baiting a Black reporter by declaring that the racial problems in Ohio and other northern states were caused by northern hypocrites and were not a response to historic inequities victimizing Black citizens. "Negroes from southern states looking for the land of milk and honey find they've been misled by northern politicians," he said.[15] His rhetoric had worked; angry pickets *and* overflow crowds greeted Wallace's speeches at both the University of Cincinnati and a downtown auditorium.[16]

Upon Wallace's entry into the Wisconsin Democratic presidential primary, the state's media and civil rights advocates "fell" swiftly into Wallace's show as the primary campaign wore on. Protests were staged most everywhere he went, action that generated more media attention than Wallace could ever afford to buy, and exposure to thousands of more voters than he might otherwise expect to reach. Whether they knew it or not, Wisconsin media were "played" in the process, right down to a united front of newspaper editors across the state who offered a last-minute series of editorials all appearing in the week of March 10 urging Wisconsin Democrats to stand up to the Wallace challenge. Editorial writers at the *Stevens Point Daily Journal* seemed to reflect the sense of disbelief that continued to swirl around Wallace's coming presence in the state. Noting that Wallace had "made a spectacle of himself" in the fight to oppose integration of the University of Alabama, the editorial moaned, "To suggest at that time that this demagogue should be a candidate for president of the United States would have been the ultimate in sick humor. But that's a fact today, thanks to the political manipulators who have fouled up the Wisconsin presidential preference primary."[17] Editors at the *Appleton Post-Crescent* cautioned a real risk remained that a strong vote for Wallace in the primary might embarrass President Johnson. "Wallace's sudden candidacy [in Wisconsin] is bound to draw some conservative votes which might have gone to the Republicans," the *Post-Crescent* surmised. "And there is no way to know how much antagonism has grown, even in Wisconsin, to some recent Negro demands. It is not popular to be against civil rights in Wisconsin, but some secret attitudes may show up in the ballot box."[18] The *Sheboygan Press* called Wallace's presence "an opportunity" and predicted failure for the Alabama interloper noting that a repudiation of his candidacy "could mean a resounding victory for the orderly process of government by law in this nation. A stinging Wallace repudiation could and would mean a clear victory for civil rights."[19] Meanwhile, on the Sunday before the primary, the *Racine Journal-Times* took up the issue of Wallace's campaign and urged its readers to vote against him. "This is no longer a regular political campaign," the Racine editorial said. "It is a moral issue" and that "repudiation of Wallace is necessary for Wisconsin and for America."[20] It was an amazing amount of column inches to give to a candidate all of the editors—and many reporters—said they loathed so much.

In Indiana, the second 1964 primary Wallace entered, the media seemed a little more circumspect and less direct in their assault on Wallace. Whether it was the state's sad history of racism or just a more thoughtful approach being employed, Indiana reporters took a fuller look at Wallace and seemed less aghast or impressed by the "show." An *Indianapolis Star* reporter covering Wallace's remarks focused in more on *how* Wallace answered questions, rather than *what* he said: "He handily answered questions on the civil rights issue, he appeared nervous and vague on other issues such as foreign affairs. He frequently rubbed his eyes and mopped his brow with a handkerchief."[21] Across town, the state's largest African American newspaper, the *Indianapolis Recorder*, followed the advent of the Wallace campaign closely but made no attempts to appear to be objective, referring to Wallace as a racist. It did, however, avoid lengthy reporting on the theatrics the Wallace campaign inspired (including NAACP pickets at his campaign headquarters), and instead analyzed that "Negroes are seeking a stronger voice in the Indiana primary [than they could in Wisconsin] since they compose approximately six percent of the state's population. In comparison, Negroes make up only two percent of Wisconsin's citizenry."[22] Further, statements from Wallace's stand-in opponent, Governor Matthew Welsh, printed by the *Recorder* seemed more serious: "We do not underestimate the challenge [of Wallace] and we intend to conduct a vigorous campaign in Indiana."[23]

If anyone doubted that the 1964 Democratic presidential primary in Indiana was a national story, they needn't look any further than the presence of CBS News patriarch Walter Cronkite anchoring his national program, *The CBS Evening News*, from an Indianapolis storefront in the days before the vote. Not to be outdone, NBC News dispatched analyst Frank McGhee to file reports for *The Huntley/Brinkley Report*, while ABC sent newsman Bill Lawrence to file live reports from Indiana. Lawrence told the *Indianapolis Star* that the Indiana primary was "the top political story of the week."[24] As Cronkite put it, the "human element" of the campaign was needed and, "You can't cover a primary from a wire machine in New York anymore." The CBS effort had included recruiting 3,500 volunteers statewide to collect vote totals on primary day from key precincts to allow the network to make early projections as the votes were still being counted.

While the national media came to town expecting a good fight, during some early appearances in Indiana the expected fireworks did not materialize. It appeared only the Pulitzer Prize-winning *Indianapolis Times* planned to take on Wallace directly, warning Hoosiers that "every vote for Wallace will be accepted throughout the world as a ringing endorsement of the ugliest race relations in America. It will be interpreted everywhere as the approval of the hate-filled violence with which a few Wallace goaded Alabamans shocked the world."[25]

Interestingly, Wallace seemed to be spoiling for a fight during a news conference in Indianapolis, perhaps hoping to create some of the sparks that had so far been missing. Wallace openly ignored questions posed to him by Black reporters from both the *Indianapolis Recorder* and the *Indiana Herald*.[26] Aides later tried to explain Wallace was offended by the "pointed" nature of the questions posed, particularly from Opal L. Tandy, publisher of the *Herald*. An

Associated Press photo showed Wallace raising his fists in the direction of Tandy as the Black journalist attempted to ask the governor a question as he exited the room. Wallace campaign aides said the governor "did not threaten Tandy" and that he was simply trying to emphasize a point.[27] Wallace's campaign was taking Indiana seriously, spending more than $100,000 for the effort, engaging the Indianapolis advertising agency of Paul Lennon to place display advertising in dozens of newspapers. In addition, Wallace planned daily five-minute radio "programs" on 41 radio stations in the state, expanding those to 15-minute "programs" in the final days before the primary. Further, although television campaigning was in its infancy in 1964, Wallace's team had enough money to purchase 30-minute slots on fourteen Indiana television stations.[28] The paid advertising would be needed as invitations to speak before civic organizations in the state were becoming difficult to obtain, many of the groups reluctant to insult the state's sitting governor. For example, an invitation for Wallace to speak before the Valparaiso chapter of the Jaycees was later withdrawn when an internal battle erupted between club members on the appropriateness of having Wallace as a speaker.[29]

If Wisconsin media had been aghast and appalled by Wallace, and Indiana media had been cautious or dismissive of him, reporters and editors in Maryland staged all-out war on Wallace with the gloves fully off. Just as he arrived in the state to start his third primary campaign, a *Baltimore Sun* editorial took exception to Wallace, calling him "ignorant," and asked, "Does Governor Wallace think Marylanders are dim-witted enough to believe that he scheduled a speech . . . in Cambridge for any other reason" than to stir racial strife?[30] Reflecting the worry and discord the Wallace campaign was inspiring in the state, the editorial writer noted,

> So it goes, drearily, dismally, dishonestly, on all subjects, an effort to play on every fear, every apprehension, every nameless worry, in the interests of a false and raggedy cause. It is candid only in its insolence; only in its profound contempt for the intelligence of Marylanders and its reckless disregard for the domestic peace of this state. A man with a more sensitive conscience than Governor Wallace's would have slept ill last night.[31]

The *Sun*'s caustic editorials were either written directly by the newspaper editorial page editor, Bradford McElderry Jacobs, or assigned by him. Jacobs was in similar form in reviewing Wallace's insistence on appearing at Cambridge, writing after the fact, "It was a splendid night for a riot. A warm spring sky, but not hot, sap rising in the poplars and in the populace."[32] The vitriolic response Wallace was receiving on the editorial pages of the state's largest newspaper did not go unnoticed. Wallace decided, as he had done before, to use the editorials as evidence of a liberal bias against him by members of the media. "Certain portions of the press are trying to obscure what the real issues are," he said, referring specifically to the *Baltimore Sun*.[33]

Editorials in the *Baltimore Afro-American*, the state's largest Black newspaper, were as expected, not supportive of Wallace's effort. Calling Wallace a man "whose mind is crooked," the paper's editors cautioned that Wallace engaged in "double talk" and claims victory even when he loses—as he did in both Wisconsin and Indiana.[34] Another editorial referred to him as "Alabama's half-pint chief executive" and said Wallace possessed "unmitigated gall to contend he had scored a 'major victory' while losing" the Wisconsin primary. Wallace's assessment of his political chances is "built on the same shaky foundation of gross falsehoods and distortions that marked his mendacious campaign interpretations of the civil rights bill."[35] The *Baltimore Afro-American* made no attempt at objectivity with the banner headline three days before the primary, noting simply in large block letters: "HELP BEAT WALLACE."[36] The day of the primary, the newspaper ran another massive headline that read: "WALLACE INSULTS US ALL."[37]

His "primary folly" completed—and apparently his point made that at least some Democrats and Americans were not fully on board with the push for civil rights, Wallace tried to stay in the conversation. For weeks, he milked the idea of whether he would continue his challenge to President Johnson all the way to the Democratic convention. Doing so ensured that he continued to get booked on national television news shows, including CBS's *Face the Nation*. Once there, Wallace brought his well-rehearsed indictment of the media and how they had covered his campaign. He noted,

> You know the press in this country draws conclusions that have no foundation
> at all. And I think the American people are sick and tired of columnists and TV
> dudes who get on the national networks, and instead of reporting the news as it
> is, and shame the devil, which is what they are supposed to do, they try to slant
> and distort and malign and brainwash this country. . . . I think the press and the
> national news media are going to get some of these liberal smiles wiped off their
> faces because we in Alabama are tired of being maligned by distorted views of
> what happens in our state, the distorted versions of what the governor of that
> state stands for, and the good people of our region stand for.[38]

Wallace offered up one of his favorite examples, noting, "There has been more violence in one subway in New York City in one night than there has been in the entire state of Mississippi in a year. But they don't talk about sending troops to the subways. They talk about sending them to Mississippi. It's a purely political gimmick." He made a distinction, he said, between how the press handled the views of southerners versus other Americans:

> You see, the press and news media has tranquilized people into not speaking out against [matters of concern] because if you do, that makes you a racist or a bigot or you are prejudiced, you are biased, or you are immoral. But it is not immoral, and you are not a bigot or a racist or biased or prejudiced just because you want to solve problems within the context of the American system.[39]

Apparently still smarting from a slight from the National Press Club (whose president had declined to give Wallace its traditional "certificate of appreciation" after speaking before the group), he blurted out, "Well, I will say here again that they can take their traditional certificate and they know what they can do with it."[40]

Without a doubt, TV journalists were beginning to understand that Wallace made for "good TV." He brought all of the elements TV news relied upon—color, controversy, and conflict. The producers of NBC's *Meet the Press* wanted their shot at giving Wallace a platform, booking him on their program on October 25, 1964, just before the national election. *Meet the Press*, a venerable NBC News institution that proclaimed itself as "America's Press Conference of the Air," was produced and moderated at the time by respected journalist Lawrence E. Spivak. Spivak took a different tact than his CBS colleagues and invited Wallace to appear along with Vermont Governor Philip H. Hoff, a Democrat who had appeared on TV with Wallace earlier in the year in Massachusetts. As was the case in their previous joint appearance, Wallace stole the show with the middle-of-the-road approach of Hoff, not prone to making inflammatory remarks, having far less impact than Wallace. Panelists on the show were a distinguished group of Washington journalists: Herbert Kaplow of NBC News, Rowland Evans of the *New York Herald Tribune*, May Craig of the Portland (Maine) *Press Herald*, and James Kilpatrick of the *Richmond* (Virginia) *News Leader*. Kaplow opened the questioning by asking if Wallace was prepared to endorse a candidate for president, and Wallace once again declined but offered an interesting reason that allowed him to take another swing at the media: "I realize that the national media has, in many instances, distorted the attitude of the people of my state and as the Governor of Alabama, I am sure that if I endorsed someone here today, whoever it was, that would be used in the next few days literally to smear that candidate to death."[41] Wallace said he did not want to "allow my liabilities to be saddled upon any candidate"—whether it was President Johnson or Senator Goldwater.

Craig asked Wallace if he truly believed he had never referred to any person as being inferior because of their race, "Then why do you want to segregate Negroes?" He replied that his position on integration of schools in Alabama reflected the views of the citizens of his state to determine their own policies on school integration. "I care nothing about what kind of school system you have in Oregon, Virginia or California, I only say that the people of my state should determine that policy," he said. "If they desire to have an integrated school system, that is their right. If they desire to have a segregated school system, I think that is their right."[42] He told Craig he had no intention of discussing her follow-up question about what percentage of "Negro blood" was required to determine a person was Black, and therefore, needed to attend a different school.

As the 1964 campaign between Johnson and Goldwater heated up, media attention quickly turned away from Wallace, his impact and influence checked for now. His sometimes-open disputes with the media would continue, especially following the violent police put-down of the 1965 marchers at Selma. At that time, Wallace took issue with how reporters were characterizing the situation and singled out Al Kuettner, a United Press International reporter assigned to cover southern states. When Kuettner asked Wallace what he thought was the cause of the violence at Selma, Wallace replied, "You represent UPI. UPI's misleading reporting is one reason for the trouble. People all over the country read the UPI stories [and that] inflames the people of the state."[43] Wallace also chastised a Kuettner story that alleged some Alabama hospitals refused to provide care to Black patients. The governor claimed, "No Negro has ever been turned away from a hospital in Alabama because he was a Negro. If I ever found out that this has happened, I would do something about it."[44]

1968: A Quixotic Effort Draws the Spotlight

The tension growing out of the push and pull of the civil rights battles playing out in Wallace's Alabama and across the South made for engaging and important reporting in its era. The coverage of those issues most always put Wallace front and center. But beyond civil rights discourse, just the quixotic effort required to get Wallace on the ballot in all fifty states for the 1968 General Election created a good story unto itself. Reporters filed dozens of stories in the last half of 1967 about Wallace's full-court press in California to get enough signatures to qualify for the ballot. In the weeks and months before, many other reporters took up the analysis of third-party candidacies in American politics and the "horse race" coverage of how effective the Wallace drive was. The *Los Angeles Times* dispatched Howard Seelye to cover one of Wallace's ballot signature events at the Garden Grove in northern Orange County. Even the setting provided Seelye good content to include (especially in an era when descriptive, even "literary" journalism was popular): "Waiting for George Wallace, the people stood on sidewalks and in the parking lot of a shopping center . . . A loudspeaker filled the air with the voice of gospel singer Wally Fowler. Card tables in front of the Wallace Campaign Headquarters were manned by deputy registrars of voters."[45]

Even journalists-in-training got in on the act, as Pat DeGraw, a journalism student at the University of Southern California, set out to follow Wallace as he traveled the state looking for signatures on American Independent Party petitions. DeGraw attended a Wallace meeting at the Jubilee Motel in Lynwood (in south central Los Angeles) and took note of the somewhat "down-home assembly, part camp meeting, part family gathering, part Grand Ole Opry, and part pure politics." No doubt a student of the emerging literary journalism style emerging in the field in the late 1960s, DeGraw's observation included

> a good hour and a half before George Corley Wallace entered the narrow meeting room of the Jubilee Motel, his followers [transported by an Alabama van] were warming up a soggy and rather sad little group of people who had come out of the rain. And when Wallace finally did come, he continued the process, bringing his elderly listeners out of another rain, supposedly more dangerous and more devastating than any Southern California flood.[46]

Presidential historian Theodore White was among those who analyzed the Wallace interactions with the media, who he said were "trying to document the Wallace campaign in words and pictures, and began to spread the image of a man not mastering disorder in the nation, but provoking it nearly everywhere he went." Indeed, media coverage continually focused on the protests and outbursts at Wallace rallies—which were once a common occurrence at Hubert Humphrey rallies as well. Protestors, however, seemed to give Humphrey some pause as the campaign wore on and turned their attention mostly to Wallace. Dissecting the Wallace rallies was a particular favorite of reporters throughout the country, some of them unaccustomed to the church "tent revival" nature of the events. Some journalists seemed to generate almost granular attention to the procedural nature of Wallace rallies meant to collect ballot signatures, voters, and cash for the campaign ahead. The *Boston Globe*'s James Stack reported, "The Wallace 'rally' was only minutes old when it became clear the former Alabama governor was here to canvas for funds and volunteer workers to unify the ultra-conservative element in the state." Stack shared with his readers the sometimes awkward and bold money grab that would punctuate the rallies.

Stack noted that at first, Wallace's promoters asked for donors willing to give $1,000 to stand and be recognized. None did. The request was lowered to $500, and again, no one stood. "There was, however, more response when 'The Wallace Girls' wrapped in campaign banners and wearing sailor straw hats, circulated pails for more modest contributions," Stack wrote. "Those were poured into a huge cardboard box, together with signed cards bearing personal information about contributors who will be contacted during the campaign."[47]

This type of coverage—long on details of what rallies looked and sounded like—and short on anything Wallace actually talked about—could irritate many of his handlers, who sometimes struggled in their interactions with journalists. Some of Wallace's Alabama advisers approached more urbane reporters from the North and East with a great deal of suspicion. Writer Pete Hamill noted that Wallace rarely fraternized with reporters, kept away from them by his handlers. Hamill surmised that Wallace was sometimes personally embarrassed that he had lambasted reporters with ugly words at his rallies and then later being asked to find the spirit to engage in cordial, respectful personal interactions with those same reporters. Hamill believed the one-on-one interactions with reporters were just too difficult for Wallace to navigate. "Y'all keep hittin it, just get my name right," was about all Wallace would share between puffs of his cigar aboard his campaign plane.[48]

Garry Wills, in his thought-provoking tome *Nixon Antagonists: The Crisis of the Self-Made Man* noted, "The newsmen who followed Wallace said they felt like patsies, straight men for the candidate's act, so much did he use them to elicit boos and jeers from the crowd."[49] A similar pathos would emerge in the 2016 Trump campaign, equally problematic and boorish. In the closing days of the 2016 campaign, *New York Times* correspondent Nick Corasaniti reported on a renewed focus on the media by Trump and his supporters. Corasaniti wrote,

> Even reporters long accustomed to the toxic fervor of Trump rallies were star-tled—and even frightened—at the vitriol of a Cincinnati crowd . . . as more than 15,000 [Trump] supporters flashed homemade signs, flipped middle fingers and lashed out in tirades often laced with profanity as journalists made their way to a crammed, fenced-in island in the center of the [rally] floor. The Trump support-ers crowded by the metal barriers protecting the area, leaned over to get in one last insult before returning their attention to the stage.[50]

Corasaniti added that Trump's attacks on the media "reached an intensity never before seen from a presidential candidate." He noted, "By attacking the news media, Mr. Trump appears to be seeking to delegitimize an industry he views as an impediment to his presidential ambitions, while riling up his base of supporters."[51] In words that could have been uttered by George Wallace four or five decades earlier, Trump told a Florida audience:

> The establishment and their media neighbors wield control over this nation through means that are very well known. Anyone who challenges their control is deemed a sexist, a racist, a xenophobe, and morally deformed. They will attack you. They will slander you. They will seek to destroy your career and your family. They will seek to destroy everything about you including your reputation. They will lie, lie, lie, and then again, they will do worse than that. They will do whatever's necessary.[52]

Despite the tension created by Wallace (and Trump) between his supporters and the media, the media was along for the ride, whether they wanted to be or not. As *Los Angeles Times* reporter (and Alabama native) Jack Nelson admitted, Wallace "was good copy on the stump; he was good copy when you interviewed him."[53]

It wasn't, however, that reporters couldn't become bored with covering another Wallace speech that sounded a lot like the ten he had given before. In one instance, a reporter seemed to cover Wallace only as an afterthought, focusing instead on the media covering Wallace. That was the case in Moline, Illinois, as *Moline Dispatch* reporter Dot Buresh grew tired of waiting for a chance to speak to Wallace and instead interviewed correspondent Douglas Kiker, his soundman Jerry Ongaro, and filmographer Gary Hallberg of NBC News. Kiker, who regularly appeared on NBC's *Huntley-Brinkley Report*, was tight-lipped but Ongaro seemed eager to provide some insights. Ongaro spoke "kindly" of Wallace and said he "believes that Wallace's jibing at the press is just part of his routine and not meant too seriously." He did express concern about repeated reports that Wallace's life was threatened on the trail.[54] "The role of the traveling press is far less than glamourous," Buresh offered. "First there are the long hours, little sleep, meals which may be a finger sandwich or a greasy sandwich in an all-night beanery."[55] Ongaro confirmed the "press pays its own way" on the Wallace campaign and estimated NBC was spending upwards of $5,000 a week in salaries, plane fares, meals, buses, and other incidentals in order to cover Wallace and his campaign. Kiker called the interview to an end, Buresh noted, as Wallace approached the lobby of the LeClaire Hotel in downtown Moline. Kiker asked Wallace if he was still tired from his rigorous campaign schedule, to which Wallace replied: "I'm not all that tired. You in the press sometimes exaggerate." Buresh was not convinced. She shared with her readers, "There is no denying the lines in the third-party candidate's face and the hollows under the eyes that were evidence of the strain of his campaign."[56]

Wallace's presence in Moline, Illinois, in late October 1968 didn't fail, however, to produce more news for reporters to chew on following a violent near-riot at a Wallace rally. One reporter, ABC News correspondent Sam Jaffee, believed he had fallen victim to Wallace's regular rants against the media as he reported the theft of a small Olivetti portable typewriter he had lugged all around the world, only to have it stolen by a protestor in an Illinois town. "It has a good deal of sentimental value to me, and I had to come to Moline to have it taken from me," Jaffee lamented. Jaffee (who eventually got his typewriter back), was among those who talked openly about the "complications" of covering the Wallace campaign described as "chaotic" and "disorganized." Reporters lamented they were "often not told when or where the former governor of Alabama will go next in his campaign swing until either the night before, or shortly before take-off."[57] Reporters in Buffalo, New York even raised a complaint about the "press credential" badges they were required to wear to board the Wallace campaign plane and to approach the candidate at campaign events. As Gannett News reported, "Newsmen covering the George Wallace presidential campaign are finding the accreditation given them by the third-party candidate is causing trouble. Each member of the entourage following Wallace must wear a small white tag with a heading in capital letters that reads, 'Wallace for President.'"[58] Reporters complained that the badge was a problem because Wallace protestors "heckle" news reporters, assuming their badge means they are part of the campaign.[59]

A *New York Times* writer surmised that "Wallace has learned to expect little sympathy from the television networks and the big-city papers and habitually pronounces the phrase 'news media' with exquisite distaste."[60] In Hammond, Indiana, Wallace got one of his loudest responses from more than 4,500 supporters when he said,

> Some of these liberal newspaper editors are saying one reason the Wallace phi-losophy is so popular is he says what the people want to hear. And they're saying it in such a manner that it sounds like what the people want is bad. Their trouble is these liberals created a Frankenstein in our country and now their chickens are coming home to roost and they don't like it.[61]

Although most of the altercations between Wallace and the media were academic, and not personal, one angry dust-up with ABC News reporter Sam Donaldson surfaced early on. In June 1968, ABC officials alleged Wallace's security guards illegally seized film they had shot of the former governor shaking hands with Robert Shelton, an imperial wizard of the Ku Klux Klan, during a campaign appearance at Eutaw, Alabama. The network claimed an unnamed Wallace aide "forcibly removed the film" from one of its cameras at the event after they refused his repeated requests to turn it over. ABC said Wallace himself ordered the security man to "take it" when the film was refused. The Associated Press reported, "The bodyguard pulled the camera from the shoulder of cameraman Charlie Jones and removed the exposed film."[62] Shelton confirmed he paid to attend the Wallace event and said, "I don't see what difference it would make if they had a picture of me shaking his hand." The Wallace people apparently thought so, however, fearing Shelton's Klan connections were not helpful to their fifty-state campaign. In his on-air report, Donaldson said,

> Wallace did this because he didn't like the fact that we had filmed him shaking hands with Robert Shelton. . . . Shelton had joined a receiving line apparently without Wallace's knowledge, walked up to the candidate while our TV light was on. Shelton was wearing a Wallace for President button, but it should be noted that George Wallace has declared he does not welcome the endorsement of the KKK.[63]

Donaldson confirmed on air that it was Wallace himself who "huddled with his closest advisers" and that the security guard threatened the cameraman saying, "You can make it easy on yourself and give it to us, or we'll take it."[64] Donaldson added, "When I protested that the film was the property of ABC and we would not give it up, Wallace said 'Take it,' and the bodyguard acted."[65] The bosses back at ABC News in New York City were not pleased and made their feelings known directly to Wallace in a telegram. In it, Elmer W. Lower, the president of ABC News said: "ABC News must protest most vigorously the action of members of your staff in confiscating and destroying news film last night in Eutaw, Alabama. This violates the basic rights of the news media to report your presidential campaign. May I have your personal assurance that there will be no repetition and that ABC News personnel will be free to cover your campaign unhindered by members of your entourage staff?"[66] Wallace offered a succinct, poorly written, nonreply via telegram, "I regret the incidence [sic] and the events surrounding the accurance [sic] of the incidence [sic] referred to in your telegram. We are happy to have ABC with us."[67]

If the dust-ups between Wallace and reporters were having a lasting effect, Wallace seemed to avoid acting punitively about it. In fact, as the 1968 campaign drew to a close, Wallace was a combination of thankful and critical of the coverage he had received. He told one group of reporters, "You folks helped make me and my movement," but then he added, "The press has indicted a whole region of people as being racists. You've looked down your nose and called southerners rednecks and peckerwoods and wool-hats and crackers and Okies."[68]

Pulitzer Prize-winner Haynes Johnson took note of Wallace's interactions with reporters, seeming self-conscious about the style of his campaign. "Wallace is aware of the contrasts between his operation and those of the other candidates and sometimes is a bit defensive about it," Johnson wrote. "He can't supply champagne, he says, to the newsmen 'the way the others do for you all.'" At other moments, Johnson found Wallace attempting to make amends, making a general promise to reporters, "I'm going to take care of 'my boys,'" he said in a tired voice after a long day of campaigning.[69]

Jack Nelson of the *Los Angeles Times* wrote that Wallace "harangued a lot of reporters over his long political career," but despite knowing Nelson was from Alabama, he said, "I didn't mind pressing him with thorny questions at press conferences," and "he relished singling me out at his political rallies for his own special brand of ridicule." Nelson said he knew Wallace's wrath for him was personal and fierce. *Alabama Journal* editor Ray Jenkins told Nelson, "A few newsmen have so incurred the Governor's wrath that he holds a permanent grudge. Nelson has written so sharply about Wallace and has pressed uncomfortable questions so relentlessly at press conferences that Wallace is given to making savage jabs at him in public as well as in private."[70]

Describing their relationship as "complicated," Nelson said Wallace

angrily resented what I wrote, but I think somewhere deep down he had a sneaking fondness for his fellow Alabamian. And he was accessible to me. . . . Still, he didn't hesitate to use me as a foil. At political rallies he would draw raucous laughter and sometimes muttered threats by pointing me out and shouting in his thick drawl, "Thay he is, out there from *The Los A-n-g-e-l-e-e-s Times*. Out there where they give blood to the Veet Cong, fly the Veet Cong flag! Look at him, ah made 'em get his hair cut!"[71]

Nelson admitted that he wrote about Wallace "in the vernacular," using apostrophes when he would drop the "g" from words ending in "ing"—which he did often. Nelson admitted he knew the vernacular he used in describing Wallace's speeches was irritating to the governor, but he did it anyway.[72] Wallace supporters would sometimes shout threats at Nelson—and other reporters—and Nelson said he felt no reassurance despite claims by bodyguards to the governor saying he had asked them to keep reporters safe.

Dan King Thomasson, a Scripps-Howard News Service reporter and editor, recalled a long ride on the Wallace campaign plane in the 1968 campaign in which he and another journalist decided to spend the time trying to "pin" Wallace down on a key issue or two:

We went up to the front of the plane and we asked Wallace, "What are you going to do if you are really elected President of the United States?" What would he do if he woke up one morning and he was President of the United States? Wallace knew he wasn't going to win . . . so we spent like five minutes trying to get him to answer directly what he planned to do if he was elected. He wouldn't answer that question directly. He became morose, and never answered it. He was angry [with us] and I am sure he bit his cigar in half. It was clear he had never thought about it. I never fully understood him from that standpoint.[73]

Thomasson said he was not convinced that Wallace believed "half of what he said." He added, though, that Wallace "would single out reporters, especially Jack Nelson, but sometimes it was me. You just got used to it." Reporters would get their moments of revenge. On long bus or plane rides with Wallace out of earshot, members of the press corps would take turns mimicking Wallace's standard stump speech in their best faked Alabama accents. "We especially liked the one about 'pseudo-intellectuals' in Washington, D.C. and 'throwing their briefcases into the Potomac River.'"[74] Thomasson was among those who found great contrast between how the press corps was treated in the Wallace campaign versus how they fared tagging along with Nixon or Humphrey. The Nixon campaign spent considerable time and money wooing reporters: "The Nixon campaign just covered you with creature comforts. With Wallace, we were lucky to get an RC cola and a moon pie. It was a great contrast." The Wallace plane, for the record, was supposed to be a no-booze-allowed zone. Further, Wallace and Humphrey shared a similar problem—perpetually running behind schedule—while the Nixon campaign ran like clockwork.[75]

Wallace's relationship with opinion columnists and editorial writers seemed to offer more hostility than his regular interactions with beat reporters. One ugly example arose just as Wallace received the good news that with a Supreme Court ruling, he had gained ballot access in Ohio (thus in all fifty states). On that same day, nationwide columnists Drew Pearson and Jack Anderson fired a damaging salvo in their column "Washington Merry-Go-Round," sharing that "For the first time in 192 years of American history, a man with an established mental disability is running for president of the United States." Pearson and Anderson wrote, "George C. Wallace, upon retiring from the Army Air Force, applied for mental disability payments and convinced the doctors that he deserved at least partial compensation."[76] Senator Wayne Morse, an Oregon Democrat, had released Wallace's confidential military medical record that showed he was determined by military doctors in 1946 to have at least a 10 percent disability. Pearson and Anderson got nasty: "Some observers who have watched the mental gymnastics of his current campaign say doctors were conservative."[77] Senator Morse said the records showed Wallace entered the military on October 20, 1942, and was honorably discharged on Dec. 8, 1945, with the grade of sergeant in the Army Air Corps. During his service, he participated in offensive air strikes against Japan and won an Air Medal and good conduct medals. The record Morse made available included a September 1945 hospitalization of Wallace for "a severe anxiety state, chronic, manifested by tension states, anxiety attacks, anorexia, and weight loss."[78] Pearson and Anderson opined that Wallace "owes it to the American people to let them know about his mental state" and that he perhaps should return to "see the Army doctors again.[79]

The press coverage of Wallace's 1968 campaign reflected the bumpy nature of how it proceeded, taking place in a year of almost unmatched tumult in the modern era. The political assassinations of Dr. King and Senator Kennedy, a Democratic National Convention marred by bloody and violent protests in Chicago, and a politically wounded incumbent President Johnson walking to the sidelines, meant 1968 was a year unlike any other.

Nelson concluded Wallace was "angry and apparently disappointed" as his campaign moved closer to Election Day, and he appeared "tired and testy after a grueling nine-day western tour." His speeches at California aerospace plants had not gone well, smaller numbers of employees willing to use their lunch hour to hear Wallace than had done so when Humphrey visited a few weeks earlier. At Aerojet General in Downey, Nelson reported that Wallace had spoken for more than 30 minutes before drawing any applause from the group of only 500 who showed up. Nelson's report included pointed exchanges between Wallace and reporters aboard his campaign plane as it left California. He told Nelson, "You folks at *The Los Angeles Times* can write that we got a cool reception here, but we got a good reception here, and we let them hear it." As he walked down the center aisle of the plane, he pointed at another reporter and said, "Aw, I know you. You don't want to see a good reception" and denied hecklers in San Diego had especially angered him. "I never get mad," Wallace said. He also singled out a reporter from *Time* magazine for a cover story that he viewed unfavorably. Nelson said he told the *Time* reporter, "I see you got psychiatrists and sociologists and anthropologists and all the other ologists analyzing me. Probably next week you'll have the zoologists analyzing me."[80]

Wallace himself would later acknowledge that his announcement of his running mate for 1968 had not gone well, and gave the media some of its best opportunities to brutally scrutinize the Wallace campaign. On October 2, 1968, Wallace stood before 200 reporters (and a live national TV audience) inside a packed ballroom of Pittsburgh's Hilton Hotel and introduced retired air force general Curtis LeMay as his running mate. Wallace and LeMay cast a serious pose over the podium (with LeMay standing many inches taller than Wallace), but their lack of compatibility, or even familiarity with one another, appeared physically evident from the start. LeMay, noticeably uncomfortable with public speaking, stood silently as Wallace extolled the retired general's virtues. Among the "virtues" shared were not ones historian Dan T. Carter said Wallace had been forewarned about. LeMay's views on the use of nuclear weapons were controversial, surely as problematic as those that had dogged Senator Goldwater in the 1964 campaign. The night before LeMay was to be announced as the running mate, Carter said "the Wallace staff spent hours preparing the outspoken LeMay on how to dodge any questions about the 'bomb' issue." Regardless, questions about use of nuclear weapons in Vietnam (and elsewhere) were quickly asked, and LeMay fell face first into the trap.[81]

Answering Jack Nelson of the *Los Angeles Times* and his query about the bomb, LeMay charged full steam ahead:

We can win this war without nuclear weapons, but I have to say that we have a phobia about nuclear weapons. I think there may be times when it would be most efficient to use nuclear weapons. However, the public opinion in this country and through the world throw up their hands in horror when you mention nuclear weapons just because of the propaganda that's been fed to them.[82]

Not done yet, LeMay rambled off into a strange soliloquy about a film he had watched about an island in the South Pacific after nuclear testing had been conducted there that showed rats and other vermin had survived the radiation exposure. Wallace, clearly pained and standing at the side, stepped toward the microphone and interrupted, "Now, let me say, gentlemen, now let me say, General LeMay hasn't advocated the use of nuclear weapons, not at all. He is just discussing nuclear weapons with you."[83] Nelson asked a follow-up question, however, about whether *if* he found it necessary to use nuclear weapons, would he keep that option in play? LeMay jumped in for a second time:

If I found it necessary, I would use anything we could dream up—anything that we could dream up, including nuclear arms, to end the war. I know I will be misquoted. It has happened before. I'll be damned lucky if I don't appear as a drooling idiot whose only solution is to drop atomic bombs all over the world. I hope we can stay out of war. But once the time comes when we have to fight, I would use any weapon in our arsenal that is necessary. . . . I think to most military men a nuclear weapon is just another weapon in the arsenal. Nuclear war would be horrible. To me, any war is horrible. To me, if I had to go to Vietnam and get killed with a rusty knife or get killed with a nuclear weapon, I would rather get killed with a nuclear weapon.[84]

Wallace repeatedly stressed he believed the Vietnam War was "winnable" with the use of conventional weapons, but he did not rule out the use of nuclear weapons. The governor said there was no disagreement in his position and that expressed by General LeMay. "All General LeMay has ever said is that you don't tell the enemy what you're going to do. But I'm already on record and he doesn't disagree with my position at all. We can win with conventional weapons and we ought to win. I do not recommend the use of nuclear weapons at all."[85] As reporters continued to goad LeMay, Wallace grew noticeably irritated and accused reporter Jack Nelson of engaging in demagoguery. Wallace repeated,

Not only do I say [nuclear weapons] are not necessary, I have said we would not use nuclear weapons in Vietnam. We would use conventional weapons because, in my judgment, from what I understand from the military, the war could be won with conventional weapons. I don't want to use nuclear weapons at all. I just want our nation to gain superiority in defensive and offensive capabilities so that we can always negotiate. We cannot stay [in Vietnam] and lose several hundred men every week for years and years to come.[86]

LeMay biographer Warren Kozak assessed that the botched news conference by LeMay confirmed "everything Wallace had feared, and every reason Wallace wanted to run alone played out in front of him." The panicked and angry look on Wallace's face revealed the almost instantaneous doubts Wallace must have felt: "Everything he had worked for and felt within his grasp suddenly dissolved, like a handful of sand in an ocean wave," Kozak wrote.[87]

Reporters noted LeMay gave rather short shrift to any remarks about why he felt compelled to run for vice president and why he wished to run with George Wallace. Most presumed he had chosen to join Wallace's campaign as part of an effort to return to the national platform to promote his military views—particularly as they related to the war in Vietnam. Wallace and his aides were anything but subtle—all but physically pushing the retired general aside to take up and shut down questions that were baiting LeMay into more and more difficult waters. Eventually, Wallace declared the news conference over and began to exit the dais with General LeMay still standing at the podium. As Los Angeles Times columnist Bill Henry offered:

It wasn't anything new for the ex-four star airman to be the center of controversy. . . . But he was hardly accustomed to being elbowed away from the microphone and having somebody try to explain what he'd just said before the words were hardly out of his mouth . . . and the general plainly didn't like it.[88]

Thomasson believed the obviously flawed "vetting" of LeMay resulted from the fact Wallace didn't want a running mate and only selected one because he had to. In the hours after LeMay's terrible debut in Pittsburgh, Thomasson noted Wallace was "visibly agitated" with how the general had spoken before reporters but accused reporters of attempting to distort LeMay's words. Regardless, "there were indications that Wallace intends to keep as close rein as possible on the volatile former Air Force Chief of Staff," and at subsequent large rallies in Indianapolis and Toledo on the same day LeMay joined the ticket, he and his "mink adorned wife" were introduced, but Wallace was the only one speaking.[89] It didn't take long for polling to reveal the mistake the LeMay selection was. Even back home in Montgomery, editorial writers were openly questioning the LeMay choice. The final straw for the editors of *The Alabama Journal* appeared to be LeMay's open support of integration (despite Wallace's assurance that he was referring to integrating the air force only). LeMay's response to a question about birth control and legalized abortion—"I support both"—also raised concerns.[90]

Wallace allowed his frustration to show publicly, brow beating reporters on his campaign plane as they left California about the kind of coverage he was getting. Wallace's aides were convinced the media had "turned" on Wallace and that was the cause of his faltering polling numbers. In the aftermath, Nelson of the *LA Times* concluded he'd "never seen Wallace so upset" and surmised it was partially attributable to the stress of his "exhausting campaign . . . [that showed] no signs that he was gaining momentum" left political analysts convinced the Wallace campaign was "sputtering."[91] Nelson's analysis was spot on—with polling numbers falling like a rock following the LeMay announcement, the end of Wallace's 1968 campaign was a foregone conclusion long before voters went to the polls. Wallace and his campaign managers may have blamed the media for their loss, but ample evidence existed that they had suffered many self-inflicted wounds along the way as well.

1972: Continuation of "the Show"

Whether Wallace would be a political factor four years later in 1972 was unknown, but what *was* known was that he would continue to be a "media star" who drew an out-sized level of attention when placed next to the impact of his campaigns to date. All of the major national media once again signed up to cover Wallace's entry into the race—this time in the Democratic preferential primaries across numerous states. Among those was ABC News, who assigned veteran newsman Steve Bell to cover Wallace's 1972 Democratic primary run on a daily basis. Bell, who had been one of the last reporters to stand next to Senator Robert F. Kennedy before he was shot and killed in June 1968, was ready for whatever the campaign could offer. Not surprisingly, it offered the rather familiar role of reporters as foils, Bell recalling he and others were frequently the butt of Wallace's jokes or remarks to his rally crowds. He recalled,

> There would be a section, relatively near the top of his speech, where he would blast the media for its coverage of him. Of course we were just on the other side of the rope, in front of the crowds, and there were some nights when the crowds would get really riled up [with the media]. Then he would always point down to us, or just open his hand down to us, and say, "Now, don't take it out on these boys, they just don't know any better." And he would calm things down a bit and go on with his speech. We were often the targets, pointed out by him to the crowds, and then "saved" by him.[92]

Bell recalled Wallace and his team would become angry when "staged media events" did not produce the kind of coverage they desired. As an example, he noted visits by Wallace to factory plant gates in his campaigns in both Wisconsin and Indiana. Bell said:

> We would interview workers coming out who had shook Wallace's hand, and we would ask them if they planned to vote for Wallace. Interesting, a lot of them said they were trying to decide between the two Georges—George Wallace and George McGovern. These were two very ideologically different candidates, but they both were attractive to anti-establishment voters.[93]

The Wallace campaign had sought more "conventional" media coverage in 1972 than he had in his previous two tries, trying visits to plant gates and smaller interactions between Wallace and voters rather than relying solely on large, boisterous rallies for coverage. Wallace's media team also tried to woo TV reporters behind the scenes, hoping for more favorable coverage, by providing off-the-record private access to the governor. Bell recalled,

> Sometimes after the last rally of the night, you'd be in your motel room and there would be a knock on the door and it would be one of the aides to Wallace saying, "The governor would like to see you." We would literally go into George's bedroom in the motel and it was always just him, none of his staff, just national news

media people, two or three of us, and George Wallace. He would talk and talk, he just couldn't wind down, and he really just wanted company and wanted to chat. We would talk about anything in the world with him. These were strictly off the record [meetings] and they seldom focused on the campaign. It was mostly him telling old war stories, just anything to get him relaxed for the night.[94]

Bill Curtis, reporting for the *CBS Evening News,* apparently was unconvinced Wallace was a different candidate in 1972 than he had been before. Covering a speech Wallace made before union workers in Indianapolis, Curtis reported, "His speeches haven't changed much, the issues provide some fertile ground for a Wallace appeal: high emotion over busing, rising taxes, a protest vote of the working man, and the claim that he said it all first."[95] One change was present in the CBS report, however, as Curtis cut away to video of George and Cornelia Wallace driving an Oldsmobile "pace car" at high speeds around the famous Indianapolis Motor Speedway to show Wallace in more "conventional" campaign settings. The campaign had done likewise days earlier in Wisconsin as Wallace hitched a ride on a snowmobile on a snowy day there. Mainline Democrats may have become concerned that Wallace was making inroads with voters who had rejected him before because of his segregationist views and strident tone of the past. In Indiana and Michigan, Wallace rival Hubert Humphrey spent thousands of dollars on television advertising that proclaimed: "When Wallace got the vote, Nixon got the White House. It wasn't meant to be that way but a lot of people got fooled." Wallace was angered by the Humphrey effort, telling an Indianapolis audience: "Many of the things said about us have been distorted. And you've had some ads on television and in the newspapers that are just as erroneous and untrue as anything I have ever heard of."[96]

Bell spent hundreds of hours in Wallace's company throughout the spring and summer of 1972 and said he could recall only one occasion when Wallace grew personally angry with him. He said the flash of anger came when Wallace confronted him about a report Bell had filed in the days following the assassination attempt on Wallace that indicated Wallace likely had no hope of being nominated given his physical condition and that his voters were using his campaign "to send a message" but were not interested in making him the party's nominee. Bell said,

His supporters were saying we are angry, look who we are voting for. We are voting for the bulldog who is barking the loudest at the national conventional candidates who shares our anger with our inability to make things happen....
My story that really made Wallace personally angry was one where I reported that many of his voters had no intention of supporting him in November. George

hated it because I pointed out that he was never going to be elected president of the United States.[97]

1976: New Image, New Issues Emerge

As the 1976 primary season approached—and Wallace was entering a third term as governor—his increasingly outspoken wife, Cornelia, was elevated to a larger role with the media. Often appearing at Wallace's side, she tried to made certain she was never photographed standing next to her now-wheelchair-bound husband, and instead was captured seated next to him, concerned the "optics" of such a look could make Wallace look weak. As part of Cornelia's role for 1976, the Wallace camp arranged for Cornelia to receive an offer to publish a personal memoir. Titled C'nelia and published by the A. J. Holman Publishing Company of Philadelphia (better known for publishing Bibles), the book detailed the long, hard drive Governor Wallace had undertaken in coming back from his bullet wounds. The idea, it seems, was to paint Wallace as a strong fighter who couldn't be kept down, but the personal stories contained in the book backfired and served to raise more questions than they resolved. United Press International reported on Cornelia's new book noting, "fighting intense pain that drove him into deep depression and lengthy crying spells, Governor George Wallace took two years to recover from near fatal gunshot wounds. . . . Wallace's two-year recovery was painful and frustrating. She says he was often overtaken by lengthy crying spells during moods of depression."[98]

Amidst the troubling picture painted of a strong man driven to "lengthy crying spells," Cornelia spoke openly about issues related to pain killers. "For a while, George became psychologically dependent on the pain injections, but when it became obvious he was asking for the shots too often, sterile water was substituted for the medicine."[99] The question of Wallace's level of physical pain was seemingly always up in the air. Wallace himself told a reporter, "I have what you call paraplegic discomfort" and had to adjust his seated position often. The governor openly stated he took Tegretol for discomfort—a prescription drug that his doctor said was neither a tranquilizer nor a pain-killing narcotic.[100] An Associated Press writer, Kendall Weaver, wrote an account, however, that matched the conclusion many reporters had reached: "George Wallace lives manfully with pain, the deadening pain of paralysis. It is a triumph of personal courage and, possibly, a fatal political liability. The pain grows daily around his middle. It is, at best, a discomfort. In idle moments it is a grim reminder that his legs, now frail, will never walk again."[101]

Passages such as that, ones that emphasized Wallace's physical disability and personal health struggles served to "wall off" the candidate, over time, from both reporters and his supporters. Wallace campaign managers grew weary of images that seemed fixated on their candidate's inability to walk, rather than his message. It was, after all, unchartered territory for any national candidate to try to traverse. Never before had a presidential candidate (sans Franklin D. Roosevelt) with such physical challenges ever presented himself on the national stage.

In Maryland, *Lowell Sun* Statehouse reporter Loring Swaim expressed the frustration many reporters noted in 1976—Wallace was generally unavailable or unwilling to do one-on-one interviews with reporters. By now he was a known commodity—and one with a lot of campaign cash in the bank—earned media was not the priority it once had been.[102] Reporters did seem to keep a great deal of their focus on Wallace's health, which they viewed as a legitimate issue for a presidential candidate to address. When a reporter would ask Wallace if he was tired from all the campaigning, Wallace would reply: "No, I'm not tired, are you?"[103] In Marion, Illinois, a small Williamsburg County seat town about fifty miles north of the Ohio River, Wallace directly addressed questions about his health and physical fitness. "Convinced that the question of his health cost him a victory in the Florida primary, Governor Wallace is working hard to lay the issue to rest in Illinois," AP writer Dennis Montgomery reported. Montgomery noted, however, that as much as Wallace and his team appeared ready to make the case that he was physically able to be president, they were unprepared to release his medical records "for fear they might be misinterpreted by reporters who lack medical training." For his part, Wallace said: "I am physically able to serve and run and if that were not true I am honest enough not to be a candidate." Regarding his medical records, he said doctors had told him he "was in good shape."[104] The Wallace response to requests for his medical records in the wake of surviving an assassination attempt seemed to be repeated decades later, when the Trump campaign became the first in modern history to refuse to release the candidate's tax returns and other financial documents. Just as Wallace had taken a "just-trust-me" approach, Trump did so as well.

The *Chicago Tribune's* Robert Davis, covering Wallace's Illinois campaign swing, raised the issue of the health of the candidate in the aftermath of a leg injury he suffered in Florida. Davis noted that campaign officials would concede privately that Wallace's health *was* an issue. A poll taken after the Florida primary revealed that two out of every five voters did not vote for Wallace because he was in a wheelchair. Davis reported,

> Because of that, Wallace campaign strategists have made some subtle campaign changes in Illinois. At the many airport stops Wallace makes to greet supporters

in small towns and to talk to local news media representatives, the white "Trust the People" jet the governor uses has been taxied around the airport runways and turned so onlookers cannot see him being carried down the steps and seated in his wheelchair.[105]

Also noted was the fact Wallace was seated in a regular desk chair for an ABC News television interview, his wheelchair nowhere in sight. Davis added that while it was not customary for Wallace to address his disability in Florida, after his loss there, "he now mentions it in nearly every speech, pointing to his rigorous schedule as proof that he is physically able to serve as president."[106] Wallace told Illinois supporters that the media were "ganging up" on him including newspaper editorial writers "who sit up in their ivory towers [and] think the average man doesn't have any intelligence and doesn't know how to walk across the street. The people are as intelligent and know as much as those who write the editorials of our country's biggest newspapers."[107] The scrutiny Wallace received *was* exacting—an Associated Press photograph moved nationally from a Wallace speech in Belleville, Illinois featured a cutline from the AP that called attention to the irony that while Wallace spoke beneath a banner proclaiming, "Trust the People," he was surrounded by a bullet proof glass separating him from his audience.[108]

For a brief period, Wallace tried a new tact by beating reporters to the punch and broaching the topic of his physical health before he was asked about it "because the news media has played up the fact that I'm in a wheelchair." He declared himself a serious contender for the Democratic nomination. He added, "Roosevelt was four terms in a wheelchair, but they didn't have television in those days," Wallace said, trying to explain the newfound focus on his disability resulting from the 1972 shooting. In a lengthy television interview for an Alabama TV station, Wallace said, "If my doctors had any doubts that I was physically unable to do anything I want to, they would tell me. . . . It would be unfair to the people of this country [to run for president] if I wasn't healthy enough to do the job."[109] Wallace even tried a bit of humor to make his point, appearing on NBC's *Meet the Press*, and telling the panelists, "Even though my legs are useless, at least I'm not paralyzed in the head [like] some of the people that have been running our government."[110] The focus on Wallace's wheelchair, however, was taking its toll. Publicly, Billy Joe Camp, Wallace's press secretary, said the governor's physical condition "is not an issue we're either going to raise or turn away from." Deputy Press Secretary Elvin Stanton, noted: "There's going to be a batch of reporters everywhere he goes, they're going to watch everything he does, and it's going to speak for itself."[111] Privately, Camp later confirmed Wallace's physical condition *was* a factor in why the 1976 campaign was relying less upon large rallies. In 1972, 4,500 people showed up to hear Wallace speak in LaCrosse, Wisconsin. Four years later, he was doing press interviews and greeting a small party of 300 supporters at the LaCrosse airport. Wallace told a Wisconsin reporter, Grant Blum from the *LaCrosse Tribune* that he was irritated with the media:

> All they showed on the television was me getting up to the podium in a wheel-chair. They've got these people feeling that Wallace is not physically able. The image they built up is he's a sick man. That's what the polls showed in North Carolina and Florida. . . . I just had an accident, I was shot. I don't have disease.[112]

As Wallace tried to make headway in Wisconsin, troubling editorials popped up back home in Alabama that caused a new drag on his campaign. Reporters peppered Wallace with questions about the newspaper editorials that essentially begged the governor to quit his presidential campaign and come home to attend to business there. The combined *Montgomery Advertiser* and *Alabama Journal*, under a front-page editorial offered by its editor and publisher, Harold E. Martin, was blunt: "Governor George Wallace should withdraw from the presidential race and devote his energies to finding the solutions to some of the critical problems facing Alabama."[113] H. Brandt Ayers, editor and publisher of the *Anniston Star*, wrote a similar editorial, offering:

> The Wallace era in American politics has ended. It was an exciting, outrageous and ultimately useful period of political readjustment . . . [but] George Wallace was never destined to lead America. . . . Hopefully, he will gracefully withdraw from further active campaigning and spend more of his time in Alabama.[114]

Clearly, the editorials irritated Wallace who told a reporter that the *Montgomery Advertiser* "has had a personal vendetta against me."[115] The *Advertiser's* editorial had some strong words in it for Wallace—

> Wallace's health is a major issue in the presidential campaign and Wallace has become almost paranoid in his desire to demonstrate that he is in good physical condition, other than being in a wheelchair. Newsmen and others traveling the campaign trail agree that he has demonstrated his stamina. It may be a sad comment on human nature that a paraplegic in a wheelchair is not accepted as a viable candidate for the presidency, but it is a fact of life, as Wallace has found out. And no amount of jokes about his opponents being paralyzed from the neck up is going to change that fact.[116]

The editorials notwithstanding, Wallace went on with a Green Bay appearance where he attempted to explain why his current campaign was skipping the big, loud rallies that had been the trademark of earlier Wallace efforts: "All I got out of the rallies was talkin' to my own people and television pictures of my wheelchair. I'm not in the business of selling wheelchairs. I'll do that when I'm done runnin' for president. . . . Nobody's got the nomination locked up, and they won't prior to the Democratic convention."[117]

As the Alabama editorials dogged him on the trail, two separate polls published in Wisconsin showed the race was essentially between Jimmy Carter and Morris Udall, with Wallace running no better than third. Still, Wallace trudged on. Reporters engaged in open conjecture that Wallace was staying on the campaign trail for reasons beyond believing he could actually be nominated by the Democratic Party. Some speculation centered on the idea that the Wallace campaign was actually serving as a form of mental and physical therapy for the candidate. Media profile articles that took on the governor's health became regular fair as the primary season wore on—some of them positive and hopeful, others damning and questioning. *Parade* magazine offered what the Wallace campaign had planned as a positive story about a new Wallace family biography ghost-written for George Wallace Jr. timed to come out during the 1976 primaries. His father wrote a revealing introduction to the work that was part of the frame his campaign hoped to install on the "new" George Wallace:

> I now view things in a different perspective. Before I was shot, I worried about things that seem trivial today, compared to the problem I now have of not being able to walk—not being a normal person. I have adapted and accepted it . . . but if I could walk the next minute and be whole again, I would have no problem in the world, no worry in the world.[118]

Wallace's personal description of himself as "not being a normal person" was a poor choice of words and seemed the antithesis of what he said he wanted to project—a man who had suffered an accident but who was in no way incapable of holding the highest office in the land. While the Wallace campaign was successful in getting its more positive frame placed on the health of their candidate via the widely read, but little-respected *Parade* magazine, other journalists, such as Ann Pincus, took a decidedly more pointed approach to Wallace's health. For the August 4, 1975, edition of the *Village Voice*, Pincus offered a blistering review of Wallace's health under an uncompromising headline, "George Wallace Couldn't Function as President—Even if Elected."[119] Picked up by newspapers across the country, Pincus's report was written after she was granted several days of access to the governor on his home turf in Alabama. She didn't hold back; she wrote openly about his noticeable hearing loss, his sometimes-drifting attention span, and countered assurances from his doctors and political aides that since he was able to serve as a full-time governor of Alabama, he would likewise be able to serve as president.

Pincus, despite her access, reported that Wallace's aides made her efforts to learn more about the governor's health as difficult as they could, including denying her a promised one-on-one interview with Wallace. Wallace's aides became aware of the focus Pincus was placing on the governor's health; she had already learned that the governor regularly took a powerful drug called Tegretol (Carbamazepine) to reduce his abdominal pain. She also reported on his use of anticoagulants to prevent blood clots and a catheter was in place since he had no control of his bowel. Wallace had undergone a series of at least eight surgeries since he was shot in 1972, most designed to either relieve his near-constant pain or to help him gain control of his bowel. Pincus reported Wallace had found

> a medicine that works for his deep depressions, a miracle drug that's faster than aspirin and turns him from an enfeebled man slumped in his wheelchair clutching his side into a vibrant, vital candidate for the presidency of the United States. The name of the drug is "Challenge." It comes from large rallies and wicked antagonists. It's the smell of greasepaint, the roar of the crowd, and it really does work. He forgets the pain and the helplessness. The "people" is the reason he has survived.[120]

Pincus said Wallace had "suffered pain, humiliation, personal degradation and embarrassment" as the result of his wounds but that he had also survived. Regardless, she found few people in Alabama willing to talk openly about the governor's physical or mental condition. When asked, "most lower their eyes when this delicate subject is broached" reminding any who inquired that "it is somehow bad manners to pry into Wallace's health" and instead offer defensive comparisons between Wallace and Franklin Roosevelt. Despite such comparisons, most admitted that Wallace was unable to keep up the busy schedule FDR followed and certainly lacked the cheery outlook Roosevelt constantly conveyed in public life. "Combine his love for campaigning with the fact that the crowds make him forget about the pain and bolster him up, add that he believes in his cause, and you have the answer of why he runs for president," Pincus assessed.[121]

What Wallace believed, however, was not the only factor to be considered. Pincus ended her article with a series of pointed and difficult questions—including asking whether the nation's voters should be asked to participate in his "mental therapy" that included making millions of dollars in federal matching campaign funds available to him? She concluded with an acknowledgment that while it was bad manners to probe into the delicate question of Wallace's physical and mental ability to serve in the nation's highest office and that he was worthy of sympathy and admiration for his struggle, "but let's not give him the presidency. That won't make it up to him for his legs."[122]

As the 1976 primary campaign went forward, Cornelia Wallace had a few of her own missteps. Some suggested that her awkward public remarks may have been an early public sign of the private marital strife emerging between the Wallaces that would eventually end their union. Sitting with a features writer for *Parade* magazine, Cornelia acknowledged that his paralysis was not helping make her husband electable:

> Without a doubt, the image of a man in a wheelchair might be acceptable in Alabama where people know and love George, but it may be not acceptable to some people in this country. Most people want their president to stand up tall and straight when he meets a head of state [from another nation]. . . . Wheelchair to many people is synonymous with sick, and you know he's not sick. He's extremely healthy, but it would take a lot of education for people to realize that.[123]

Cornelia raised eyebrows a second time in Indiana when responding to questions about her husband's stamina for political campaigning. Mrs. Wallace, apparently granting interviews on her own without consulting the campaign, told *Washington Star* reporter Betty Beale that she had personally lost any enthusiasm for campaigning, and she seemed to be joining the doomsday chorus haunting her husband, describing his campaign through thirty-three primaries as "a long haul" and reminding reporters that he hadn't won a single contest and only a handful of delegates. "I would be relieved if we were home, but George doesn't seem to have any trauma [about campaigning]," Cornelia shared. "Part of the reason [he campaigns so much] is to dispel the feeling that he wasn't well enough to be president. But two out of five people in Florida thought he wasn't physically able to be president, and one out of three in North Carolina. If he continues maybe they will finally get the message that he's healthy."[124]

Depending upon the setting, Wallace himself could be remarkably candid about his condition based on his near-death experience. He seemed to try to strike a balance between being open and forthcoming and in putting the issue aside. In one interview, he said: "I've had some mental stress and some anguish, and sometimes I have wondered "Why did this happen to you?"—but I accepted the fact that I was not going to walk, save a miracle, and I have adjusted my life, I have accepted it, and so I really don't worry about it."[125]

Wallace would even bring up the subject in his campaign rallies:

I can understand that people can question about my health, but Franklin Roosevelt was elected president four times in a wheelchair, and as Al Smith said one
time, "We're not electing an acrobat." If you needed an acrobat to be president, I
would not be qualified. But you don't need an acrobat to be president.[126]

Despite trying to make comparisons to the beloved FDR, and trying every other
tact—openness, shields from the media, and even pre-emptive strikes on the
health issue—the emphasis on the issue persisted. In the wake of his devastating
Florida loss to Jimmy Carter, *The New Yorker's* Elizabeth Drew asked Wallace
if the loss was tough to take: "Oh no, honey. Nothing's that tough. After you've
been shot five times and suffered the loss of walking, what's a loss? Not being
able to walk, but I'm living. I thought I was going to die as soon as I was hit.
So losing a campaign—my goodness, that's not your life."[127]

Losing primaries, however, did not cause Wallace to leave the campaign
trail and reassess his chances. He pressed on to Wisconsin and Indiana, but
the trouble he was having connecting seemed to show. *Indianapolis Star* writer
William M. Shaw covered a "fly in" news conference at the Weir Cook airport
just a day before the Indiana primary and noted some differences:

The governor was smiling broadly when he emerged from his gleaming DC-9
campaign jet with "Trust the People" emblazoned across the tail, but the general
tone of his remarks indicated his poor delegate showing in recent primaries is
taking its toll. He no longer talks of winning the Democratic presidential nomination. Instead, he emphasizes that because of his efforts the party platform will
reflect "the views of the great middle class". . . . He said he will remain an active
candidate, however, and has no intention of dropping out of the race, despite
being third.[128]

Shaw asked Wallace whether he had grown discouraged. "Wallace replied in
an almost fatalistic manner: 'I never get discouraged. With the things that have
happened to me, I never get discouraged unless, of course, someone walked
up and stuck a thirty-eight in my face.'"[129] While in Indiana, a *New York Times*
report indicated the candidate appeared "fatigued and bored" and distressed by
the number of his supporters deserting him for Ronald Reagan running in the
Republican primary. He addressed Reagan's impact on his campaign directly,
conceding some of his campaign staff and volunteers "had went over to Mr.
Reagan," believing Reagan had a better chance of winning that did Wallace.
Regardless, Wallace said, "I would expect my supporters [in Indiana] to vote

for me. I don't expect them to crossover but I hope some of the Republicans cross over to support George Wallace."[130]

Days later, when most reporters had predicted Wallace would withdraw, he popped up again in Michigan, hoping to revive any last hope he could for votes and delegates. Assessing Wallace's remaining effort in Michigan, *Lansing State Journal* State Capitol reporter Jerry Moskal wrote,

> Those Michigan voters who gave George Wallace's presidential ambitions a hit four years ago now appear on the brink of letting him down for good. The belief not only permeates the thinking of political observers in the state but reaches right into Wallace's Michigan campaign operations as well.[131] *Lansing State Journal* Capitol reporter Pat McCarthy painted a rather bleak picture of the Wallace campaign stop in Lansing: It wasn't the same. The response wasn't there, because the crowd wasn't there. He was defensive about his health and about voters deserting him for a Republican. Governor George Wallace still fired off the catch phrases that captured the "us against them" tone of his previous campaigns, but somehow the banty rooster aggressiveness of his earlier days has faded. . . . Wallace said "I feel kindly toward the people who voted for me [in 1972 after he was shot], but I'm not looking for sympathy." Wallace lashed out at the media for "muckraking and lies" about his health. . . . The sparse crowd, the repeated assertion that he was a "viable" candidate, the emphasis on running second to Carter, and yes, the wheelchair, all left the impression that the 1972 glory days of George Wallace in Michigan must remain a fond memory.[132]

Wallace believed, however, it was important to actively campaign, to show up in as many states as possible to ask for the vote, and to demonstrate that his physical ability to serve was intact. Others, including those close to him, quietly whispered in confidence that campaigning in 1976 had taken on some form of mental therapy for Wallace who was decidedly bored with his duties back home as governor and longed for the glory days now long past.[133]

Just as it had in 1972, Wallace's campaign for the Democratic nomination came to an end in Maryland. His world had changed dramatically in the four years since he left Holy Cross Hospital in Silver Spring, Maryland, while recovering from multiple gunshot wounds. In the weeks and months leading up to the May 18, 1976, Maryland primary, it became abundantly clear that Wallace was not going to win the nomination or be any factor whatsoever. A month before the primary, Wallace's campaign workers in Maryland talked to reporters as they closed out the main campaign office at a Baltimore office building. They insisted the campaign was "restructuring, but not abandoning" the Maryland effort.[134] The curtailed effort in Maryland made sense. A *Washington Post* report from Cumberland found 50 registered voters who said they had voted for Wallace four years earlier in 1972 planned to support Carter in 1976. *The Post* survey found that Wallace still enjoyed support from four out of 10 voters in the Cumberland area, "but that's well off the 85 percent vote he received there in the 1972 primary."[135] One in four voters surveyed by the *Washington Post* expressed concern about Wallace's paralysis, but thought that "a lessening of racial tensions [in Maryland] has also hurt [Wallace's] campaign."[136] A *Baltimore Sun* poll of Democratic voters found the Maryland contest had settled on two candidates (neither of them Wallace) with 31 percent supporting Carter, and 28 percent backing California Governor Jerry Brown.[137] In the wake of such results, Wallace campaign officials announced two previously scheduled stops in both Silver Spring and Laurel were being canceled.[138] Two days later, the campaign announced the governor would appear in Wheaton less than 24 hours before the primary polls opened in the state. Reporters outnumbered supporters at the Wallace news conference conducted inside his heavily guarded and nearly abandoned campaign office.

Myrna MacPherson of the *Washington Post* wrote an analysis of the end of the Wallace era on the national scene and found his wife, Cornelia, ready to place blame on some of Wallace's campaign aides. She said Alabama advisers had "bungled" the campaign for 1976. "You're not allowed too many mistakes in this game," she said. Cornelia explained, "George Wallace is like the hen that laid the golden egg—and [his Alabama campaign aides] are the farmers who don't know how to pick it up." She complained that campaign advertising and appearances permitted too many images of "them loading him in and out of airplanes and rolling him to platforms."[139] Cornelia said she had tried to do her part. During an interview on the nationally syndicated *Mike Douglas Show*, she told viewers that the shooting had changed her husband: "He'd always been an aggressive, rowdy little fella, kind of a diamond in the rough. He's more mellow now, polished. His edges are smoothed off."[140] She said her ideas for how to portray Wallace for the '76 campaign had been rejected, saying,

> They should've shown him swimming in the pool, driving the boat up at the lake. They could've stood him up in his braces or leaned him up against a fence post on the farm and had him say, "This is where I was brought up. My father was a dirt farmer." He can do the same thing Jimmy Carter did. . . . Anyway, about George, they didn't do much to overcome his wheelchair image. In retrospect, I think he would have been better off staying at home and letting them show TV films expressing his views.[141]

Before the end of 1976, widespread rumors of troubles in the marriage of George and Cornelia broke wide open in the media. Their divorce became final in January 1978. Cornelia said the 1976 campaign had left both her and George "somewhat sour." Cornelia admitted she harbored significant fears in the years following the shooting and that her smiles on the campaign trail were often forced. "I didn't enjoy the rallies anymore," she said. "I found myself searching the crowd and faces. A couple of times I pointed out [to security officers] unusual people. I think it's a natural reaction to what happened four years ago. It's one of the tragic side effects."[142] Wallace's daughter Peggy Wallace Kennedy looks back on the 1976 campaign with regret. "[The campaign] was a challenge, it certainly was," she said. "He was tired [and] I don't think his heart was in it. I think he ran just because of the Wallace machine. He certainly was not physically fit to run in that campaign."[143] Wallace's diminished physical condition was costly, allowing men such as Carter and Reagan, who were not battling a physical disability, to articulate his views more powerfully. Nixon analyst and adviser Pat Buchanan believed Wallace's "handicap" cost him the nomination altogether: "For someone like Wallace [his] appeal really is that he has a tremendous amount of animal energy and dynamism. If you can't stand up there at that podium, it is a tremendous disadvantage."[144]

CHAPTER 6

Politics of Success and Failure

So why did Donald Trump succeed in 2016 and win the Electoral College and become president of the United States, while such a mountaintop remained a destination that eluded George Wallace in more than a dozen years of trying? There are likely as many answers to that question as there are stars in the sky, but some more salient explanations rise to the fore in helping understand how two candidates, remarkably similar in their demagoguery, yet separated by a half century in political cycles (1964–2016) reached such vastly different ends. Comparing the political approach both Wallace and Trump took into the arena provides many similarities: both men were interested in revenge against and ostracizing identified out-group enemies, and both often promoted themselves as more important than any viable policy that might exist (or that they might propose) to improve American's lives. Wallace's example was to assist in advancing key elements of "the lost cause" for the allegedly "wronged southern states" under the guise of preserving states' rights, while Trump, for example, opposed the Affordable Care Act ("Obamacare") mostly on the basis of who proposed it. Despite repeated claims by Trump (and the entire Republican ticket) that they would "repeal and replace" the ACA, it was never replaced with a similar form of universal health care for the nation and instead was stripped of key components (such as the individual mandate) they and their financially connected backers disliked. Further, Trump took scapegoating even further than Wallace, advocating expelling or keeping Muslims, Mexicans, and other "others" out of the nation, while Wallace focused on keeping power out of minority hands. Both men advocated jailing those who opposed or dared to challenge government leaders.[1] Trump extended this idea with a "third world twist" to suggesting during a presidential debate and numerous rallies

that his opponent, Hillary Clinton, should be imprisoned. While both Wallace
and Trump relied upon the "spectacle" of their campaign rallies, Trump used
spectacle to greater effect than Wallace could in large part because of the dramatically different nature of media in contemporary times. Trump rallies gave
him the "freedom to do and say whatever he wants" where his own personal
"braggadocio and mockery [were] welcome features, a show of strength," noted
Anna M. Young.[2] Likewise, 24-hour news channels and online digital media
platforms existed to carry Trump's words sans any editing or commentary.
Whereas Trump could command an hour or more of broadcast time, Wallace
was competing for two- or three-minute segments on the evening network and
local news. In the years *when* Wallace could draw a rally-sized crowd, during
the 1964, 1968, and 1972 campaigns (but clearly not in 1976), the coverage of
Wallace's message was filtered through what the media reported on them after
the fact. Trump rallies became a form of "entertainment" television for cable
and online news—attention Wallace's rallies no doubt would have attracted
if such mediums existed in his era. Ultimately, perhaps the greatest obstacle
facing Wallace that he could not overcome was the fact of who he was and the
gaping lack of campaign resources, resources that Trump brought to his effort
in 2016 from his own pocket with seemingly no limit. As he had throughout
his life, Trump was able to "buy" the access he needed, whereas Wallace had to
"earn" his as most traditional politicians have done. While Wallace relied on
news conferences for earned media, Trump generally eschewed interactions
with reporters that would require him to elaborate upon or reconcile any so-
called "policy positions" he might promote. When he did meet with reporters,
Trump engaged in time-consuming name calling and challenges, in August
2015 telling Spanish-language Univision reporter Jorge Ramos to "sit down" and
"go back to Univision" (a phrase strikingly familiar to an epithet used against
many Latinx Americans who are told "Go back to Mexico!") before Ramos was
forcibly removed from the room by Trump associates. Wallace met regularly
with reporters but could not always count on positive outcomes.

A further complication, of course, in comparing the campaigns and rhetoric
of Wallace and Trump is the significant difference in the eras in which they
occurred. The American electorate has continued, as always, to change and
evolve. No one could accurately argue voters in 1968 hold much resemblance
to those of 2016. Anna Young offers also that the politics of the Trump era has
moved into an unprecedented time of emphasis on the aesthetic with voters
closely following what politicians wear, what social media they use, slogans
and catchphrases, lifestyles—but may know very little about the candidate's
policy positions or voting records.[3] Donald Trump, coming directly from the
entertainment industry and having no prior political experience, brought this

media aesthetic to the fore in greater measure than perhaps even the most famous entertainer-turned-politician, Ronald Reagan. While Reagan brought his immense talent as a speaker and attractive presenter to the arena, he also rode a wave of conservative reform with specific policy positions that drew voters in (and in Reagan's era was arguably necessary to get past voter doubts that an entertainment or media figure should be considered a serious political figure). Wallace held no such appeal. In fact, his lack of charisma was often obvious, with more than one writer comparing him to late-night film noir villains played by the likes of Edward G. Robinson. Wallace's "aesthetic" was always based in the original moniker assigned him—"the fightin' lil judge" from Alabama—and only softened temporarily in the 1972 campaign cycle before he met a fate as painful as one of Robinson's characters.

In lieu of the paid media—or digital media—that Trump could command, Wallace had to submit to a parade of reporters seeking to do "profile" pieces on him. The process for such articles, allowing reporters to spend long periods of time with the candidate and giving them access to sources in and out of the campaign was a risky proposition. Journalistic freedom meant Wallace could do little to control what was written or said about him, and unlike Trump, he lacked the digital media to fire back unfiltered to his supporters. A 1968 visit to Alabama assigned Scottish Canadian writer Paul Cowan (writing for the *Village Voice*) was typical with Cowan attempting to bring perspective to Wallace's forays out of the Deep South in preparation for his third-party challenge. In July of that year, Cowan tagged along as Wallace "barnstormed through the small cities that surround Boston" gathering more signatures than needed to meet the Massachusetts ballot access requirements. Cowan wrote about his doubts whether Wallace was in Massachusetts to boost the ballot access effort or to start a new form of American revolution, one aligned with the first American revolution. And while Wallace's ballot-access drive was carried out with little to no violence, the linkages to the American Revolution of 1776 could not be ignored when in 2021 Trump forces used "1776" as a battle cry for their violent and deadly attack upon the US Capitol on January 6, 2021, as Trump's re-election defeat was affirmed by Congress.[4] Cowan said Wallace was consistent in his approach, offering in almost every speech in the commonwealth that "what we are demanding in our state is exactly what your forefathers demanded in Massachusetts: the right to self-government." In his era, Wallace's words were mostly just words—few expected anyone to actually rise up with violence to force their will. Decades of changes in political rhetoric, and the digitized nature of all things political, meant an entirely different element was in play in 2021. The centerpiece of Wallace's rhetoric was still meant to portray him as "the common man's candidate, the one person in public life who speaks for the taxi driver, the beautician, the steel worker, the barber against 'those pinheads in ivory towers who write guidelines telling you when to get up in the morning and when to go to bed at night when they can't even park a bicycle straight themselves.'[5] Trump's demagogic rhetoric went far further, successfully inciting violence and insurrection.

By 1968, Pete Hamill, a former reporter and columnist for the *New York Post*, had begun to gain a solid reputation as one of the most fluent and colorful "literary journalists" on the market. Known for a tough and tight turn of a phrase, he had sat out a newspaper printers' strike in the 1960s by writing longer form stories for magazines. Doing so had further enhanced his embrace of the new journalistic writing style emerging in this era. "Little" George C. Wallace from Alabama made for good copy and was irresistible to *Ramparts* magazine, who dispatched Hamill to profile Wallace. Again, it was exposure and coverage that put Wallace into the legitimacy category for president but came fraught with the analysis and perspectives of the individual writer. In this case, it's clear the brusque Hamill came away unimpressed by the "Wallace aesthetic." He wrote of the governor:

> He stands there smiling, clutching a cigar in a horn holder, a small, round-headed man with the air of a dandy about him. He wears his suits cut tight, with highly polished shoes, carefully trimmed fingernails, a handkerchief making a white arrowhead in his breast pocket. He looks like a caricature, with his Vitalis-sleek hair combed straight back. Black eyebrows dominate his small, Cagney-like features and have a way of making him look Satanic when he lowers the head and looks up from under them. The back of his neck was raw on the day I first met him, as if he had just come from a barbershop.[6]

Theodore White offered his requisite examination of Wallace that focused on many aspects of the man, including his physical dimensions. He noted that Wallace had emerged on the national scene in 1963 at an opportune time for the growth of the civil rights movement and the technological media advancement represented in television news. He wrote of "the over-cropping black eyebrows" Wallace sported, dubbing him "a scrapper" from his boxing past. Aboard a Wallace campaign plane, White described the scene with

> George Wallace in the forward compartment, in an aisle seat . . . a man obviously nervous in flight, with perhaps some remembered carry-over from rocking and tumbling his B29s had taken during [World War II]. A big gold ring glistened on his finger, and in repose his somber face glowered. Occasionally he would run a comb through his sleek glossy hair, halfway between chestnut and jet black; his

eyes close-set were shrunken into deep, dark hollows under the great eyebrows. He was a very little man, almost a frail man, above all a nervous man, his hands twitching when he spoke, shifting from pocket to pocket as he rose.[7]

Washington Star reporter Haynes Johnson (a Pulitzer Prize winner who later joined the *Washington Post* for the bulk of his career) joined the parade of reporters who followed Wallace during the 1968 campaign to write a lengthy three-part profile. Johnson said he found that "despite all his self-assurance, his natural pugnaciousness and drive, George Wallace seems at times ill at ease." Johnson quoted Wallace from "a moment of candor" as remarking, "I haven't got so good a personality." He also described an awkward moment when Wallace's handlers set up an event that clearly was not to the candidate's liking. Reporters were invited in to watch Wallace make telephone calls to supporters in Washington state who had successfully got his name on the ballot, but Wallace seemed to freeze. He snapped to the reporters and photographers nearby, "I can't even think with all you sitting around here looking at me." Some of Wallace's problems could be found, Johnson said, in the fact that "he pushes himself at a harder pace than the other two presidential candidates"— describing a typical campaign day starting as early as 6:30 a.m. and not ending until 2:30 a.m. the next morning. "His campaign is solely a George Wallace operation and it reflects all his conflicting strains, and personal strengths and weaknesses," Johnson wrote. "As he has remarked, 'I'm the chief man.' He is also the chief strategist, promoter and guiding force."[8] Part of Wallace's success in 1968, Johnson believed, was in the growing familiarity Americans were gaining of him as he struggled to reach beyond the one-dimensional "character" of himself broadcast in grainy black-and-white television news reports about racial strife:

> Strangely, for all the concern and tumult he creates, Wallace is gaining support because he does not present the threatening image of the old-time demagogue. There is none of the glowering and menace of a Joe McCarthy. Wallace, in person, smiles and laughs. He teases his hecklers and reminds them that there are two sides to free speech.... He strikes a patient, tolerant stance in the middle of a disturbance.... He always thanks people for coming, and apologizes for making them wait or having to stand in the sun. He makes them believe he cares.[9]

Journalist William S. White, a former AP and *New York Times* correspondent, whose national column was sold by United Feature Syndicate to more than 175 newspapers, claimed that the George Wallace of 1968 was "a revolutionary change" from his start. White theorized, "the new George Wallace" was "gain-

ing momentum at a rate that should frighten both the major parties" but that
a peak was at hand. He noted,

> For the fact is that the George Wallace of yesterday who seemed to evoke mainly
> only the passions of racial antagonism and the plain know-nothingism that
> thrives among the less educated of both North and South, is a Wallace that is no
> more. . . . Two great realities have been evident here. The first is that Wallace has
> changed. He is soft-pedaling any lingering racist line and is instead speaking out
> now not to alienate, but rather in the support of Negro voters. Simultaneously,
> he is far less certain now about all the top issues of the day, notably the war in
> Vietnam.[10]

White concluded Wallace's effort to "transform himself" from "a far-out shouter
on the far-right wing to a reasonable facsimile of any ultra-conservative, highly
free-enterprise politician" made him a lukewarm version of himself. White
wondered aloud whether the "new Wallace" could "*send* the crowds so well as
the old Wallace had done?"[11]

The media profiles produced on Wallace came through a veil of distrust, and
may not have been the truly personal, in-depth examinations they purported
to offer. Wallace historian Dan T. Carter said Wallace felt deep distrust and
anger toward members of the "Yankee press" for alleged unfair coverage of all
aspects of southern life. "There was a grain of truth in Wallace's complaints,"
Carter noted. "Some journalists allowed their prejudice to overcome their bal-
anced judgment at times."[12]

While reporters who maintained a healthy skepticism of Wallace greatly
outnumbered those who privately supported his viewpoints, there were a few
well-placed journalists who appeared to offer favorable coverage of Wallace. One
of those was national columnist Paul Harvey, whose newspaper column was
carried by 300 US newspapers, who was apparently so ingratiating that Wallace
briefly considered Harvey as a potential running mate in 1968. In March 1968,
Harvey was helpful in explaining the delicate position Wallace found himself
in—desperate to get his national campaign for president underway, while his
wife, Lurleen, was facing the final days of her long battle with cancer. Harvey
said, many were commenting: "George Wallace can't win. Why, with his wife
so seriously ill, does he continue to stump the nation espousing a hopeless
cause?"[13] Harvey answered his own question:

> In the beginning, Wallace intended for himself the role of gadfly. He was hope-
> ful that his candidacy would threaten to siphon off so many conservative votes
> that one or both major parties would make concessions to the South. That was

his purpose and plan. Things have changed since his campaign was launched. . . . within recent months, suddenly the longshot candidate from Alabama has three things going for him: Vietnam, crime and race. . . . Now, instead of just a gadfly seeking to influence the platforms and the slates of the big party kingmakers, George Wallace emerges in a position from which he may have much influence on the next president of the United States.[14]

The "rest of the story" man predicted that it was highly possible Wallace could be "in a position to deliver the presidency to either nominee." In the House of Representatives where a deadlocked race would go, "Wallace could drive a very hard bargain. He has promised no secret, back-room deals" and would require full disclosure on appointments and concessions nominees would make. "Then, to the highest bidder, he would deliver the key to the White House."[15] Harvey challenged the proposition that Wallace was "a race-baiter" and said he was a man "dedicated to the proposition that a malignant big government in Washington, D.C., is a more immediate threat to historic American institutions than is Moscow—and that toughness is the only deterrent for troublemakers, abroad or at home."[16]

Southern reporters were a particularly reliable source for stories about the growing competence of the Wallace campaign. Other reporters wrote about Wallace, but most reporters in southern locales could be counted on to produce positive stories—ones that would likely help keep donors sending money to the campaign in the belief that it was not a wasted cause. One of the most reliable writers was Tom Ethridge, originator of the "Mississippi Notebook" column he wrote for both the *Jackson Clarion Ledger* and the *Jackson Daily News*, published by the Hederman family. Described as "a Confederate-waving . . . archconservative, race-baiting defender of Mississippi and Southern values," Ethridge promoted Wallace's strength nationally.[17] Wallace has "enormous 'grass roots support' as a result of his progressive Americanism, support of free enterprise and strong stand against crime, communism, federal encroachment and one-world radicalism," Ethridge wrote.[18] James Free, the Washington, DC correspondent for the *Birmingham News*, traveled with Governor Wallace to Fargo, North Dakota, and declared his rally there, drawing about 4,000 faithful, as the most "far out dateline on George Wallace's campaign. . . . which is a long, long way indeed from Wallace's Deep South stronghold." Free posed the loaded question: "What does the strength of the Wallace party mean so far as the future is concerned?" In North Dakota, it meant that Wallace was speaking to issues that mattered to rural, conservative white voters there, ones that Nixon and Humphrey were not articulating.[19]

Despite the mixed results the "profile pieces" gained them, the Wallace camp continued to "work" reporters for such articles in place of expensive paid advertising. The only exception to the "earned media" approach required in the Wallace era was the campaign-financed film shown at ballot signature and fundraising events across the country—portions of which were edited down into 15- and 30-minute paid television commercials on local independent and network affiliate television stations across the nation. The laborious task of producing such a film, let alone buying and scheduling time for it to run on literally hundreds of television stations across the nation, stands in stark contrast to a 140-character tweet that can be composed and broadcast within seconds.

Scholar Paul J. Achter noted that the consideration of the rhetoric of demagogic political figures—such as Wallace and Trump—should consider not only the traditional examination of the words used, but also the images or representations of the figure.[20] While this expanded view likely assisted Trump—especially given his financial and personal success as a businessman and entertainer—it was a preclude that was impossible for Wallace. The Alabama politician, more ambitious and certainly harder working than Trump, could not cast the same type of persona or image as the star of primetime TV's *The Apprentice*. No one really aspired to be what George Wallace was. While his up-from-the-bootstraps story had a traditional American appeal, it was the kind of "back story" that was already growing dated in an era exposed to the mien of the privileged Kennedys, who, like Trump, exuded success that was to be envied and even fantasized about—not resented. Wallace (and Nixon as well) never seemed to let go of their resentment of their "betters" and find their place with them (as arguably others such as Bill Clinton did). As a result, a rhetoric of resentment flowed forth, one that attracted a following because it seemed to give voice to unresolved feelings and fears, but one that ultimately resolved little. As author Jody Carlson noted, Wallace's rhetoric was fully expressive but was "not designed to move in any productive way toward getting more power for the people, but to make them feel more powerless instead."[21]

In Wallace's time, many speculated in fear about the prospects of a Wallace presidency—no matter how remote the possibility might seem. Many of Wallace's most fervent opponents shivered at the vision of what a "President Wallace" would be like, but in the post-Wallace years, Americans may have had glimpses of a Wallace presidency throughout parts of the subsequent Republican administrations of Nixon, Reagan, and Trump. All three "Wallace successors"—Nixon, Reagan and Trump—successfully co-opted the "southern strategy" to electoral success but in the case of Nixon and Reagan, they did so mostly minus any open racial discord. Nixon and Reagan, certainly politicians influenced by the traditional and powerful role presidents played in the post–World War II era, may have tapped into Wallace tactics to gain public office, but both governed in a manner Wallace could not have achieved. Wallace, his boredom with policy and management being well known, would not have pursued the domestic or foreign policy agendas demanded of a president in the same way Nixon and Reagan did. Perhaps the demands of the Cold War left them no choice, but Nixon and Reagan *did* attempt to wrestle with the forces opposed to democracy in the world and did so with larger American ideals undergirding their efforts. In other words, they were presidents carrying out the tasks of their jobs within the context of their human frailties. With Donald Trump, we gained perhaps a more accurate picture of what a Wallace presidency would have looked like, essentially a president who doesn't want to do the job. With Trump we witnessed a commander-in-chief with little interest in the actual "work" of the job but in love with the accoutrements that go with it. Basking in the trappings of the office is part of the needs fulfillment Trump seemingly meets by nearly constant campaigning (and watching over and over again past campaign and debate performances on tape) living out what Jonathan Swan of Axios.com dubbed Trump's desire to "luxuriate in the moments he believes are evidence of his brilliance."[22] Smaller-scale reminders of that existed throughout the Wallace era—even his closest aides admitting the governor was frequently bored with the duties of the job—*New York Magazine* noting that "on [Wallace's] priority list he always puts the nuts-and-bolts management of Alabama far below the needs of the next campaign."[23] Further, just as Wallace symbolically stood in the schoolhouse door, only to back down, Trump projected and later withdrew several proposals popular with his base of supporters, only to abandon them later (a most recent example being Trump's announced 2020 plan to deport all international students who were not taking in-person classes due to the COVID-19 pandemic, a policy position withdrawn as quickly as it was offered).

There are, then, many factors that contributed to the ultimate failure of George Wallace—referred to by some as "America's greatest loser"—and some are ones he could not escape. The *Alabama Journal* ruminated as Wallace exited the national political stage in 1976 that his "gravest mistake" was to link his ambitions to the politics of racial prejudice. Noting that politicians who came along after the civil rights movement had progressed were relieved of having to face pressures to respond in a lesser, more base manner, as the *Journal* noted, "Once Wallace had socked [the] tarbaby [of racial prejudice], there was no extricating himself."[24] But more than a lesson in the consequences of giving in to the temptations of prejudice and exploiting fear, Wallace's rhetoric is instructive to understanding the words that continue to permeate the American political scene. They remind us of how powerful and easily strung are words that become a tight noose around the neck of democracy, choking off discussion, deliberation, consideration, and certainly compromise. The demagogic rhetoric that remains gives easy answers that fit nicely into a digi-tized "information society" and relieve us of further thinking or feeling. And while the gilded nature of such a time may look lovely—even suggesting an aesthetic that seems authentic and fulfilling—it ultimately is just a long shadow over what could be and reminds us of the easily manipulated spaces that keep Americans separated one from another.

EPILOGUE

In January 1979, George Wallace was coming to the end of eight consecutive years as governor of Alabama and was publicly all smiles as he indicated he was stepping out of public life, having backed Republican-turned-Democrat Fob James to succeed him in the governor's chair. He took a position as a fundraiser for the University of Alabama at Birmingham and made a handful of speeches on their behalf. Insiders, however, reported Wallace fell into a deep depression once out of the political spotlight. As biographer Jeff Frederick indicated, "Wallace grew increasingly depressed, lost physical strength, and became more isolated. By 1982, friends and associates were eager to get Wallace back into electoral politics, convinced his deteriorating health and spirits would be buoyed by a new campaign."[1]

Perhaps a return to public life was in his mind as he surprised many by taking a meeting with now US representative John Lewis of Georgia. Lewis, who as a young man had been beaten and bloodied by Alabama police at the Edmund Pettus Bridge in Selma in 1965 acting under Wallace's orders, wrote about his meeting with Wallace many years afterward:

> I could tell he was a changed man; he was engaged in a campaign to seek forgiveness from the same African-Americans he had oppressed. He acknowledged his bigotry and assumed responsibility for the harm he had caused. He wanted to be forgiven. . . . When I met George Wallace, I had to forgive him, because to do otherwise—to hate him—would only perpetuate the evil system we sought to destroy.[2]

In 1981, Wallace entered his third (and final) marriage to thirty-two-year-old Lisa Taylor, nearly three decades his junior. She had been in love with Wallace since she was a young woman, singing as one half of Mona and Lisa, a singing duo that accompanied Wallace's 1968 campaign. The marriage didn't last, a divorce decree for the couple being entered in 1987; however, the third Mrs. Wallace was along as George, now sixty-three-years-old, gave in to need and instinct and entered the 1982 race for governor. He won a narrow victory in the Democratic primary over former lieutenant governor George McMillan (with Wallace surprising many by capturing about a third of all Black votes in the process). Political analysts carefully studied Wallace's 1982 success, noting that he was perhaps the last southern Democrat who could successfully draw back into the fold "Reagan Democrats" who had abandoned the party for the GOP, all the while attracting a respectable portion of the state's Black vote. The 1982 version of Wallace was, by all accounts, a kinder, gentler version, one campaign ad offering: "We need George Wallace as governor again. He is a compassionate man who understands the needs of the average working man and woman. He cares about all our people—young and old, rich and poor, black and white."[3]

In November 1982, Wallace won 69 percent of the vote over a popular Republican mayor of Montgomery, Emory Folmar, and carried 62 of the state's 67 counties. His victory only temporarily delayed, however, a Republican wave taking over Alabama for succeeding election cycles. During a mostly unremarkable four years as governor, Wallace appointed a record number of African Americans to positions in his administration and state boards and commissions. In May 1984 he also signed into law Alabama's official designation of a state holiday honoring the late Rev. Dr. Martin Luther King Jr. (Alabama's version falling on an already existing state holiday observance for Confederate General Robert E. Lee).[4] A year earlier, Wallace welcomed the Rev. Jesse Jackson to the Governor's Mansion prior to Jackson's speech before the Alabama legislature. Jackson, a candidate for the 1984 Democratic presidential nomination, met with his once former foe, Wallace, for about twenty minutes and described the meeting as "amiable" and one that opened a discussion "in an atmosphere of searching for common ground." While photographs were taken of the two men together, reporters were not admitted to the meeting, and Jackson later relayed, "It's obvious he's been sick," but "he's getting better."[5]

While Wallace's spirits were raised considerably with another term in the governor's office, his physical health began to show signs of serious problems. Gone were dramatic demonstrations, such as he gave in 1973 when he stood clutching handrails as he addressed the state legislature. Repeated hospitalizations for infections and other nagging health problems persisted, although many expected Wallace would run again in 1986. However, his January 1986 State of the State address prompted serious reservations. Legislators and reporters called Wallace's "pell-mell speech" rambling and disorganized. One Democratic legislator (who asked that his name not be used) told a reporter, "His words were very slurred. Overall, it was poorly delivered. There were a couple of worried moments that he would lose his speech, but this was a partisan crowd, and they weren't disappointed."[6] Three months later, Wallace ended all speculation and gave a tearful April 2, 1986, speech to members of the legislature announcing at age 66 he was retiring from public life, once and for all:

> I would like to be a part of the future myself. But during the past few days I have done a lot of personal evaluation and much soul searching. Some of you younger may not realize that I paid a pretty high price back in 1972. Those five bullets gave me a thorn in the flesh as they did the Apostle Paul. And I prayed that they should be removed, but they were not. I realized that in my own mind that although I am doing very good at the present time, as I grow older the effects of my [health] problems may grow more noticeable. I feel that I must say I have climbed my last political mountain, but there are still some personal hills that I must climb. But for now, I must pass the rope and the pick to another climber and say, "Climb on! Climb on to higher heights! Climb on until you reach the very peak." Then look back and wave at me, for I too will still be climbing. My fellow Alabamians, I bid you a fond and affectionate farewell.[7]

In his remaining years, Wallace continued to welcome political figures from both parties seeking to be in his company for whatever advantage it may hold among Alabama and other conservative voters. Jesse Jackson returned to Wallace's side in 1987 as he prepared a second run for the White House in 1988.[8] In 1993, after fellow southerner, Arkansas governor Bill Clinton was elected president, Wallace asked for Clinton's help in convincing federal officials to reopen the investigation into the 1972 shooting by Arthur Bremer that had left him paralyzed. Wallace wrote to Clinton, "A reopening of this investigation would uncover new evidence and answer questions my family and I have involving this most tragic event." Wallace said he didn't believe Bremer "acted alone" and wanted more answers. A spokesman for Clinton said the president had received Wallace's request and was "taking it under advisement."[9] The need for more answers had not overshadowed Wallace's desire to publicly forgive Bremer and to repeat his desire to meet his would-be assassin in person. No such meeting would ever occur, although Wallace and members of his family wrote to Bremer on more than one occasion. In one of Wallace's letters to Bremer, the former governor wrote, "I am a born-again Christian. I love you. I hope that we can get to know each other better. We have heard of each other a long time." Bremer wrote no reply.[10] Wallace stated publicly in 1985 he did not oppose parole for Bremer, though he noted the irony that his shooter may "walk the streets freely" but that he could not. Later, in 1997 as the Maryland Parole Commission considered again a parole for Bremer, Wallace wrote to them:

There are still many unanswered questions and mysteries surrounding Bremer's attempt on my life, and until he discusses his version of the events—something which he has never done—I am afraid they will go unanswered. . . . By the time Bremer is released from prison in the next century, I will be gone from this Earth. In the meantime, I pray that the Lord will give him solace as well as the strength to become a positive member of society.[11]

Bremer eventually was released from prison in 2007, after serving 35 years of his sentence. He never granted interviews about his case and lives quietly in rural Maryland. As he expressed open forgiveness for Bremer's violent act, Wallace took other public steps to seek the redemption his career (and likely his heart and mind) needed. In March 1995, the former governor, now showing fragility at age 75, held the hands of Southern Christian Leadership Conference president Joseph Lowery as 200 marchers re-enacted the march from Selma to Montgomery and sang, "We Shall Overcome." Lowery told Wallace: "You are a different George Wallace today. We serve a God who is able to make the desert blossom. He can make crooked places straight. He can make the high low and he can exalt the lowly. *You* have come a long way, yes, and *we* have come a long way."[12]

Wallace, suffering from almost complete hearing loss and unable to sit completely upright in his wheelchair, communicated with Lowery and others using a legal pad with handwritten notes. When the marchers were assembled, Wallace was too weak to read his own statement, so Lowery read it for him. Here was the fiery man who had once stood on the same spot to declare his total commitment to segregation, instead now offered in the twilight of his life a simple message of reconciliation: "Those were different days and we are all in our own way different people. We have all learned hard, important lessons in the 30 years that passed. . . . May your lessons never be forgotten and may our history always be remembered."[13] George C. Wallace died on September 13, 1998, at Jackson Hospital in Montgomery, Alabama. He was seventy-nine years old.

NOTES

Introduction

1. Singer, Paul, and Slack, Donovan. (2016, May 4). "Tale of the Tape: The 16 Contenders Trump Has Knocked Out." *USA Today*. Retrieved online at: https://www.usatoday.com/story/news/politics/onpolitics/2016/05/04/trump-knock-out-contenders-republican-nomination-president/83850800/.

2. Martin, Jonathan, and Rappeport, Alan. (2015, July 19). "Donald Trump Says John McCain is No War Hero, Setting Off Another Storm." *New York Times*. Retrieved online at: https://www.nytimes.com/2015/07/19/us/politics/trump-belittles-mccains-war-record.html.

3. Johnson, Jenna. (2015, Dec. 7). "Trump Calls for 'Total and Complete Shutdown of Muslims Entering the United States." *Washington Post*. Retrieved online at: https://www.washingtonpost.com/news/post-politics/wp/2015/12/07/donald-trump-calls-for-total-and-complete-shutdown-of-muslims-entering-the-united-states/.

4. Elliott, Debbie. (2016, April 22). "Is Donald Trump a Modern-Day George Wallace?" NPR Radio *All Things Considered*. Retrieved online at: https://www.npr.org/2016/04/22/475172438/donald-trump-and-george-wallace-riding-the-rage.

5. Elliott, Debbie. (2016, April 22). "Is Donald Trump a Modern-Day George Wallace?" NPR Radio *All Things Considered*. Retrieved online at: https://www.npr.org/2016/04/22/475172438/donald-trump-and-george-wallace-riding-the-rage.

Chapter One

1. Young, Anna M. (2018). "Rhetorics of Fear and Loathing: Donald's Trump's Populist Style." In *Faking the News: What Rhetoric Can Teach Us about Donald J. Trump*. Ryan Skinnell (ed). LaVergne, TN: Ingram Book Company, pp. 23, 29.

2. Wallace remarks quoted in Greenhaw, Wayne. (1976). *Watch Out for George Wallace*. Englewood Cliffs, NJ: Prentice-Hall, Inc., pp. 31–32.

3. Lowndes, Joseph E. (2008). *From the New Deal to the New Right: Race and Southern Origins of Modern Conservatism*. New Haven, CT: Yale University Press, p. 78.

4. Speech of Donald Trump, Youngstown State University, Youngstown, OH, Aug. 15, 2016. Transcript retrieved from: https://www.politico.com/story/2016/08/donald-trump-terrorism-speech-227025.

5. Transcript of WNAC-TV Broadcast, "In Search of a Solution," originally aired Nov. 3, 1963. Transcript from the McClain Library & Archives, University of Southern Mississippi, Box M308, Box 2, Folder 15.

6. Associated Press, Nov. 4, 1963; United Press International, Nov. 4, 1963.

7. Bevard, Charles W., Jr. (1963, Nov. 4). Wallace in Boston. *The Crimson*. Retrieved online at: https://www.thecrimson.com/article/1963/11/4/wallace-in-boston-ppresident-kennedy -will/.

8. Transcript of WNAC-TV Broadcast, "In Search of a Solution," originally aired Nov. 3, 1963. Transcript from the McClain Library & Archives, University of Southern Mississippi, Box M308, Box 2, Folder 15.

9. Transcript of WNAC-TV Broadcast, "In Search of a Solution," originally aired Nov. 3, 1963. Transcript from the McClain Library & Archives, University of Southern Mississippi, Box M308, Box 2, Folder 15.

10. *Boston Globe*, Nov. 5, 1963.

11. *Arizona Daily Star* (Tucson, AZ), Jan. 10, 1964.

12. *Arizona Daily Star* (Tucson, AZ), Jan. 10, 1964.

13. Speech of Gov. George C. Wallace, Harvard University, Cambridge, MA, Nov. 3, 1963. Transcript from the McClain Library & Archives, University of Southern Mississippi, Box M308, Box 1, Folder 15.

14. Speech of Gov. George C. Wallace, Harvard University, Cambridge, MA, Nov. 3, 1963. Transcript from the McClain Library & Archives, University of Southern Mississippi, Box M308, Box 1, Folder 15.

15. Speech of Gov. George C. Wallace, Harvard University, Cambridge, MA, Nov. 3, 1963. Transcript from the McClain Library & Archives, University of Southern Mississippi, Box M308, Box 1, Folder 15.

16. Wallace, George C. (1976). *Stand Up for America*. Garden City, NY: Doubleday & Co., Inc., p. 102.

17. *Minneapolis Star-Tribune*, Feb. 17, 1964.

18. Donald Trump tweet, June 2, 2002; Donald Trump campaign rally remarks, Charlotte, NC, March 2, 2020. Retrieved online at: https://factba.se/transcript/donald-trump-speech -kag-rally-charlotte-north-carolina-march-2-2020.

19. *Minneapolis Star-Tribune*, Feb. 17, 1964.

20. Donald Trump remarks, CNN Republican Presidential Town Hall, Columbia, SC, Feb. 18, 2016; Donald Trump quoted by Jeremy Diamond, CNN.com, March 6, 2016; and Donald Trump quoted by Tim Harris, RealClear Politics, Feb. 9, 2016.

21. Skinnell, Ryan. (2018). "What Passes for Truth in the Trump Era: Telling It Like It Isn't." In *Faking the News: What Rhetoric Can Teach Us about Donald J. Trump*. Ryan Skinnell (ed). LaVergne, TN: Ingram Book Company, p. 89–90.

22. *Milwaukee Sentinel*, March 17, 1964.

23. *Milwaukee Sentinel*, March 17, 1964.

24. *Green Bay (WI) Press-Gazette*, March 17, 1964.

25. *Green Bay (WI) Press-Gazette*, March 17, 1964.

26. Rohler, Lloyd. (2004). *George Wallace: Conservative Populist*. Westport, CT: Praeger, p. 35.

27. *Indianapolis Star*, April 16, 1964.

28. Gov. George C. Wallace speech, Ball State Teachers College, Muncie, IN, May 1, 1964. Retrieved online at: https://dmr.bsu.edu/digital/collection/HistFilmVid/id/9.

29. Associated Press, May 1, 1964.

30. *Birmingham Post-Herald*, May 15, 1964.

31. *Birmingham Post-Herald*, May 15, 1964.

32. *Baltimore Sun*, May 9, 1964.

33. *Baltimore Sun*, March 30, 1964.

34. *Baltimore Sun*, May 16, 1964.

35. Steudeman, Michael J. (2018). "Demagoguery and 'The Donald's' Duplicitous Victimhood." In *Faking the News: What Rhetoric Can Teach Us about Donald J. Trump*. Ryan Skinnell (ed). LaVergne, TN: Ingram Book Company, p. 7.

36. Rohler, Lloyd. (2004.) *George Wallace: Conservative Populist*. Westport, CT: Praeger, pp. 37–38.

37. *Doylestown (PA) Daily Intelligencer*, Oct. 6, 1964.

38. *Los Angeles Times*, Dec. 17, 1967.

39. Lowenthal, Leo, and Guterman, Norbert. (1948). "Portrait of the American Agitator." *Public Opinion Quarterly*, Autumn 1948, p. 420.

40. Guillott, J. (Director), and Naill, Norman E. C. (Executive Producer). (1967). "*George Wallace & California: The Beginning.*" [Video file]. Retrieved online Aug. 21, 2018 from: https://www.c-span.org/video/?4089521/george-wallace-campaign-film Produced by Fidelity Film Productions, Dallas, TX.

41. Associated Press, May 4, 1967.

42. Associated Press, May 4, 1967.

43. *North Tonawanda (NY) News*, Oct. 5, 1968.

44. Associated Press, May 4, 1967.

45. Walker, Samuel E. & Archbold, Carol A. (2020). *The New World of Police Accountability*. Los Angeles: Sage Publications, p. 43.

46. Associated Press, Oct. 5, 1968.

47. *Birmingham News*, May 2, 1967.

48. Associated Press, June 17, 1967.

49. Associated Press, June 17, 1967.

50. United Press International, Sept. 17, 1968.

51. *Northwest Arkansas Times* (Fayetteville), Oct. 15, 1968.

52. *Los Angeles Times*, Dec. 9, 1967.

53. *San Bernardino (CA) County Sun*, Dec. 14, 1967.

54. Speech of Richard Nixon, Republican National Convention, Miami, FL, Aug. 8, 1968. Retrieved online at: http://www.4president.org/speeches/nixon1968acceptance.htm.

55. Speech of Richard Nixon, Republican National Convention, Miami, FL, Aug. 8, 1968. Retrieved online at: http://www.4president.org/speeches/nixon1968acceptance.htm.

56. Speech of Richard Nixon, Republican National Convention, Miami, FL, Aug. 8, 1968. Retrieved online at: http://www.4president.org/speeches/nixon1968acceptance.htm.

57. Humphrey, Hubert H., and Sherman, Norman. (1991) *Hubert H. Humphrey: The Education of a Public Man, My Life and Politics*. Minneapolis: University of Minnesota Press, p. 279.

58. Humphrey, Hubert H., and Sherman, Norman. (1991) *Hubert H. Humphrey: The Education of a Public Man, My Life and Politics*. Minneapolis: University of Minnesota Press, p. 283.

59. Rohler, Lloyd. (2004). *George Wallace: Conservative Populist*. Westport, CT: Praeger, p. 96.

60. Papers of Gov. George C. Wallace, Governors George C. & Lurleen B. Wallace Collection, Alabama Department of Archives and History, Montgomery, AL, Box 42, Folder 8.

61. Lowenthal, Leo, and Guterman, Norbert. (1948). "Portrait of the American Agitator," *Public Opinion Quarterly*, Autumn 1948, pp. 418, 421–22.

62. *Raleigh News & Observer*, April 30, 1972.

63. *Raleigh News & Observer*, April 30, 1972.

64. *Tampa Bay (FL) Times*, Jan. 14, 1972.

65. Gov. George C. Wallace live interview with Frank McGee, NBC *Today Show*, Miami, FL, March 14, 1972. Retrieved online at: https://www.youtube.com/watch?v=yJrqsOh9Hno.

66. Gov. George C. Wallace live interview with Frank McGee, NBC *Today Show*, Miami, FL, March 14, 1972. Retrieved online at: https://www.youtube.com/watch?v=yJrqsOh9Hno.

67. *Washington Post*, Feb. 7, 1972.

68. *Boston Globe*, Feb. 8, 1972.

69. Gov. George C. Wallace live interview with Frank McGee, NBC *Today Show*, Miami, FL, March 14, 1972. Retrieved online at: https://www.youtube.com/watch?v=yJrqsOh9Hno.

70. Lowndes, Joseph E. (2008). *From the New Deal to the New Right: Race and Southern Origins of Modern Conservatism*. New Haven, CT: Yale University Press, p. 79.

71. Text of President Richard M. Nixon March 16, 1972 television address, American Presidency Project. Retrieved online at: https://www.presidency.ucsb.edu/documents/address-the-nation-equal-educational-opportunities-and-school-busing.

72. Text of President Richard M. Nixon March 16, 1972, television address, American Presidency Project. Retrieved online at: https://www.presidency.ucsb.edu/documents/address-the-nation-equal-educational-opportunities-and-school-busing.

73. Buchanan, Patrick J. (2017). *Nixon's White House Wars: The Battles That Made and Broke a President and Divided America Forever*. New York: Crown Publishing Group, Inc., p. 133.

74. *Terre Haute (IN) Tribune-Star*, April 25, 1972.

75. *Birmingham Post-Herald*, Aug. 9, 1975.

76. *Washington Post*, April 7, 1975.

77. *Washington Post*, April 7, 1975.

78. *Pittsburgh Post-Gazette*, Jan. 20, 1976.

79. *Lowell (MA) Sun*, Feb. 15, 1976.

80. *Lowell (MA) Sun*, Feb. 15, 1976.

81. *Lowell (MA) Sun*, Feb. 18, 1976.

82. *Lowell (MA) Sun*, Feb. 21, 1976.

83. *Lowell (MA) Sun*, Feb. 21, 1976.

84. Associated Press, April 25, 1976.

85. Former governor Michael Dukakis telephone interview with the author, Feb. 12, 2012.

86. George Wallace campaign advertisement, *Playground Daily News* (Fort Walton Beach, FL), March 7, 1976.

87. Associated Press, March 13, 1976.

88. United Press International, March 15, 1976.

89. *Decatur (IL) Daily Review*, March 12, 1976.

90. Associated Press, March 27, 1976.

91. Associated Press, March 27, 1976.

92. Associated Press, March 27, 1976.

93. Economist magazine, May 8, 1976.

94. Wills, Garry. (2004). *Lead Time: A Journalist's Education*. Boston, MA: Houghton Mifflin Company, p. 259.

95. *Anderson (IN) Herald-Bulletin*, April 28, 1976.

96. *Terre Haute (IN) Tribune*, April 23, 1976.

97. Roberts-Miller, Patricia. (2017). *Demagoguery and Democracy*. New York: The Experiment, LLC, p. 65.

98. Gunn, Joshua. (2007). "Hystericizing Huey: Emotional Appeals, Desire and the Psychodynamics of Demagoguery." *Western Journal of Communication* 71 (1), p. 1–27; Grant, Stephanie. (2008). *Map of Ireland*. New York: Simon & Schuster, Inc., p. 27.

Chapter Two

1. Roberts-Miller, Patricia. (2017). *Demagoguery and Democracy*. New York: The Experiment, LLC, pp. 1–2.

2. Donald Trump interview, CBS News "*60 Minutes*," originally broadcast July 17, 2016. Transcript reprinted by the *Washington Post*, July 18, 2016. Retrieved online at: https://www.washingtonpost.com/news/the-fix/wp/2016/07/18/donald-trump-is-way-more-humble-than-you-could-possibly-understand/.

3. Statement and Proclamation of Gov. George C. Wallace, University of Alabama, Tuscaloosa, AL, June 11, 1963. Transcript from the Alabama Department of Archives and History. Retrieved online at: https://archives.alabama.gov/govs_list/schooldoor.html.

4. *Montgomery (AL) Advertiser*, Sept. 16, 1963; *Birmingham (AL) News*, Sept. 16, 1963.

5. *Montgomery (AL) Advertiser*, Sept. 16, 1963; *Birmingham (AL) News*, Sept. 16, 1963.

6. President John F. Kennedy, Statement by the President on the Sunday Bombing in Birmingham, Sept. 16, 1963. Indexed by Gerhard Peters and John T. Woolley, The American Presidency Project. Retrieved online at: https://www.presidency.ucsb.edu/node/235791.

7. Gallagher, Gary W. (2000). *The Myth of the Lost Cause and Civil War History*. Bloomington: Indiana University Press, p. 1.

8. Speech of Gov. George C. Wallace, Harvard University, Cambridge, MA, Nov. 3, 1963. Transcript from the McClain Library & Archives, University of Southern Mississippi, Box M308, Box 1, Folder 15.

9. Johnson, Paul Elliott. (2017). "The Art of Masculine Victimhood: Donald's Trump's Demagoguery." *Women's Studies in Communication* 40 (3), p. 238.

10. *Baltimore Sun*, March 30, 1964.

11. *Baltimore Sun*, March 30, 1964.

12. *Baltimore Sun*, March 30, 1964.

13. *Indianapolis Star*, April 16, 1964.

14. Associated Press, April 19, 1964.

15. Associated Press, April 29, 1964.

16. United Press International, April 22, 1964.

17. United Press International, April 22, 1964.

18. United Press International, April 22, 1964.

19. *South Bend (IN) Tribune*, April 24, 1964.

20. *Valparaiso (IN) Vidette-Messenger*, April 27, 1964.

21. *Terre Haute (IN) Tribune-Star*, April 30, 1964.

22. *Indianapolis News*, April 25, 1964.

23. Associated Press, April 26, 1964.

24. Associated Press, April 24, 1964.

25. Associated Press, May 2, 1964.

26. Associated Press, May 2, 1964.

27. Associated Press, May 9, 1964.

28. *Baltimore Sun*, May 11, 1964.

29. *Cumberland (MD) Evening Times*, May 7, 1964.

30. *Baltimore Sun*, May 8, 1964.

31. Roberts-Miller, Patricia. (2017). *Demagoguery and Democracy*. New York: The Experiment, LLC, pp. 44–45.

32. *Chicago Tribune*, Sept. 16, 1964.

33. *Chicago Tribune*, Sept. 17, 1964.

34. *Montgomery (AL) Advertiser*, March 7, 1965.

35. *Alabama Journal* (Montgomery, AL), March 8, 1965.

36. United Press International, March 8, 1965.

37. Miller-Roberts, Patricia. (2017). *Demagoguery and Democracy*. New York: The Experiment, LLC, pp. 87–88.

38. Speech of Ronald Reagan, "A Time for Choosing," Oct. 27, 1964, Los Angeles, CA. Retrieved online at: https://www.americanrhetoric.com/speeches/ronaldreaganatimefor choosing.htm.

39. Associated Press, May 21, 1967.

40. Associated Press, May 21, 1967.

41. *New York Times*, June 19, 1967.

42. *New York Times*, June 19, 1967.

43. Associated Press, Sept. 7, 1968.

44. 1968 Wallace Campaign Files. George C. Wallace Papers, Box 9, Folder 9. Alabama Department of Archives and History, Montgomery, AL.

45. *San Bernardino (CA) County Sun*, Dec. 14, 1967.

46. *San Bernardino (CA) County Sun*, Dec. 14, 1967.

47. *Fremont (CA) Argus*, Dec. 15, 1967.

48. 1968 Wallace Campaign Files. George C. Wallace Papers, Box 2, Folder 10. Alabama Department of Archives and History, Montgomery, AL.

49. *Santa Cruz (CA) Sentinel*, Dec. 12, 1967.

50. *Santa Rosa (CA) Press-Democrat*, Dec. 13, 1967; *San Mateo Times*, Dec. 13, 1967; *San Bernardino County Sun*, Dec. 13, 1967.

51. *Chula Vista (CA) Star-News*, Dec. 7, 1967.

52. *Los Angeles Times*, Nov. 1, 1967.

53. *Chula Vista (CA) Star-News*, Dec. 10, 1967.

54. *Chula Vista (CA) Star-News*, Dec. 10, 1967.

55. *Long Beach (CA) Independent*, Jan. 4, 1968.

56. Guillott, J. (Director), and Naill, Norman E. C. (Executive Producer). (1967). *George Wallace & California: The Beginning*. [Video file]. Retrieved online Aug. 21, 2018 from: https://www.c-span.org/video/?4089521/george-wallace-campaign-film Produced by Fidelity Film Productions, Dallas, TX.

57. Associated Press, Feb. 8, 1968.

58. *Nevada State Journal* (Reno, NV), Jan. 10, 1968.

59. *Orlando Evening Star*, Jan. 13, 1972.

60. Associated Press, May 1, 1972.

61. United Press International, April 30, 1972.

62. *Indianapolis Star*, May 3, 1972.

63. *Detroit Free Press*, May 12, 1972.

64. *Detroit Free Press*, May 14, 1972.

65. CBS Evening News, May 2, 1972. Retrieved online at: https://www.youtube.com/watch?v=LxUIAMba-hE.

66. Associated Press, April 14, 1972.

67. Associated Press, April 14, 1972.

68. Associated Press, April 15, 1972.

69. *Detroit Free Press*, April 16, 1972.

70. *Detroit Free Press*, May 4, 1972.

71. Associated Press, May 25, 1975.

72. *Detroit Free Press*, Feb. 4, 1976.

73. Thimmesch, Nick. (1975, June 9). "The Grass-Roots Dollar Chase: Ready on the Right." *New York Magazine*, p. 58.

74. Thimmesch, Nick. (1975, June 9). "The Grass-Roots Dollar Chase: Ready on the Right." *New York Magazine*, p. 58.

75. United Press International, April 22, 1976.

76. *Northwest Florida Daily News* (Fort Walton Beach, FL), March 7, 1976.

77. Associated Press, Feb. 28, 1976.

78. *Los Angeles Times*, April 1, 1976.

79. Anderson, Patrick. (1994). *Electing Jimmy Carter: The Campaign of 1976*. Baton Rouge: Louisiana State University Press, p. 6.

80. *Alabama Journal* (Montgomery, AL), June 9, 1976.

81. *Montgomery Advertiser*, June 13, 1976.

82. *Montgomery Advertiser*, June 13, 1976.

83. Walter Mondale email interview with the author, April 6, 2016.

84. James Free "Exit Interview" conducted on Dec. 16, 1980, archive of the Jimmy Carter Presidential Library. Retrieved online at: https://www.jimmycarterlibrary.gov/assets/documents/oral_histories/exit_interviews/Free.pdf.

85. Walter Mondale email interview with the author, April 6, 2016.

86. Walter Mondale email interview with the author, April 6, 2016.

Chapter Three

1. Roberts-Miller, Patricia. (2017). *Demagoguery and Democracy*. New York: The Experiment, LLC, p. 61.

2. Edelman, Murray. (1988). *Constructing the Political Spectacle*. Chicago: University of Chicago Press, pp. 12, 26.

3. Associated Press, July 11, 1968.

4. United Press International, Jan. 24, 1968.

5. *Anniston (AL) Star*, Sept. 20, 1968.

6. *Anniston (AL) Star*, Sept. 20, 1968.

7. Roberts-Miller, Patricia. (2017). *Demagoguery and Democracy*. New York: The Experiment, LLC, p. 63.

8. Candidacy announcement by Donald Trump, Trump Tower, New York, NY, June 15, 2016. Retrieved online at: https://time.com/3923128/donald-trump-announcement-speech/.

9. Wingard, Jennifer. (2018). "Trump's Not Just One Bad Apple: He's the Product of a Spoiled Bunch." In *Faking the News: What Rhetoric Can Teach Us about Donald J. Trump*. Ryan Skinnell, ed. LaVergne, TN: Ingram Book Company, p. 41.

10. Speech by Gov. George C. Wallace, South Carolina Broadcasters Association meeting, Myrtle Beach, SC, July 15, 1963. Transcript from the McCain Library & Archives, University of Southern Mississippi, M308 Box 1, Folder 12.

11. Speech by Gov. George C. Wallace, South Carolina Broadcasters Association meeting, Myrtle Beach, SC, July 15, 1963. Transcript from the McCain Library & Archives, University of Southern Mississippi, M308 Box 1, Folder 12.

12. Speech of Gov. George C. Wallace, Miami Area Kiwanis Clubs, Miami, FL, July 24, 1963. Transcript from the McCain Library & Archives, University of Southern Mississippi, M308, Box 1, Folder 13.

13. *Minneapolis Star-Tribune*, Feb. 18, 1964.

14. Associated Press, March 23, 1964.

15. *Washington Daily*, University of Washington, Jan. 15, 1964.

16. *New York Times*, Oct. 19, 2016.

17. Davis, Patricia G. (2017). "Reversal of Injury in the Obama Era: *Shelby County v. Holder*, Resentment, Moral Authority and the Discursive Construction of White Victimhood. *Rhetoric Review* 36 (4), pp. 320–31.

18. *Milwaukee Journal*, April 3, 1964.

19. *Milwaukee Journal*, April 3, 1964.

20. United Press International, March 13, 1964.

21. Associated Press, March 18, 1964.

22. *Wisconsin Jewish Chronicle*, March 27, 1964.

23. *Stevens Point (WI) Journal*, April 1, 1964.

24. United Press International, March 24, 1964.

25. Fowler, R. B. (2008). *Wisconsin Votes: An Electoral History*. Madison: University of Wisconsin Press.

26. Associated Press, May 3, 1964.

27. Associated Press, May 3, 1964.

28. Associated Press, May 3, 1964.

29. Associated Press, May 3, 1964.

30. Associated Press, May 3, 1964.

31. Associated Press, May 3, 1964.

32. George C. Wallace, May 1, 1964 Speech, Ball State Teachers College, Muncie, IN. Transcript from Ball State University Libraries, Archives & Special Collections.

33. George C. Wallace, May 1, 1964 Speech, Ball State Teachers College, Muncie, IN. Transcript from Ball State University Libraries, Archives & Special Collections.

34. *Salisbury (MD) Times*, May 12, 1964.

35. *Jackson (MS) Clarion-Ledger*, June 26, 1964.

36. Speech of Gov. George C. Wallace, Political Campaign Rally, Jackson, MS, June 25, 1964. Transcript from McClain Library & Archives, University of Southern Mississippi, M308, Box. 1, Folder 31.

37. Speech of Gov. George C. Wallace, Political Campaign Rally, Jackson, MS, June 25, 1964. Transcript from McClain Library & Archives, University of Southern Mississippi, M308, Box. 1, Folder 31.

38. Remarks of President Lyndon B. Johnson, East Room, White House, July 2, 1964. Transcript provided by the American Presidency Project, retrieved online at: http://www.presidency.ucsb.edu/ws/index.php?pid=26361.

39. *Anniston (AL) Star*, July 5, 1964.

40. *Anniston (AL) Star*, July 5, 1964.

41. United Press International, July 5, 1964.

42. Speech of Gov. George C. Wallace, Independence Day Rally, Atlanta, GA, July 4, 1964. Transcript from McClain Library and Archives, University of Southern Mississippi, M308, Box 1, Folder 34.

43. Remarks of Gov. George C. Wallace, CBS News *Face the Nation* broadcast of July 19, 1964. Transcript from the McCain Library and Archives, University of Southern Mississippi, M308, Box 2, Folder 18.

44. Remarks of Gov. George C. Wallace, CBS News *Face the Nation* broadcast of July 19, 1964. Transcript from the McCain Library and Archives, University of Southern Mississippi, M308, Box 2, Folder 18.

45. White, Theodore H. (1969). *The Making of the President 1968*. New York: Atheneum Publishers, p. 344.

46. George C. Wallace remarks, *Meet the Press*, NBC. Originally broadcast June 30, 1968. Lawrence E. Spivak, host.

47. *Alabama Journal* (Montgomery, AL), June 5, 1968.

48. *Alabama Journal* (Montgomery, AL), June 5, 1968.

49. Associated Press, June 14, 1968.

50. Associated Press, June 12, 1968.

51. Guillott, J. (Director), and Naill, Norman E. C. (Executive Producer). (1967). *George Wallace & California: The Beginning*. [Video file]. Retrieved online Aug. 21, 2018 from: https://www.c-span.org/video/?4089521/george-wallace-campaign-film Produced by Fidelity Film Productions, Dallas, TX.

52. White, Theodore H. (1969). *The Making of the President 1968*. New York: Atheneum Publishers, p. 364.

53. *New York Times*, Aug. 19, 1968.

54. *Boston Globe*, Oct. 1, 1968.

55. *Boston Globe*, Oct. 1, 1968.

56. Young, Anna M. (2018). "Rhetorics of Fear and Loathing: Donald Trump's Populist Style." In *Faking the News: What Rhetoric Can Teach Us about Donald J. Trump*. Ryan Skinnell, ed. LaVergne, TN: Ingram Book Company, p. 34.

57. *Detroit Free-Press*, Oct. 2, 1968.

58. *Detroit Free-Press*, Oct. 2, 1968.

59. *Flint (MI) Journal*, Feb. 10, 2008.

60. Associated Press, July 7, 1968.

61. Associated Press, July 7, 1968.

62. *New York Times*, Aug. 19, 1968.

63. Associated Press, Dec. 20, 1971.

64. John J. Synon national column, from *Cottonport (LA) Leader*, Jan. 14, 1971.

65. "Settin' the Woods on Fire," Daniel McCabe & Paul Stekler, directors. (2000). *American Experience* [PBS Television Series]. Retrieved online at: https://vimeo.com/116273297.

66. "Settin' the Woods on Fire," Daniel McCabe & Paul Stekler, directors. (2000). *American Experience* [PBS Television Series]. Retrieved online at: https://vimeo.com/116273297.

67. "Settin' the Woods on Fire," Daniel McCabe & Paul Stekler, directors. (2000). *American Experience* [PBS Television Series]. Retrieved online at: https://vimeo.com/116273297.

68. Carter, Dan T. (2000). *The Politics of Rage: George Wallace, the Origins of the New Conservatism, and the Transformation of American Politics*. Baton Rouge: Louisiana State University Press, p. 416.

69. Peggy Wallace Kennedy telephone interview with the author, Feb. 21, 2016.

70. Dan King Thomasson, interview with the author, Dec. 18, 2015.

71. Associated Press, Feb. 28, 1972.

72. Associated Press, April 16, 1972.

73. Associated Press, May 5, 1972.

74. Associated Press, May 5, 1972.

75. *Philadelphia Inquirer*, April 23, 1972.

76. *Philadelphia Inquirer*, April 23, 1972.

77. *Franklin (IN) Daily Journal*, April 26, 1972.

78. *Indianapolis Star*, April 26, 1972.

79. *Franklin (IN) Daily Journal*, April 26, 1972.

80. Evans & Novack column, *Tucson (AZ) Citizen*, Feb. 28, 1976.

81. Evans & Novack column, *Tucson (AZ) Citizen*, Feb. 28, 1976.

82. Lowndes, Joseph E. (2008). *From the New Deal to the New Right: Race and Southern Origins of Modern Conservatism*. New Haven, CT: Yale University Press, pp. 87–88.

83. Lowndes, Joseph E. (2008). *From the New Deal to the New Right: Race and Southern Origins of Modern Conservatism*. New Haven, CT: Yale University Press, p. 87.

84. Associated Press, May 18, 1976.

85. Johnson, Paul Elliott. (2017). "The Art of Masculine Victimhood: Donald Trump's Demagoguery." *Women's Studies in Communication* 40 (3), p. 230.

Chapter Four

1. Lardner, George & Loh, Jules. (1969, May 1). "The Wonderful World of George Wallace." *Esquire* magazine.

2. Edelman, Murray. (1988). *Constructing the Political Spectacle*. Chicago: University of Chicago Press, p. 30.

3. Kellner, D. (2017). "Guy Debord, Donald Trump, and the Politics of Spectacle." Briziarelli, M. and Armano, E. (eds.) *The Spectacle 2.0: Reading Debord in the Context of Digital Capitalism*. London: University of Westminster Press, p. 1.

4. Edelman, Murray. (1988). *Constructing the Political Spectacle*. Chicago: University of Chicago Press, p. 120.

5. Yates, Heather E. (2019) *The Politics of Spectacle and Emotion in the 2016 Presidential Campaign*. Cham, Switzerland: Springer Nature Switzerland AG, p. 18.

6. Edelman, Murray. (1988). *Constructing the Political Spectacle*. Chicago: University of Chicago Press, p. 120.

7. Edelman, Murray. (1988). *Constructing the Political Spectacle*. Chicago: University of Chicago Press, p. 123.

8. The Hill, Oct. 14, 2016. Retrieved online at: https://thehill.com/blogs/ballot-box/presidential-races/301147-cnn-president-airing-so-many-full-trump-rallies-was-a.

9. Hollywood Reporter, Feb. 29, 2016. Retrieved online at: https://www.hollywoodreporter.com/news/leslie-moonves-donald-trump-may-871464.

10. *Montgomery Advertiser*, Nov. 3, 1963.

11. United Press International, Oct. 16, 1963.

12. *Montgomery Advertiser*, Nov. 3, 1963.

13. Associated Press, Nov. 3, 1963.

14. *Boston Globe*, Nov. 5, 1963.

15. *Boston Globe*, Nov. 5, 1963.

16. Speech of Gov. George C. Wallace, Harvard University, Cambridge, MA, Nov. 3, 1963. Transcript from the McClain Library & Archives, University of Southern Mississippi, Box M308, Box 1, Folder 15.

17. Speech of Gov. George C. Wallace, Dartmouth College, Hanover, NH, Nov. 5, 1963. Transcript from the McClain Library & Archives, University of Southern Mississippi, Box M308, Box 1, Folder 16.

18. *Boston Globe*, Nov. 6, 1963.

19. *Anniston (AL) Star*, Nov. 7, 1963.

20. The Sophian, Smith College, Northampton, MA, Nov. 7, 1963. Article from Smith College Special Collections, Young Library, Northampton, MA.

21. The Sophian, Smith College, Northampton, MA, Oct. 15, 1963. Article from Smith College Special Collections, Young Library, Northampton, MA.

22. The Sophian, Smith College, Northampton, MA, Nov. 7, 1963. Article from Smith College Special Collections, Young Library, Northampton, MA.

23. Associated Press, Nov. 7, 1963.

24. The Sophian, Smith College, Northampton, MA, Nov. 7, 1963. Article from Smith College Special Collections, Young Library, Northampton, MA.

25. Speech of Gov. George C. Wallace, Brown University, Providence, RI, Nov. 7, 1963. Transcript from the McClain Library & Archives, University of Southern Mississippi, Box M308, Box 1, Folder 17.

26. Speech of Gov. George C. Wallace, Brown University, Providence, RI, Nov. 7, 1963. Transcript from the McClain Library & Archives, University of Southern Mississippi, Box M308, Box 1, Folder 17.

27. Speech of Gov. George C. Wallace, Brown University, Providence, RI, Nov. 7, 1963. Transcript from the McClain Library & Archives, University of Southern Mississippi, Box M308, Box 1, Folder 17.

28. Rohler, Lloyd. (2004). *George Wallace: Conservative Populist*. Westport, CT: Praeger, p. 97.

29. *Montgomery Advertiser*, Nov. 24, 1963.

30. Associated Press, Jan. 8, 1964.

31. Associated Press, Jan. 9, 1964.

32. *Los Angeles Times*, Jan. 11, 1964; Archives of the Communication Studies Department, University of California, Los Angeles.

33. *Los Angeles Times*, Jan. 11, 1964; Archives of the Communication Studies Department, University of California, Los Angeles.

34. Associated Press, Jan. 13, 1964.

35. Associated Press, Jan. 15, 1964.

36. *Capital Journal* (Salem, OR), Jan. 14, 1964.

37. *Capital Journal* (Salem, OR), Jan. 14, 1964.

38. *Capital Journal* (Salem, OR), Jan. 14, 1964.

39. *Capital Journal* (Salem, OR), Jan. 14, 1964.

40. *Capital Journal* (Salem, OR), Jan. 14, 1964.

41. *Montgomery Advertiser*, Jan. 15, 1964.

42. *Washington Daily*, University of Washington, Jan. 15, 1964.

43. Associated Press, Jan. 15, 1964.

44. *Montgomery Advertiser*, Jan. 17, 1964.

45. *Minneapolis Star-Tribune*, Feb. 18, 1964.

46. *Appleton (WI) Post-Crescent*, March 18, 1964.

47. *Milwaukee Sentinel*, March 19, 1964.

48. Haney, R.C. (1978, Summer). "Wallace in Wisconsin: The Presidential Primary of 1964." *Wisconsin Magazine of History* 61 (4).

49. Associated Press, March 23, 1964.

50. *Milwaukee Sentinel*, March 25, 1964.

51. *Milwaukee Sentinel*, March 25, 1964.

52. *St. Norbert (WI) Times*, April 3, 1964 (courtesy of Mulva Library, St. Norbert College).

53. *Milwaukee Journal*, April 3, 1964.

54. *Milwaukee Journal*, April 3, 1964.

55. *Milwaukee Journal*, April 3, 1964.

56. *Milwaukee Journal*, April 3, 1964.

57. *Milwaukee Journal*, April 3, 1964.

58. *Milwaukee Journal*, April 6, 1964.

59. *Milwaukee Journal*, April 6, 1964.

60. *Milwaukee Journal*, April 6, 1964.

61. *Kenosha (WI) News*, April 9, 1964.

62. *Milwaukee Journal*, April 6, 1964.

63. *Milwaukee Journal*, April 6, 1964.

64. *Indianapolis Star*, April 14, 1964.

65. *Indianapolis Star*, April 16, 1964.

66. Edelman, Murray. (1988). *Constructing the Political Spectacle*. Chicago: University of Chicago Press, p. 125.

67. *Indianapolis Star*, April 16, 1964.

68. *Indianapolis Star*, April 16, 1964.

69. Associated Press, April 21, 1964.

70. Associated Press, April 21, 1964.

71. United Press International, April 24, 1964.

72. United Press International, April 24, 1964.

73. United Press International, April 24, 1964.

74. *Indianapolis News*, April 24, 1964.

75. *Indianapolis News*, April 24, 1964.

76. *Indianapolis News*, April 24, 1964.

77. United Press International, April 24, 1964.

78. *Indianapolis Recorder*, May 2, 1964.

79. Associated Press, April 29, 1964.

80. United Press International, April 31, 1964.

81. United Press International, April 31, 1964.

82. *South Bend (IN) Tribune*, April 31, 1964.

83. George C. Wallace, May 1, 1964, Speech, Ball State Teachers College, Muncie, IN. Transcript from Ball State University Libraries, Archives & Special Collections.

84. *Baltimore Sun*, March 12, 1964.

85. *Baltimore Sun*, May 1, 1964.

86. *Baltimore Sun*, May 1, 1964.

87. *Baltimore Sun*, May 1, 1964.

88. *Baltimore Sun*, April 9, 1964.

89. *Baltimore Sun*, April 9, 1964.

90. *Salisbury (MD) Times*, May 12, 1964.

91. *Salisbury (MD) Times*, May 12, 1964.

92. Associated Press, May 11, 1964.

93. *Baltimore Sun*, May 12, 1964.

94. *Baltimore Afro-American*, May 12, 1964.

95. *Baltimore Sun*, May 9, 1964.

96. *Baltimore Sun*, May 9, 1964.

97. *Birmingham Post-Herald*, May 15, 1964.

98. *Baltimore Sun*, May 17, 1964.

99. Lardner, George, and Loh, Jules. (1969, May 1). "The Wonderful World of George Wallace." *Esquire* magazine.

100. Associated Press, May 21, 1967.

101. *Chula Vista (CA) Star-News*, Dec. 10, 1967.

102. *Freemont (CA) Argus*, Dec. 15, 1967.

103. United Press International, Nov. 4, 1967.

104. Associated Press, March 4, 1968.

105. Associated Press, March 5–6, 1968.

106. *Nashville Tennessean*, Aug. 5, 1968.

107. Peggy Wallace Kennedy telephone interview with the author, Feb. 21, 2016.

108. Peggy Wallace Kennedy telephone interview with the author, Feb. 21, 2016.

109. Peggy Wallace Kennedy telephone interview with the author, Feb. 21, 2016.

110. Lyman, Brian. (2018, Aug. 17). "Stand Up for America: George Wallace's 1968 Presidential Campaign was Chaotic—and Prophetic." *Montgomery Advertiser*. Retrieved online at: https://www.montgomeryadvertiser.com/story/news/politics/2018/08/17/stand-up-america-george-wallaces-chaotic-prophetic-campaign/873126002/.

111. Yates, Heather E. (2019) *The Politics of Spectacle and Emotion in the 2016 Presidential Campaign*. Cham, Switzerland: Springer Nature Switzerland AG, p. 18.

112. Dan King Thomasson telephone interview with the author, Dec. 18, 2015.

113. *Chicago Tribune*, Oct. 1, 1968.

114. *Chicago Tribune*, Oct. 1, 1968.

115. *Los Angeles Times*, Oct. 1, 1968.

116. *Boston Globe*, Oct. 1, 1968.

117. *Detroit Free-Press*, Oct. 2, 1968.

118. *New York Times*, Oct. 1, 1968.

119. *Detroit Free-Press*, Oct. 2, 1968.

120. United Press International, Oct. 31, 1968.

121. Associated Press, Oct. 30, 1968.

122. Associated Press, Oct. 30, 1968.

123. Bartlett, Charles. (1968, Oct. 29). *Zeal for Wallace Fading: Exposure Was the Enemy*. Publishers-Hall Syndicate.

124. *Cincinnati Enquirer*, Sept. 28, 1968.

125. *Hammond (IN) Times*, Aug. 18, 1968.

126. *Orlando Sentinel*, Sept. 23, 1968.

127. *Orlando Sentinel*, Sept. 23, 1968.

128. *Indianapolis News*, Sept. 26, 1968.

129. *Cincinnati Enquirer*, Sept. 28, 1968.

130. United Press International, Sept. 26, 1968.

131. *Chicago Tribune*, Oct. 1, 1968.

132. Associated Press, Oct. 24, 1968.

133. Associated Press, Oct. 15, 1968.

134. Associated Press, Oct. 15, 1968.

135. United Press International, Oct. 17, 1968.

136. United Press International, Oct. 17, 1968.

137. Associated Press, Oct. 14, 1968.

138. Associated Press, Oct. 14, 1968.

139. *Newsday*, Oct. 26, 1968.

140. *Newsday*, Oct. 26, 1968.

141. *Des Moines Register*, Oct. 11, 1968.

142. *Des Moines Register*, Oct. 11, 1968.

143. *Des Moines Register*, Oct. 11, 1968.

144. *Des Moines Register*, Oct. 11, 1968.

145. Carter, Dan T. (2001). "Good copy." In Robert H. Giles and Robert W. Snyder (eds.). *1968: Year of Media Decision*. New Brunswick, NJ: Transaction Publishers, p. 38.

146. United Press International, Oct. 25, 1968.

147. *New York, Times*, Oct. 25, 1968.

148. *New York, Times*, Oct. 25, 1968.

149. *New York Times*, Oct. 25, 1968.

150. George Wallace, October 24, 1968 speech transcript, Madison Square Garden, New York City. University of Michigan Archive. Retrieved online at: http://www-personal.umd .umich.edu/~ppennock/doc-Wallace.htm.

151. Lardner, George, and Loh, Jules. (1969, May 1). "The Wonderful World of George Wallace." *Esquire* magazine.

152. Loh, Jules. (1972, Oct. 1). "Lonesome George." *Esquire* magazine.

153. Associated Press, May 10, 1972.

154. Arthur Bremer Personal Diary, recovered from his vehicle by FBI, May 16, 1972. Dearborn references, p. 249–56. Retrieved online at: https://archive.org/details/nsia-Bremer ArthurDiaryBookof/.

155. Arthur Bremer Personal Diary, recovered from his vehicle by FBI, May 16, 1972. Dearborn references, p. 249–56. Retrieved online at: https://archive.org/details/nsia-Bremer ArthurDiaryBookof/.

156. Arthur Bremer Personal Diary, recovered from his vehicle by FBI, May 16, 1972. Dearborn references, p. 249–56. Retrieved online at: https://archive.org/details/nsia-Bremer ArthurDiaryBookof/.

157. Arthur Bremer Personal Diary, recovered from his vehicle by FBI, May 16, 1972. Dearborn references, p. 249–56. Retrieved online at: https://archive.org/details/nsia-Bremer ArthurDiaryBookof/.

158. Associated Press, May 11, 1972.

159. United Press International, May 11, 1972.

160. *Traverse City (MI) Record-Eagle*, May 11, 1972.

161. Arthur Bremer Personal Diary, recovered from his vehicle by FBI, May 16, 1972. Cadillac references, p. 256–58. Retrieved online at: https://archive.org/details/nsia-Bremer ArthurDiaryBookof/.

162. Arthur Bremer Personal Diary, recovered from his vehicle by FBI, May 16, 1972. Cadillac references, p. 256–58. Retrieved online at: https://archive.org/details/nsia-Bremer ArthurDiaryBookof/.

163. *New York Times*, May 29, 1972.

164. *New York Times*, May 29, 1972.

165. Arthur Bremer Personal Diary, recovered from his vehicle by FBI, May 16, 1972. Cadillac references, p. 259. Retrieved online at: https://archive.org/details/nsia-Bremer ArthurDiaryBookof/.

166. Arthur Bremer Personal Diary, recovered from his vehicle by FBI, May 16, 1972. Cadillac references, p. 261. Retrieved online at: https://archive.org/details/nsia-Bremer ArthurDiaryBookof/.

167. *Birmingham News*, May 7, 1972.

168. *New York Times*, May 7, 1972.

169. Associated Press, May 15, 1972.

170. *Chicago Daily News*, May 27, 1972.

171. *New York Times*, May 29, 1972.

172. Associated Press, May 16, 1972.

173. *Baltimore Sun*, May 16, 1972.

174. Steve Bell telephone interview with the author, Jan. 4, 2015.

175. *Baltimore Sun*, May 16, 1972.

176. *Baltimore Sun*, May 16, 1972.

177. *Baltimore Sun*, May 16, 1972.

178. *Baltimore Sun*, May 16, 1972.

179. Federal Bureau of Investigation, Archived Report on the Assassination Attempt on George Wallace. Retrieved online at: https://archive.org/details/AssassinationAttemptOn GeorgeWallace/page/n1.

180. WALA-TV Report, Mobile, Ala., 1996. Retrieved online at: https://www.youtube .com/watch?v=oWmtPlcLwag&feature=youtu.be.

181. Wallace, George C. (1976). *Stand Up for America*. Garden City, NY: Doubleday & Co., Inc., p. 3–4.

182. Wallace, George C. (1976). *Stand Up for America*. Garden City, NY: Doubleday & Co., Inc., p. 6.

183. Steve Bell telephone interview with the author, Jan. 4, 2015.

184. Peggy Wallace Kennedy telephone interview with the author, Feb. 21, 2016.

185. Peggy Wallace Kennedy telephone interview with the author, Feb. 21, 2016.

186. Wallace, George, Jr., and Gregory, James. (1975). *The Wallace's of Alabama: My Family*. Chicago: Follett Publishing Co., p. 206.

187. Wallace, George, Jr., and Gregory, James. (1975). *The Wallace's of Alabama: My Family*. Chicago: Follett Publishing Co., p. 214.

188. Peggy Wallace Kennedy telephone interview with the author, Feb. 21, 2016.

189. Peggy Wallace Kennedy telephone interview with the author, Feb. 21, 2016.

190. Steve Bell telephone interview with the author, Jan. 4, 2015.

191. *Iowa City (IA) Press-Citizen*, July 3, 1972.

192. *Iowa City (IA) Press-Citizen*, July 3, 1972.

193. Steve Bell telephone interview with the author, Jan. 4, 2015.

194. ABC Evening News report, archival video of July 7, 1972. Retrieved online at: https:// www.youtube.com/watch?v=cdhqD7IfW9M.

195. *Montgomery (AL) Advertiser*, July 8, 1972.

196. Associated Press, July 8, 1972.

197. Associated Press, July 8, 1972.

198. United Press, International, July 2, 1972.

199. *New York Times*, July 12, 1972.

200. *New York Times*, July 12, 1972.

201. *New York Times*, July 12, 1972.

202. *New York Times*, July 12, 1972.

203. *New York Times*, July 12, 1972.

204. *Orlando Sentinel*, July 12, 1972.

205. *Anniston (AL) Star*, July 12, 1972.

206. *Montgomery Advertiser*, July 12, 1972.

207. Wallace, George C. (1976). *Stand Up for America*. Garden City, NY: Doubleday & Co., Inc., pp. 165–66.

208. Associated Press, Feb. 16, 1976.

209. *Manchester (CT) Journal-Inquirer*, Feb. 25, 1976.

210. *Manchester (CT) Journal-Inquirer*, Feb. 25, 1976.

211. *Lowell (MA) Sun*, Feb. 21, 1976.

212. *Lowell (MA) Sun*, Feb. 15, 1976.

213. *Lowell (MA) Sun*, Feb. 15, 1976.

214. *Lowell (MA) Sun*, Feb. 15, 1976.

215. United Press International, Feb. 3, 1976.

216. United Press International, March 31, 1976.

217. United Press International, March 31, 1976.

218. Associated Press, April 2, 1976.

219. Associated Press, May 13, 1976.

220. United Press International, May 18, 1976.

221. *Detroit Free Press*, May 15, 1976.

222. Gannett News Service, May 18, 1976.

223. Gannett News Service, May 18, 1976.

224. United Press International, May 18, 1976.

225. United Press International, May 18, 1976.

226. United Press International, May 18, 1976.

227. *Pittsburgh Press*, May 18, 1976.

228. Stuckey, Mary E. (2017, June 15). "The Politics of Spectacle." Current Commentary, Political Communication. *Communication Currents*. Washington, DC: National Communication Association.

Chapter Five

1. Yates, Heather E. (2019). *The Politics of Spectacle and Emotion in the 2016 Presidential Campaign*. Cham, Switzerland: Springer Nature Switzerland AG, pp. 19–20.

2. Carlson, Jody. (1981). *George C. Wallace and the Politics of Powerlessness: The Wallace Campaigns for the Presidency, 1964–1976*. New Brunswick, NJ: Transaction Books, p. 278.

3. Carlson, Jody. (1981). *George C. Wallace and the Politics of Powerlessness: The Wallace Campaigns for the Presidency, 1964–1976*. New Brunswick, NJ: Transaction Books, p. 278.

4. Carlson, Jody. (1981). *George C. Wallace and the Politics of Powerlessness: The Wallace Campaigns for the Presidency, 1964–1976*. New Brunswick, NJ: Transaction Books, p. 278.

5. Carter, Dan T. (2001). "Good copy." In Robert H. Giles & Robert W. Snyder (eds.). *1968: Year of Media Decision*. New Brunswick, NJ: Transaction Publishers, pp. 38–39.

6. Remarks of Richard M. Nixon, Beverly Hilton Hotel, Los Angeles, CA, Nov. 6, 1962. Retrieved online at: https://www.nixonfoundation.org/2017/11/55-years-ago-last-press -conference/.

7. Sugars, Stephanie. (2019, Jan. 30). "From 'fake news' to 'enemy of the people': An anatomy of Trump's tweets. Committee to Project Journalists. Retrieved online at: https:// cpj.org/2019/01/trump-twitter-press-fake-news-enemy-people/.

8. Shafer, Jack. (2015, Aug. 10). "Donald Trump: American Demagogue." Politico.com. Retrieved online at: https://www.politico.com/magazine/story/2015/08/dont-write-trumps -obit-yet-121232.

9. Achter, Paul J. (2018). "Great Television: Trump and the Shadow Archetype." In Ryan Skinnell (ed.). *Faking the News: What Rhetoric Can Teach Us about Donald J. Trump.* LaVergne, TN: Ingram Book Company, pp. 108–9.

10. Achter, Paul J. (2018). "Great Television: Trump and the Shadow Archetype." In Ryan Skinnell (ed.). *Faking the News: What Rhetoric Can Teach Us about Donald J. Trump.* LaVergne, TN: Ingram Book Company, p. 119.

11. Speech by Gov. George C. Wallace, South Carolina Broadcasters Association meeting, Myrtle Beach, SC, July 15, 1963. Transcript from the McCain Library & Archives, University of Southern Mississippi, M308 Box 1, Folder 12.

12. Speech by Gov. George C. Wallace, South Carolina Broadcasters Association meeting, Myrtle Beach, SC, July 15, 1963. Transcript from the McCain Library & Archives, University of Southern Mississippi, M308 Box 1, Folder 12.

13. Speech by Gov. George C. Wallace, South Carolina Broadcasters Association meeting, Myrtle Beach, SC, July 15, 1963. Transcript from the McCain Library & Archives, University of Southern Mississippi, M308 Box 1, Folder 12.

14. Speech of Gov. George C. Wallace, Brown University, Providence, RI, Nov. 7, 1963. Transcript from the McClain Library & Archives, University of Southern Mississippi, Box M308, Box 1, Folder 17.

15. *Dayton (OH) Daily News*, Feb. 11, 1964.

16. Associated Press, Feb. 12, 1964.

17. *Stevens Point (WI) Journal*, March 10, 1964.

18. *Appleton (WI) Post-Crescent*, March 10, 1964.

19. *Sheboygan (WI) Press*, March 11, 1964.

20. *Racine (WI) Journal-Times*, April 5, 1964.

21. *Indianapolis Star*, April 16, 1964.

22. *Indianapolis Recorder*, April 11, 1964.

23. *Indianapolis Recorder*, April 11, 1964.

24. *Indianapolis Star*, May 6, 1964.

25. United Press International, April 18, 1964.

26. *Indianapolis Recorder*, April 18, 1964.

27. *Indianapolis News*, April 15, 1964.

28. *Indianapolis Star*, April 18, 1964.

29. Associated Press, April 27, 1964.

30. *Baltimore Sun*, May 12, 1964.

31. *Baltimore Sun*, May 12, 1964.

32. *Baltimore Sun*, May 12, 1964.

33. *Baltimore Sun*, May 9, 1964.

34. *Baltimore Afro-American*, April 11, 1964.

35. *Baltimore Sun*, May 8, 1964.

36. *Baltimore Afro-American*, May 16, 1964.

37. *Baltimore Afro-American*, May 19, 1964.

38. Remarks of Gov. George C. Wallace, CBS News *Face the Nation* broadcast of July 19, 1964. Transcript from the McCain Library and Archives, University of Southern Mississippi, M308, Box 2, Folder 18.

39. Remarks of Gov. George C. Wallace, CBS News *Face the Nation* broadcast of July 19, 1964. Transcript from the McCain Library and Archives, University of Southern Mississippi, M308, Box 2, Folder 18.

40. Remarks of Gov. George C. Wallace, CBS News *Face the Nation* broadcast of July 19, 1964. Transcript from the McCain Library and Archives, University of Southern Mississippi, M308, Box 2, Folder 18.

41. Remarks of Gov. George C. Wallace, NBC News *Meet the Press* broadcast of Oct. 25, 1964. Transcript from the McCain Library and Archives, University of Southern Mississippi, M308, Box 2, Folder 19.

42. Remarks of Gov. George C. Wallace, NBC News *Meet the Press* broadcast of Oct. 25, 1964. Transcript from the McCain Library and Archives, University of Southern Mississippi, M308, Box 2, Folder 19.

43. United Press International, March 15, 1965.

44. United Press International, March 15, 1965.

45. *Los Angeles Times*, Dec. 10, 1967.

46. *Los Angeles Times*, Dec. 9, 1967.

47. *Boston Globe*, June 29, 1968.

48. Hamill, Pete. (1968, October 26). Travels with the Right: Wallace. *Ramparts*, pp. 45–48.

49. Wills, Garry. (1970). *Nixon Antagonists: The Crisis of the Self-Made Man*. Boston, MA: Houghton Mifflin Company, p. 37.

50. New York Times, Oct. 14, 2016. Retrieved online at: https://www.nytimes.com/2016/10/15/us/politics/trump-media-attacks.html.

51. New York Times, Oct. 14, 2016. Retrieved online at: https://www.nytimes.com/2016/10/15/us/politics/trump-media-attacks.html.

52. New York Times, Oct. 14, 2016. Retrieved online at: https://www.nytimes.com/2016/10/15/us/politics/trump-media-attacks.html.

53. Carter, Dan T. (2001). "Good copy." In Robert H. Giles & Robert W. Snyder (eds.). *1968: Year of Media Decision*. New Brunswick, NJ: Transaction Publishers, p. 39.

54. *Moline (IL) Daily Dispatch*, Oct. 22, 1968.

55. *Moline (IL) Daily Dispatch*, Oct. 22, 1968.

56. *Moline (IL) Daily Dispatch*, Oct. 22, 1968.

57. *Moline (IL) Daily Dispatch*, Oct. 22, 1968.

58. Gannett News Service, Oct. 5, 1968.

59. Gannett News Service, Oct. 5, 1968.

60. *New York Times Magazine*, Sept. 22, 1968.

61. *New York Times*, Aug. 19, 1968.

62. Associated Press, June 27, 1968.

63. Associated Press, June 27, 1968.

64. Associated Press, June 27, 1968.

65. Associated Press, June 27, 1968.

66. Elmer W. Lower June 27, 1968 telegram to George C. Wallace. 1968 Wallace Campaign Files. George C. Wallace Papers, Box 12, Folder 13. Alabama Department of Archives and History, Montgomery, AL.

67. George C. Wallace, June 28, 1968 telegram to Elmer W. Lower. 1968 Wallace Campaign Files. George C. Wallace Papers, Box 12, Folder 13. Alabama Department of Archives and History, Montgomery, AL.

68. *Washington Post*, Oct. 8, 1968.

69. *Washington Star*, Oct. 1, 1968.

70. Nelson, Jack. (2013). *Scoop: The Evolution of a Southern Reporter*. Jackson: University of Mississippi Press, p. 128.

71. Nelson, Jack. (2013). *Scoop: The Evolution of a Southern Reporter*. Jackson: University of Mississippi Press, p. 129.

72. Nelson, Jack. (2013). *Scoop: The Evolution of a Southern Reporter*. Jackson: University of Mississippi Press, p. 130.

73. Dan King Thomasson, interview with the author, Dec. 18, 2015.

74. Dan King Thomasson, interview with the author, Dec. 18, 2015.

75. 1968 Wallace Campaign Files. George C. Wallace Papers, Box 5, Folder 9. Alabama Department of Archives and History, Montgomery, AL.

76. *Washington Post*, Oct. 16, 1968.

77. *Washington Post*, Oct. 16, 1968.

78. *Washington Post*, Oct. 16, 1968.

79. *Washington Post*, Oct. 16, 1968.

80. *Los Angeles Times*, Oct. 16, 1968.

81. Carter, Dan T. (2001). "Good copy." In Robert H. Giles & Robert W. Snyder (eds.). *1968: Year of Media Decision*. New Brunswick, NJ: Transaction Publishers, p. 41.

82. United Press International, Oct. 3, 1968.

83. Carter, Dan T. (2001). "Good copy." In Robert H. Giles & Robert W. Snyder (eds.). *1968: Year of Media Decision*. New Brunswick, NJ: Transaction Publishers, p. 42.

84. United Press International, Oct. 3, 1968.

85. Associated Press, Oct. 6, 1968.

86. Associated Press, Oct. 6, 1968.

87. Kozak, Warren. (2009). *Curtis LeMay: Strategist and Tactician*. Washington, DC: Regnery Publishing, p. 375.

88. *Los Angeles Times*, Oct. 6, 1968.

89. Scripps-Howard News Service, Oct. 4, 1968.

90. United Press International, Oct. 24, 1968.

91. *Los Angeles Times*, Oct. 16, 1968.

92. Steve Bell telephone interview with the author, Jan. 4, 2015.

93. Steve Bell telephone interview with the author, Jan. 4, 2015.

94. Steve Bell telephone interview with the author, Jan. 4, 2015.

95. CBS Evening News, May 2, 1972. Retrieved online at: https://www.youtube.com/watch?v=LxUIAMba-hE.

96. CBS Evening News, May 2, 1972. Retrieved online at: https://www.youtube.com/watch?v=LxUIAMba-hE.

97. Steve Bell telephone interview with the author, Jan. 4, 2015.

98. United Press International, March 12, 1976.

99. United Press International, March 12, 1976.

100. *Washington Post*, March 12, 1975.

101. Associated Press, Oct. 3, 1975.

102. *Lowell (MA) Sun*, Feb. 15, 1976.

103. United Press International, Feb. 21, 1976.

104. Associated Press, March 13, 1976.

105. *Chicago Tribune*, March 15, 1976.

106. *Chicago Tribune*, March 15, 1976.

107. United Press International, March 11, 1976.

108. Associated Press, March 11, 1976.

109. *Washington Post*, March 12, 1975.

110. United Press International, March 29, 1976.

111. Associated Press, Oct. 3, 1975.

112. *LaCrosse (WI) Tribune*, March 29, 1976.

113. *Montgomery Advertiser*, March 28, 1976.

114. *Anniston (AL) Star*, March 28, 1976.

115. Associated Press, March 30, 1976.

116. *Montgomery Advertiser*, March 28, 1976.

117. *Green Bay (WI) Press-Gazette*, March 30, 1976.

118. *Parade Magazine*, March 29, 1975.

119. *Village Voice*, Aug. 5, 1975.

120. *Village Voice*, Aug. 5, 1975.

121. *Village Voice*, Aug. 5, 1975.

122. *Village Voice*, Aug. 5, 1975.

123. *Parade Magazine*, June 13, 1976.

124. *Indianapolis Star*, April 20, 1976.

125. Daniel McCabe & Paul Stekler (directors). (2000). *American Experience: "George Wallace: Setting the Woods on Fire."* Originally broadcast—PBS, April 23–24, 2000.

126. Daniel McCabe & Paul Stekler (directors). (2000). *American Experience: "George Wallace: Setting the Woods on Fire."* Originally broadcast—PBS, April 23–24, 2000.

127. Perlstein, Rick. (2014). *The Invisible Bridge: The Fall of Nixon and the Rise of Reagan.* New York: Simon & Schuster, p. 622.

128. *Indianapolis Star*, May 4, 1976.

129. *Indianapolis Star*, May 4, 1976.

130. Associated Press, May 4, 1976.

131. *Lansing (MI) State Journal*, May 6, 1976.

132. *Lansing (MI) State Journal*, May 13, 1976.

133. Peggy Wallace Kennedy telephone interview with the author, Feb. 21, 2016.

134. *Baltimore Sun*, April 9, 1976.

135. Associated Press, April 12, 1976.

136. Associated Press, April 12, 1976.

137. Associated Press, May 18, 1976.

138. *Baltimore Sun*, May 11, 1976.

139. *Washington Post*, June 10, 1976.

140. Associated Press, March 19, 1976.

141. *Parade Magazine*, June 13, 1976.

142. *Long Beach (CA) Press-Telegram*, July 19, 1976.

143. Peggy Wallace Kennedy telephone interview with the author, Feb. 21, 2016.

144. Daniel McCabe & Paul Stekler (directors). (2000). *American Experience: "George Wallace: Setting the Woods on Fire."* Originally broadcast—PBS, April 23–24, 2000.

Chapter Six

1. Steudeman, Michael J. (2018). "Demagoguery and Donald Trump's Duplicitous Victimhood." In Ryan Skinnell (ed.). *Faking the News: What Rhetoric Can Teach Us about Donald J. Trump*. LaVergne, TN: Ingram Book Company, p. 11.

2. Anna M. Young. (2018). "Rhetorics of Fear and Loathing: Donald Trump's Populist Style." In Ryan Skinnell (ed.). *Faking the News: What Rhetoric Can Teach Us about Donald J. Trump*. LaVergne, TN: Ingram Book Company, p. 32.

3. Anna M. Young. (2018). "Rhetorics of Fear and Loathing: Donald Trump's Populist Style." In Ryan Skinnell (ed.). *Faking the News: What Rhetoric Can Teach Us about Donald J. Trump*. LaVergne, TN: Ingram Book Company, pp. 24–25.

4. Cowan, Paul. (1968, July 18). "Wallace in Yankeeland: The invisible revolution." *Village Voice*, pp. 1, 17–19.

5. Cowan, Paul. (1968, July 18). "Wallace in Yankeeland: The invisible revolution." *Village Voice*, pp. 1, 17–19.

6. Hamill, Pete. (1968, October 26). Travels with the Right: Wallace. *Ramparts*, pp. 45–48.

7. White, Theodore H. (1969). *The Making of the President 1968*. New York: Atheneum Publishers, p. 348.

8. *Washington Star*, Oct. 1, 1968.

9. *Washington Star*, Sept. 30, 1968.

10. United Feature Syndicate, Sept. 16, 1968.

11. United Feature Syndicate, Sept. 16, 1968.

12. Carter, Dan T. (2001). "Good copy." In Robert H. Giles & Robert W. Snyder (eds.). *1968: Year of Media Decision*. New Brunswick, NJ: Transaction Publishers, p. 40.

13. *Jackson (MS) Clarion-Ledger*, March 10, 1968.

14. *Jackson (MS) Clarion-Ledger*, March 10, 1968.

15. *Jackson (MS) Clarion-Ledger*, March 10, 1968.

16. *Jackson (MS) Clarion-Ledger*, March 10, 1968.

17. Mississippi Encyclopedia. Retrieved online at: https://mississippiencyclopedia.org/entries/tom-ethridge/.

18. *Jackson (MS) Clarion-Ledger*, June 22, 1968.

19. *Birmingham News*, Oct. 13, 1968.

20. Achter, Paul J. (2018). "Great Television: Trump and the Shadow Archetype." In Ryan Skinnell (ed.). *Faking the News: What Rhetoric Can Teach Us about Donald J. Trump*. LaVergne, TN: Ingram Book Company, p. 111.

21. Carlson, Jody. (1981*). George C. Wallace and the Politics of Powerlessness*. New Brunswick, NJ: Transaction Books, p. 275.

22. Swan, Jonathan. (2018, Aug. 5). "The TiVo Presidency: Trump Relives Trump." Sneak Peak column, Axios.com. Retrieved online at: https://www.axios.com/newsletters/axios-sneak-peek-c6e1a552-57e0-492f-ae7b-ac9059ae1f44.html.

23. Brill, Steven. (1975, March 17). "George Wallace Is Even Worse Than You Think He Is." *New York Magazine*, p. 46. Retrieved online at: https://books.google.com/books?id=SekC AAAAMBAJ&pg=PA46&lpg=PA46&dq=George+Wallace+bored+with+being+governor &source=bl&ots=KISIrmRqFE&sig=ACfU3U2uA3zbPljL2zzAYwlLyTvqipPNyA&hl=en&sa =X&ved=2ahUKEwjpwquyhcfqAhUYFzQIHdl_ALoQ6AEwEHoECAoQAQ#v=onepage&q =George%20Wallace%20bored%20with%20being%20governor&f=false.

24. *Alabama Journal*, June 11, 1976.

Epilogue

1. Frederick, Jeff. (2007). *Stand Up for Alabama: Governor George Wallace.* University of Alabama Press: Tuscaloosa, AL, pp. 375–76.

2. *New York Times*, Sept. 16, 1998.

3. Frederick, Jeff. (2007). *Stand Up for Alabama: Governor George Wallace.* University of Alabama Press: Tuscaloosa, AL, p. 378.

4. *Alabama Journal* (Montgomery, AL), May 9, 1984.

5. *Montgomery Advertiser*, May 24, 1983.

6. Associated Press, Jan. 15, 1986.

7. Daniel McCabe & Paul Stekler (directors). (2000). *American Experience: "George Wallace: Setting the Woods on Fire."* Originally broadcast—PBS, April 23–24, 2000; *Montgomery Advertiser*, April 3, 1986.

8. United Press International, July 21, 1987.

9. Associated Press, June 29, 1993.

10. *Washington Post*, Dec. 3, 2015.

11. *Baltimore Sun*, Sept. 15, 1998.

12. Associated Press, March 11, 1995; Montgomery Advertiser, March 11, 1995.

13. Associated Press, March 11, 1995; Montgomery Advertiser, March 11, 1995.

INDEX

ABOUT THE AUTHOR

Andrew E. Stoner, PhD, is an Indiana native and author of a dozen books, including the first biography of journalist Randy Shilts, along with a variety of political history and true-crime books. A graduate of Franklin College of Indiana, Ball State University, and Colorado State University, he is a former newspaper reporter and deputy press secretary for Indiana governor Frank O'Bannon. He is associate professor of communication studies at California State University, Sacramento.